The Single Mother's Social Club

The Single Mother's Social Club

Inspiration and advice on ~~surviving~~ *embracing* single parenthood

Jacinta Tynan

murdoch books

Sydney | London

To my darling Jasper and Otis. You are my reason.

Published in 2021 by Murdoch Books,
an imprint of Allen & Unwin

Murdoch Books Australia
83 Alexander Street, Crows Nest NSW 2065
Phone: +61 (0)2 8425 0100
murdochbooks.com.au
info@murdochbooks.com.au

Murdoch Books UK
Ormond House, 26–27 Boswell Street,
London WC1N 3JZ
Phone: +44 (0) 20 8785 5995
murdochbooks.com.uk
info@murdochbooks.com.uk

Sections of this book originally appeared, in somewhat different form,
in *Sunday Life*, *Whimn* and *Kidspot*.

Quote on page 5 reprinted by permission of HarperCollins Publishers Ltd,
© 2017, Pema Chödrön

A catalogue record for this
book is available from the
National Library of Australia

A catalogue record for this book is available from the British Library

ISBN 978 1 92235 121 0 Australia
ISBN 978 1 91166 804 6 UK

Cover and text design by Emily O'Neill
Typeset by Susanne Geppert
Printed and bound in Australia by Griffin Press

10 9 8 7 6 5 4 3 2 1

Contents

INTRODUCTION

Welcome to the Club

This is not quite what I had in mind for my life – a single mother to two young children, renting a small apartment while I wait for my 'real' life to begin. Yet, it's the only way it could have gone, because it's made me who I am.

That's the thing about single motherhood: it's high pressure, high stakes, relentless and, at times, achingly lonely. But it can also be profoundly liberating, elevating us to our highest potential. When you're raising children on your own or as a co-parent, there's nowhere to hide. We don't get to pass the baton when another adult walks in the front door in time for dinner (or, preferably, to make dinner). We can't afford to take our eyes off the ball, not for a single minute. Even when our kids are with their other parent (if they have one), they're still at the top of our minds. There's so much resting on us, all of the time.

But this, too, is a gift. Single motherhood is an invitation to step up and grow and be the mother and the woman you aspire to be. It's a portal to your evolution. With no one to defer to, the only way through is to go within.

I'm not the person I was before I left home with my beautiful boys, aged four and six at the time. I've struggled and railed against reality. I've doubted myself – my eligibility and my essence – and had many sleepless nights fretting over my ability to carry my children through. And wondering how I would pay the rent. Still, I've done it. I'm doing it.

I've been scared and stripped back, completely untethered to any foundation. But along the way, I've softened and been emboldened, gaining strength I didn't realise was lacking until I needed to call upon it.

This is the side of single mothers that I see: stunningly capable, big-hearted warriors taking on the role of their lives, whether it was the plan or not. It's this story I wanted to tell – not just my own, but that of the many single mums I have met and sought out along the way who are living proof that this is an *opportunity* for a richer life.

Single-parent households are the fastest growing family group in Australia – the vast majority of these with women at the helm. The paths through which they have arrived here are as divergent as their circumstances – via separation and divorce, leaving or being left by someone they loved enough to have children with; through the death of the other parent; or the increasing number of women choosing to have babies on their own. But, for all our differences, there's a universal narrative. It goes something like this: At first we fall apart. There's grief, anger, blame. We're not sure if we'll pull through. Eventually we breathe. We recalibrate and assess how we're going to make this work. Then gradually we unfurl and rise up. We recover and rebuild. And one day we realise this is what it took to bring us back to ourselves, with our children looking to us – and sometimes only us – to lead the way. First destruction, then a reset and, ultimately, creation. Three intrinsic phases of every gripping story arc in history, each phase informing the other.

Ours is a tale of surrender and self-discovery, inner strength and excited anticipation about our unmapped futures. Of more meaningful relationships with our kids and ourselves. Not just adapting to our new normal, but wholeheartedly embracing it.

This book is my attempt to share this perspective of single motherhood – to inspire those who are living it, embolden those who are contemplating living it, and enlighten those who don't quite know what to make of us.

I have written this book through the lens of my lived experience and that of many of my single mum friends, and the women I interviewed. I am well aware that this account won't be reflective of everyone's individual circumstances or perspectives. How could it be? But I sincerely hope it provides a context for women to recognise themselves, to feel seen and validated. It's through the stories of others that we see ourselves.

* * *

A NOTE ON NAMES: I have spoken with dozens of single mothers for this book: co-parents, solo parents, single mothers by choice who conceived their babies via donor (some anonymous, some known), and widows. Many are friends, many others I had never met but I sought them out to hear their unique stories of how they came to single motherhood, and how they make the best of it.

Some women were happy to share their insights unmasked. Understandably, many others preferred to protect their privacy and that of their children. To that end, names appear in full for women who are using their real identities. Experts and writers who share their knowledge and expertise are also named. For everyone else, names have been changed. I thank them all for their generous contribution.

Part One:
DESTRUCTION

'Fear is a natural reaction
to moving closer to the truth.'

PEMA CHÖDRÖN,
When Things Fall Apart

CHAPTER 1

How Did I Get Here?

The day I became a single mother felt like a regular Tuesday. Except, after I dropped my two young boys to school and preschool, I went back home and started a new life.

I had pledged to both of my sons at their births, six and four years earlier – a loving whisper in their tiny shell ears – to do the right thing by them, to always have their backs. Staying the course, keeping our family together, was no longer fulfilling that promise. Implementing the change took months – years, really. There was no precise moment when the reordering began. Those days when your life changes course are not always easy to track. They're rarely definitive but rather are an incremental build-up of days, the correlation – the joining of the dots – only becoming apparent in retrospect. It's only when we find ourselves already well entrenched in the change that we are forced to stop and ask the hard question: *How did I get here?*

For the sake of an easy narrative, I can pinpoint becoming a single mother to the day that my sons and I left home. That was when ambiguity fell away.

We moved into our new home on a steamy summer Tuesday, ten days before Christmas. It was a small rental apartment at the other end of the same suburb as the home we had shared as an 'intact family' (a term used to describe the inferred more-appealing antithesis of 'single parent', even though it might be intact by appearance only). I deliberately booked the Airtasker removal van for a Tuesday because it was the one day of the week when my youngest, Otis, was at preschool and his brother, Jasper, was at school and I wasn't working. That gave me five hours to pack our belongings, ready for a smooth progression to our reconfigured life. I was under pressure to get the job done before the 3.05 p.m. school bell so the boys wouldn't be a party to the disentanglement.

I had broken the news at dinnertime the night before, pulling up a toddler chair at the boys' miniature orange table as they shovelled spaghetti into – and beside – their mouths with their plastic bulldozer- and excavator-shaped cutlery. It was a significant announcement heralding an irredeemable turning point in their young lives. I was nervous about how they'd react, conscious that this moment could form lasting scars for years to come. And sad, too, that it had come to this.

To my great relief, my young sons seemed to take the news in their stride. Jasper just wanted to know if the new place had a pool. (It didn't.) Otis wanted to know if he could bring 'Brown Bear'. (Of course!)

I had been promising my kids – reassuring them – for a while that the tension we'd been living with wouldn't be forever. (Although they didn't have the vocabulary to call it that; they called it 'yelling', which was just as accurate.) I'd dragged them with me to countless 'open for inspections' most Saturdays and some Wednesdays for months, to apartments all over our locality, but I hadn't divulged that the search mission was actually for us. The prospect of change before a change actually happens is far too disconcerting for young minds lodged firmly in the present. I told them I was 'looking for a friend'. Blessedly, at that age they didn't ask too many questions, delighted to explore the bare rooms and cupboards in all those vacant units.

No doubt the boys knew on some level that something was afoot, although I hid the removal boxes in the basement. Concepts are far more palatable to kids than reality. I didn't want them to have a glaring visual of this move – of furniture being shifted from one home to another – lest it sear into their memories and become a symbol of the upheaval they were subjected to, not yet even close to realising I was doing it for their own good.

That eventful Tuesday morning, one of the 'school mums' (the mums of Jasper's kindy friends and the only women I really knew in the area) turned up to help. Leaving her six-week-old twins at home with a babysitter, Lisa was at my door with pastries and sleeves rolled up. I cried when I opened the door, overwhelmed by her kindness and with the dawning enormity of what I was executing. Not just the change of address, but the irreversible changing of our lives.

Starting Over

I brought the boys home to our new apartment after school. They tore through the empty rooms, staking out their territory like newborn puppies, squabbling over who would sleep where, whose corner was whose. They assumed it was a hotel, not a permanent offering – a welcome naïveté protecting them from the stark reality of the monumental shift in their orbit that had just transpired.

Our first night as a freshly minted family of three, we stayed with my brother Ticka's family because our electricity wasn't yet connected. I was quite happy about that. It was like a brief transition point, one night with a 'real family' with the comfort of weekday commotion and care – the excuse to linger in denial a little longer – before our life began anew.

It wasn't until the next night that we really began the business of starting over.

The boys' regular babysitter, Lizzie, brought dinner. She greeted me at our rental with a teetering pile of ready-to-go pasta meals to get us through the next few days. 'I didn't think you'd feel like cooking,' Lizzie said brightly. She was right about that. And I cried again, sobbing shamelessly in her arms on the street outside our apartment block. This young girl who'd minded my children most Saturdays since their infancy – while I worked – was in this moment taking care of me. I was swept up by the full circle-ness and big-heartedness of the exchange.

Lizzie lent us a TV, too. Thank goodness for that because we didn't have one. We didn't have a couch, either. Or a bed for the boys. I'd brought a couple of camp mattresses from home; they could sleep on them until I could get the money together for bunk beds for their empty bedroom. But we did have a fridge – I'd raced out to buy one the day before, on sale at Harvey Norman, on my way back from signing the lease, and had it delivered straight away. A fridge, I reasoned, was more important than a bed because my boys might be able to sleep anywhere at their ages, but they needed cold milk for breakfast.

We ate one of Lizzie's pasta dishes for dinner, heated up on the stove (we didn't have a microwave). The three of us sat on the floor among all the removal boxes, pretending everything was normal. After I read the boys a story (keeping at least one thread of consistency with this nightly ritual) and got them to sleep (one in my bed, one on the mattress beside my bed), I sat on the lounge-room floor where a couch might eventually go and instinctively wrapped my arms around my knees, holding myself in – containment. Tears came quickly. I tried to gauge my emotional state, the first chance I'd had to do this in days – years, really. *Am I okay?* I asked myself. *Yes, I believe I am.* So, what was it then? Why was I crying? Why the deep sighs? Why was I making myself small in the expanse of a vacant room when I would've been quite warranted in the circumstances to be leaping around in exaltation to any music of my choosing without anyone around to judge? Or watching whatever I fancied on our borrowed TV? Why was I not celebrating my freedom? I was, but I felt more inclined to sit still. To be still. Being still is a luxury when you've been on edge.

I soon realised that what I was feeling was relief – relief that I had made it here with my boys, that we got to start again. Not everyone gets to start again.

On that first night of our new beginning, I stayed propped up against the wall in the unfurnished lounge room, knees bundled close to my chest, for some time, getting used to my new surrounds. My new way. From that night forward, I only needed to answer to me. I was adjusting. Recalibrating. Decompressing. I was also panicking. *I'm a single mother now. God! Am I up for this?* My mind was racing and I had to yank it back, arresting my wayward thoughts. *You've got this. You've done harder things*, I reminded myself. But had I really?

The momentousness of what I'd just orchestrated was suddenly unavoidably real. It was staring me in the face. That's why I was making myself small in contrast to the potential overwhelm of my current reality. In taking this action – fronting up with my Airtasker van of household chattels to a twelve-month lease apartment – I had unleashed a divergent course for myself and two young people who had no say in it. From this day our three lives would head in an alternate trajectory.

I am a single mum. My boys are being raised by a single mum. This is all my doing. It's not good or bad. It just is. For now I had suspended judgement, along with my life – the life I hadn't anticipated for me or my children.

Not Plan A

Nobody expects to find themselves in this situation. Not parents who had children together with all the best intentions of going the distance but then didn't, for any of myriad reasons. Nor parents whose partner has died. Single mothers by choice might be the exception – those courageous women who set out from the get-go to raise a child on their own. But even then, as one of my friends who had her baby via an anonymous donor said, 'It wasn't plan A', although it was a more desirable plan than not being a mother at all. Or, as another friend said, 'It's not your first choice but it becomes the better choice.'

Raising children by yourself, or even with a co-parent, no matter how cooperative they may be (or not), is not how it's designed to work. Whether we're co-parenting (two parents who collaborate and communicate with each other about the kids), parallel parenting (two parents who run it their way when the kids are with them) or solo parenting (bringing up children with no other parent in the picture, by choice or not), it's a lot to take on.

At some point most of us wonder how we ended up here. I know how I got here. Ending my relationship with the father of my children was the hardest thing yet it seemed the only thing left to do. I wanted anything but this – raising two children on my own, not being able to be the family they deserve. But after years of trying to find another way it became the last remaining option to live in truth. I believe it was the right thing to do by my precious and impressionable little boys, but it's not exactly how I imagined things panning out when I gave birth. And many of the single mothers I speak to feel the same, baffled about how they wound up in this place.

'I remember lying awake all night looking at the ceiling and just being terrified, but staying really still, thinking, *Don't move*, and wondering, *How am I going to do this?*' said Lara, who left the father of her two kids when they were five and seven. 'We're brought up in a society that worships the nuclear family. I saw how hard it was for my sisters who are single mothers, financially but also really lonely and isolated and I thought, *I don't want that for me.*'

'I was devastated because it was like the death of the dream family,' said Anika, a mum to two kids aged two and four when she separated. 'Suddenly I was becoming my mum, who was a single mum. My biggest fear was that I was going to be skint like when we were growing up. There was the juggling of bills, my mum waitressing at night, being babysat by anyone who was available. I felt guilty about the emotional fallout on the children, wondering if I was screwing it up. They'd ask, "Why doesn't Daddy live here anymore?" But there wasn't a choice. The idea of living that way was unfathomable. I was dying inside.'

'I had those moments where I was like, *Hang on, this wasn't meant to be my life*,' said Gigi, who was 27 when she had her son and became a single mum a week later. 'I grew up in a nice suburb, went to a good school. I was meant to have the white picket fence with the nuclear family. But you have to get over that pretty quickly.'

'Our breakdown happened when I was seven months pregnant with our second child,' said Aisha Novakovich, a mother of two boys. 'I fell into a hole of darkness and I didn't know how I would make it through the night. I felt my heart breaking. It was the loss of the dream of having a family because I didn't grow up with one myself after my father died. I felt like I lost part of my own soul. Now I was looking into a new reality, I was scared. Even though while we were married my husband wasn't always present, just having someone there I thought would be better than having no one at all.'

'I wouldn't relive that first twelve months for anything,' said Zoe, whose son was five when her husband ended the marriage. 'You literally pat yourself on the back that you get out of bed, get your child to school, get to the office, that you show up for life. And I drank a river's worth of vodka.'

'I had my first and only panic attack that day after he left,' said Joy, a divorced mum of three. 'I walked around the markets and I couldn't see properly and I felt shaky. I felt like everybody was staring at me, that everybody knew I was a single mum.'

Lisa Corduff and her husband amicably 'parted ways' to allow him to focus on recovery from his ongoing mental health struggles. Eight months later, while Lisa was still coming to terms with the end of the marriage, her ex-husband died, leaving her to raise their three children on her own. 'I experienced a massive amount of grief when my marriage evolved, letting go of what you imagine your life is going to be,' she said. 'I was brought to my knees by that ending. But I also felt quite empowered. But the finality of death is a whole other ball game. I had looked forward to co-parenting, the kids getting the best of each of us. And to have that taken away – the kids have lost their father in the physical realm – it takes everything to a whole new level.'

Kelly Exeter's husband of fourteen years, Ant, was killed suddenly in a freak accident, leaving her to raise their two young children as a single mother. 'As a naturally anxious person, I'd lived with the worry of losing Ant for so long that when it actually happened, it almost wasn't a surprise,' she said. 'My brain was like, *Oh there it is, that thing you always feared*. But, for all the fears of losing Ant, I never skipped ahead to what life without him would actually be like on a practical level. (I knew on an emotional level it would be unbearable.) At first I didn't really feel like a single parent. Every decision I made, I knew exactly what he would have thought. I felt like we were still parenting together. It was only after a year or so that I started having to make decisions where I wasn't sure what he'd say or think. That was really confronting and perhaps the first time I felt really lost and alone.'

Even mothers who sign up for single motherhood from the start – so-called single mothers by choice – also often pause to consider how this became their reality. After finding herself single at 39,

Bek chose to have a baby on her own with an anonymous donor, this alternate path striking her with searing clarity during a silent vipassana meditation retreat. 'I knew I wanted a baby. It was a gut thing. And I would have a baby by myself if I didn't meet someone. I didn't want to miss out on the experience. A few months later I froze my eggs and embyros with donor sperm to keep my options open.' At 44, Bek was in a relationship with a man who didn't want more kids, so she had one of her frozen embryos implanted. 'I wanted a baby so I made it happen,' she said. 'We're conditioned to think we want marriage and kids as if that's the only model but there are other ways.'

Other women, like my aunt, Catherine, are undaunted by the prospect of single parenthood. After arriving back in Australia with her infant son in 1980 and leaving his father behind in Argentina, where they'd been living, she felt relief. 'It was extremely emotional at the airport but when I got on the plane I was over the moon. All I thought was, *I'm going home*,' she said.

Young mum Jasmine said that while it was far from her 'life goal', her pregnancy at eighteen gave her the purpose she was so desperately seeking. 'When I saw those two pink lines on the pregnancy test, I felt something in me change. I went from having nothing to everything. It brought me back to reality and gave me the will to live and a meaning to life. It's been a really good thing for me, even though I was so young and alone. My son saved me.'

Jo Abi calls it the 'honeymoon phase' of single motherhood. 'I was elated,' she said. 'I couldn't take the smile off my face. I felt free and unburdened. I'd been wanting to leave, needing to leave for so long and I never thought I'd have the money or the strength to go. When I finally did it I was so proud of myself. I stayed in the relationship because I thought it was the best thing for my children. Then I realised that I had to leave because that was the best thing for my children.' Jo said that the post-separation honeymoon didn't last, but she's still happier than before. 'I soon realised that difficulty gets replaced with other difficulties. But I prefer these difficulties.'

How Does It Feel on the Other Side?

Many women grieve the loss of a dream, of not being able to deliver on the nuclear family idyll for their kids.

'It took a long time for it to sink in,' said Joy. 'Six months into it I'd be walking down the street thinking, *This is my reality.* I assumed we'd be together for the long haul. Because I come from a split family, I'd worked hard to make sure that didn't happen to me, that I'd chosen well and it would go the distance. You want to give your kids what you didn't have in childhood. I always wanted rollerskates, never got them, and I couldn't wait to get my kids rollerskates, but the two parents living together at home they didn't get. I couldn't do it.'

'I was so confident at first that I could be a single mum,' said Sally Burleigh, a mum to two kids aged one and three when she separated from her husband. 'I knew at the time that I could support my kids financially, nurture them, raise them, love them, I could do it all. But then there were times after we split, it was always late at night when they were in bed, I was in bed, everything's quiet, and you suddenly think, *Did I break up a family?* I felt so much guilt over not giving them a nuclear family, a family unit I had grown up with. I don't care what anyone says, children need a family unit. They want their mum and dad together.'

'This was not what was meant to happen, this was not my life plan,' said Michelle Broadbent, a mum to two young girls when her husband left. 'I fought tooth and nail and spent way longer than I should have still in the marriage because I wanted to hold the family together. I didn't want my children to be from a broken home. My parents split up and I never wanted that for them.'

'It definitely wasn't the plan,' said Stella, a mum to two kids under twelve when her marriage ended. 'But I know I did the right thing.

We've both re-partnered and I'm very happy, but that doesn't mean I don't have moments where I think life would've been much easier for the kids if I'd stayed for their sake. But staying in a marriage where even one parent's terribly unhappy is hardly good role modelling for the kids. Especially if you're in a position where the mother is being belittled. They'll think it's what marriage looks like.'

'It dawned on me that there were no longer two of us supporting our kids, that when I had the boys in my care it was solely up to me,' said Louisa, a mum to twins, after separating from their other mother. 'It was a big realisation, but at the same time I thought this is wonderful, that I get to spend quality time with my boys.'

'I'd been planning the move for a while,' said Jo. 'But the first time I felt the reality of it I was at a dance concert with my daughter and I kept looking to turn to someone and say, "How gorgeous is she!" to someone who loves her as much as me. But there was nobody there. It was a massive moment of realisation that I was a single mum now and the buck stops with me and there'd be many more moments like this in the future, delighting in my children on my own. I was sad but I also felt like, *This is the way it's got to be.* I mourned it that night then I had to look forward and be stronger.'

Digging Deep

No matter how we got here, or how thrilled – or not – we are about it, this cataclysmic shift in circumstances where we wind up as solo parents or co-parents to our children is tough going. We're often tripped up by sadness, lament, grief and anger, while feeling overwhelmed and duty-bound by our newly defined role, and hampered, in most cases, by limited financial means. Yet there is so much resting on us getting this right. The stakes are high.

Like any big life change, it's cause for introspection, an invitation to dig deeper, to sift through the choices we made along the way that led us here. The problem is, there's not always time for that. With children to take care of, it's not so easy to indulge in self-analysis or catch a ride on downward-spiralling emotions. As a single mother, we have no option but to get up and get on with it.

'This is no picnic for anyone,' said Shakti, who split with the father of her son when she was pregnant. 'I had many moments of going, *Mmm, how did I get here? This is not how I pictured it.* But you're so overwhelmed with being present and getting done what needs to be done that there's no time to process what's happening and to unpack it until you're in a state where things are reasonably steady and you're like, *Okay, now I can try and understand how it happened, because it's useful for self-knowledge.*'

Inez, who's a single mum twice over (having two kids with two separate dads, eight years apart), said that she's been led to contemplate her own role in it all. 'I did have a moment of, *Here I go again, raising kids on my own, going through a separation, custody, finances,*' she recalled. 'I'm the common denominator, so I have learned a few lessons along the way.'

Change Is Not All Bad

I had begun my own incessant soul-searching many years earlier. It had become somewhat of a hobby (enough emotional pain will do that to you). But this was a whole new ball game, because this time I wasn't just accountable to myself. Every move I made would impact my two little boys who, though they may not have known it at the time, were looking wide-eyed to me for guidance, banking on me to get it right. And I had just pulled the Reggie Robot rug right out from under them. I was the person responsible for upending their lives and there was no way they could yet see it was for the best. This cognisance may not sink in until adulthood, if ever. I had to claw back their trust. But I wasn't sure how to go about doing that –

not that first night, anyway. I wasn't sure how to do anything, really. So I stayed where I was, in the stillness, not daring to make a move lest it be the wrong one.

It wasn't the logistics that fazed me. Hauling my two boys around pretty much on my own had been my norm since they were born, apart from the two nights a week I went to work. But I was worried about how this new order would work, and the inevitable impact it would have on all of our lives. There were so many uncertainties and even more unknowns.

It was incumbent upon me to educate myself in the lexicon of single motherhood. Shared time arrangements. Parenting plans. Financial statements. Child support. A house to be sold and divvied up. Extended periods without my boys for the first time ever. Finding ways to explain all this to my kids as they grow curious and start to ask questions. Shielding them from the inevitable fallout of this life-altering wrench. Managing my own thwarted expectations as to how my life might look.

The biggest misapprehension of all was that I was over the worst of it, that this leap I'd taken – to the other end of the same suburb, although it may as well have been to the moon – was the end of the struggle. Moving out of home couldn't have been a more definitive delineation between my previous existence – a mother in a nuclear family with a mortgage, a garden and a trampoline – and this one – a single mum of two, renting an apartment the size of our old living room with a borrowed TV and no couch or bed for my kids. One thing I did know was that I was not going to come out of this the same. When I considered my passivity, my stagnation, my propensity to put up with anything (a therapist once told me, 'My wish for you is you learn to tolerate less'), this would not be a bad thing. I sort of expected that the rest would unfold organically from here.

What I soon learned is that the part where you change your life is not where the change happens. And that change is not all bad.

In the midst of my trepidation and fear I was vaguely excited about what might lie ahead – the possibility of rediscovering who I was before all this: joyful, curious, spontaneous, trusting, treading lightly. I was hopeful that my boys would get to see that side of me, too. They would witness me modelling courage, honouring myself as I hope they will always do, too. Giving them a chance at a more harmonious childhood. In choosing single motherhood, I could be the mother they need, and the woman I really am.

Be here now. I heard the words and I wasn't sure if they were coming from within me or above me, but I heard them loud and clear. That was all that was required of me, that night at least. To be here now. A call to presence. A reprieve from ruminating on the past, panicking about what might come next.

Eventually, after what seemed like hours, when the stillness became pointless and kind of boring, I crept quietly into bed in my new bedroom, stepping carefully over Jasper twisted in his robot doona on the mattress on the floor, and edging in beside Otis, who had commandeered the bed in his heavy, peaceful sleep.

'This is it,' I whispered into the night.

'Trust me,' I whispered to my boys. It wasn't the last time I'd feel the need to ask that of them. But first I had to learn to trust myself.

SINGLE MOTHER WISDOM

- Changing your life is rarely sudden, but incremental. Take one small step forward (or away) and you'll know what to do next.

- Many women stay with the other parent for the sake of their kids, but an unhealthy relationship can have a profound effect on children, too. Don't kid yourself that staying the course is necessarily the best option.

- It can seem incredibly daunting and overwhelming to leave a relationship, especially when you have children. But there is help available (see page 299).

- Countless women have walked this road before you, leaving dysfunctional relationships for the sake of themselves and their kids. You are not alone.

- Having a baby on your own is a brave choice. But it's becoming more common as more and more women are opting for mother-hood (via donor sperm, adoption or surrogacy) over holding out for love. They rarely look back.

- Grief is common for single mothers, at the start at least. There's the loss of the dream of an 'intact' family unit, often the ideal (and only) narrative that we're fed from birth. This applies to all single mothers – separated, divorced, widowed and single mothers by choice. But we soon come to learn that we're not worse off. We might even be better off.

- Sometimes sitting still is all that's required in any moment.

CHAPTER 2

Stepping Up

Ever since the day I moved out of the family home with my two young children and lived separately from their father, I've considered myself a 'single mother'. It's the common parlance for women like me: mothers who are no longer with the other parent of their children. Many single mothers take issue with the label. There's a lingering stigma attached to single motherhood – unwelcome and misaligned – denoting misfortune and hardship, and a sense of being a little less worthy of our place in the world. But, in the absence of a more appropriate appellation, we'll take it. Depending on the circumstances that brought us here, some of us even celebrate it.

The single mother landscape has changed dramatically in recent years. There is an increasing number of single mothers by choice – a result of advancements in IVF and accessibility to sperm donation – meaning many more women are technically raising children on their own, choosing motherhood over holding out for love. As playwright Alexandra Collier, herself a solo mother by choice, told Clementine Ford in the Big Sister Hotline podcast, 'I love that these women are grabbing their reproductive futures in their hand and going, "I'm going to do this regardless of what my relationship status is." Also, as the shame around being a single mum has dissipated somewhat since our own mothers became mothers, and women are more financially independent, they're prepared to leave the fathers of their children if the relationship isn't working.

Whatever the circumstances, life can be tough going for mums who are parenting on their own. As one divorced single mum friend said, 'Single mothers struggle, whatever way you cut it.'

This is even true for mothers with ex-partners who are considered co-parents. Mothering (single or otherwise) is a full-time gig. From stocking the fridge to sports schedules, homework and birthday parties, our children are always top of mind. Consistent research shows that it's predominantly women who carry the emotional and logistical load – the blueprint for family life – whether our kids are there or not. That's not co-parenting. That's single mothering.

According to psychologist Kirsty Levin, founder of The Parents Village, 'A single parent is anyone with sole responsibility for children for extended periods of time and not in a relationship with the other parent.' That's pretty much all of the women I know who are parenting on their own (at least partially), for whatever reason.

You're Not a Single Mother if Your Husband Is Away

Women in partnerships often lean in conspiratorially and tell single mothers they know how we feel because their husband is away on a boys' weekend or interstate for work. The difference is, he's coming back. Not only is there someone else paying or contributing to the mortgage or rent, there's also another adult in the home (or with a scheduled return date) with a vested interest in the wellbeing of your joint children. Another adult phoning in to check all is well or pick up lamb chops on the way home.

'With custody comes the physical, mental, emotional and spiritual responsibility for the kids. And most likely all the bills,' wrote futurist Michelle Newton in an article for *The Huffington Post* titled 'Stop Saying You're A Single Mum When You're Not'. 'As a soccer dad said on the sidelines: "It's like they are on point the whole time."'

Michelle argued that 'when married mums with absent husbands slap single mums in the face with the "it's-like-I'm-a-single-mum" line', they contribute to reinforcing the stigma and shame that often surrounds single mothers.

'Unless you're in that club of truly being a single mum and having to hustle hard and fight for survival without a partner who's got your back, don't say you are one,' said Aisha. 'You don't have that psychological support, someone to debrief with, to share life and its struggles. When other women say, "My husband is a FIFO worker and I feel like a single mum", that comes with its own struggles, sure, but there's no comparison. If your husband is working, at least he's bringing home an income. When you're a single mum, it all falls on you. You're the nurturer, the breadwinner, everything.'

Making It Work

It's not just the endless logistics you have to contend with as a single mother, and the almost inevitable financial strain that makes it so onerous, it's also the emotional load of being the only adult in charge.

'I am going crazy, and no one can help me,' wrote Suzanne Finnamore in *Split: A Memoir of Divorce*. 'This is what really happens to wives who are left with small children. I never fully appreciated this fact before.' You can't possibly know what it's like to be a single mother until you are one. I certainly didn't.

By necessity, single mothers tend to become resourceful and innovative and eternally adaptable. They're both parents in one, their eyes never off the game. They are all in, a force to be reckoned with.

Most of us have no choice but to work for money. That aside, we quite like maintaining careers we've worked hard to establish. It's the same with many partnered mothers, of course, but the notable differentiation with single motherhood is, it's all on us. We're forced to kick into survival mode.

Aisha was pregnant with her second child and in the middle of her second university degree when her husband left suddenly. 'My son had reflux so I would breastfeed six times a night whilst preparing for a tutorial the next day and try to sound intelligent and kill it with my marks. It was so difficult.' She now juggles her career as a lawyer with running her Muslim fashion label, Modest Fashion Australia, while raising her two kids on her own. She said she's had to expect less of herself. 'You can't do world domination and look after a sick child at the same time.'

'I had to think pretty quickly about survival, about being able to support my child,' said Gigi, whose son was a baby when she split with his father. 'I had to figure out how to be the breadwinner while being one hundred per cent responsible for my son. It was the mindset of, *This is on me, it's on my shoulders.* You develop a lioness-like mentality.' Neen Weir, a widow and mother of three, calls it being 'a sole trader'.

As single mothers, it's imperative that we find or create work that enables us to be there for our kids, or allocate part of the budget to pay someone to help take care of them, if we can afford that, because there's often no one else. Single mums call these 'single mum jobs' – jobs with flexible hours and understanding bosses who let you work from home if your child is sick or babysitting arrangements fall over, and give you time off in school holidays. These jobs are as elusive as the Holy Grail.

Being a TV newsreader wasn't a bad single mum job. Ever since my children were very young, I worked on Friday and Saturday nights until one o'clock in the morning, often while the boys were with their dad. Working nights meant I could be there during the day for my kids – I was lucky enough to be at every school drop-off and most pick-ups. I got to every assembly, sports carnival and Book Week parade. It was always a mad scramble to find babysitters on a Saturday night on a 'mum weekend' and it was a big chunk out of my pay, but it was a compromise I had to make to keep my career afloat.

Sometimes I had no alternative but to take my boys with me to work. They would sit in the newsroom watching TV and eating McDonald's (a ploy to keep them occupied) while I presented live news from an open studio just a few metres away. I insisted that under no circumstances should they speak to me but, at their young ages, there was no guarantee they would comply.

One memorable Friday afternoon during the coronavirus lockdown of 2020, they were forced to wait in the foyer for six hours while I was presenting the news, rushing out between news bulletins to ply them with peanut butter sandwiches hastily slapped together from the newsroom kitchenette. We were in the middle of a global pandemic and the pressure was on to deliver up-to-date, round-the-clock news bulletins. But, in my world, there were more pressing matters at hand: 'When can we go home?' my boys asked every time I ducked out to check on them. 'We're sooo bored!' I tried reasoning with them. 'Mummy needs to work so we can have a home and do fun things. Please try to be patient,' I implored. To my horror, the next time I stepped out of the newsroom I found that, with nothing better to do, they were catapulting off the couch just as my boss took a phone call mere metres away. I wasn't present for them – how could I be? I wasn't present in my job, either, and I wasn't sure how much longer I could make it work.

It turned out that was my second-last shift at work before I was retrenched. I'll never know if this timing was a coincidence.

I'm certainly not the only woman to find the juggle of working and single parenting a near-impossible stretch. 'It felt like a house of cards that might fall down any moment,' explained media executive Fiona Nilsson, a solo parent to a daughter. 'I was working 60 hours a week and bringing up a child by myself. You feel overwrought and there's no one to help. My job was a refuge as a single mum. It gave me independence and allowed me to support myself. My daughter would often sleep in my office while I was working or hang out at work with me. You do what you have to do.'

'Every time I have a job I have to scramble,' said Francesca, a solo parent to a young daughter whose father lives overseas. 'I'm passionate about my work and I want to show up fully but it's hard when you've got to balance that with the needs of your child. I'm the only parent she's got.'

Katrina Blowers, a fellow news presenter and journalist, has had to take her kids with her many times when she was called out to report on a story and was unable to find anyone to mind them. 'I'll never forget when I had to cover the story of Prince Frederik coming to a Brisbane nightclub and his entourage were exempted from the tough ID rules at the door,' Katrina said. 'I didn't have a babysitter and was forced to take my kids with me *to the nightclub* so I could negotiate with the owner for CCTV footage of the prince. He was delightful and gave my kids lemonade, but I felt like my two worlds were colliding.'

For many of us, the reality of single parenting means having to change tack, as for Shakti, who had to give up her beloved acting career to raise her young son. 'Acting isn't feasible as a single parent,' she said. 'It would cost me money to do a play while paying for babysitting and getting home at midnight. You might be doing a "guesty" on *Home and Away* and your call time changes at the last minute. The payoff I got from acting stopped being worth it. I grieved that hard. I've stepped into writing and yoga since having my son, which works well and brings me joy in a different way.'

We've Got This

As single mothers, we get the opportunity to see what we're made of. And what we find is that we're more adept than we realised – not just at making it work, but at keeping the whole ship afloat. You don't know this about yourself until you're in it.

Determined that my kids weren't going to grow up feeling like they were missing out on anything, and to make the transition to single-parent life as seamless as possible, the first Christmas after we moved out, I took them to the petrol station with me to select a live tree. They were experts at the choosing but, understandably, not so much at strapping the tree on the roof and hauling it up to our top-floor apartment. Rather than resenting the lack of assistance, it's a memory I will always treasure – a symbolic single-handed tree raising, like a stake in the ground (in the corner of the lounge room) for our revised family of three.

Journalist Melissa Wilson was still breastfeeding her baby son and had a toddler when she and her husband separated. She said that she's not sure how she made it through. 'During that first week I was crying to my mum, "I don't know how this is physically possible." I couldn't work out how to get my baby out of the bath and dressed and breastfed while watching his sister in the bath. My mum – who had four kids and is very pragmatic – advised me to "find little short cuts". She said, "Each day you'll find things that will make it easier and you'll just make it happen somehow." And she was right. I had to learn that no one else will do it for me. I ended up taking the top off the change table and leaving the baby on the floor while I bathed my two-year-old. I look back and see how competent I was when pushed to my limits and at rock bottom. I rose up from the depths of despair.'

Lisa Corduff had an epiphany before her marriage ended, that she was up for whatever lay ahead. 'I held on to my marriage for years because I was scared of being alone and I told myself I wouldn't be okay without him,' she said. 'Then I had this distinct moment where I looked at my son in the car one day and thought, *If I had to do this on my own, I know I'll be okay.* Within three weeks my husband was in a bad way, and he never came home again. I don't want to be in this position, but now that I know I can do this, it feels like I can do anything. I've seen myself in a way that I never had before. I was probably always capable, but now I know for sure.'

No matter how we arrived here, single motherhood is a calling of sorts. It's an invitation to step up, to challenge ourselves beyond what we ever imagined we were capable of. It may not be the life we had planned. It may be even better.

SINGLE MOTHER WISDOM

- There are many different versions of single mothers: separated, divorced, widowed, solo mothers. The one constant is women raising children on their own (or at least partially) who aren't in a relationship with the other parent. They're all legitimate and they all face struggles . . . and joys.

- People who aren't single mums often don't get it, but that's okay – there are plenty of other single mums around who do.

- Juggling single motherhood and a career can be tough, yet most of us need to work and many of us want to work. The ideal is to find or create work with flexible hours and conditions. It can often feel like cutting corners and like you're hanging on by a thread, but it's worth pushing through. Fortunately, many employers are becoming more understanding about the particular demands of single parenting.

- Becoming a single mum is an opportunity to see what you're made of. It's an invitation to step up.

CHAPTER 3

Single Mother Stigma

Long before I became a single mother myself, I quietly envied them. Several of my journalist colleagues separated from their partners over the years, a kind of coming of age as they stepped into their power. (Or perhaps it was due to all that shift work.) But instead of offering condolences, I was more inclined to congratulations. I noted that I didn't feel any semblance of pity, just admiration and mild awe.

When I heard that a friend had split with her husband, reclaiming her maiden name for good measure, I was taken aback by the flash of envy I had for her change in circumstances. (If ever there was a sign that I was hanging in there for the wrong reasons, this was it.)

It had never entered my head that breaking up a marriage or partnership was a shameful move to make. There was the inconvenience and the letdown, sure. The crushing disappointment of a dream thwarted, the self-recrimination for not being able to save your family for the sake of your kids. But I never considered the stigma. It never really occurred to me until a year or so after I left home, when I was sitting on the bleachers in the dying winter light at my son's soccer training with a bunch of other mothers, all married.

One of these women – who I didn't know – made an offhand remark about the changing face of the suburb where we lived thanks to 'all the single mothers'. She went on to explain her hypothesis that 'they' were lured here by the glut of apartments. She seemed deeply put out by this. It took me a moment to realise that she meant me. She was affronted by the likes of me.

There's wide consensus that two parents in a healthy, functional dynamic is the ideal set-up for kids. All the social studies helpfully point this out and, sure, you would if you could. But I had always admired women who found the fortitude to extricate themselves from sub-par, dysfunctional relationships. Or who decided to have a baby on their own. Whether the end of the relationship was their doing or not, I saw the courage in it.

Back in 1988 when my own mum became a single mother after my parents' 23-year marriage ended in divorce, she felt the whiff of disapproval from others. 'I always said you'd be better off being a widow than divorced. You're more accepted as a widow than a divorcee,' she told me much later.

But dwelling on things wasn't an option for Mum. With six kids aged from twelve to 21, she said she 'had to put one foot in front of the other and get on with it', adding, 'I didn't have time to wallow in anything.' In her mid-forties, after more than twenty years out of the workforce – apart from single-handedly running my dad's medical practice – she 'learned computers' and got herself a job. She earned not one but three post-graduate degrees and forged a successful career in nursing management until she retired in her mid-seventies.

Mum's younger sister, Catherine, had become a single mother several years earlier, raising her son on her own from when he was two years old. To me, Aunty Kate was a bohemian free spirit, a bright enigma who ran her own race, with a whip-smart bilingual toddler in tow.

It could have gone either way for her at that time. Judgement of women who had babies 'out of wedlock' was still rife in the early 1980s. But landing back in Australia on the back of the second-wave feminist movement, and moving to the heart of the anything-goes Sydney inner city, where the grammar school offered a 25 per cent discount for single parents, she and her son blended right in.

As a single mother, Aunty Kate found herself part of a group of women who were also raising children on their own. To her surprise, they were often the envy of her coupled friends. She recalls one friend, happily married with three kids, secretly admitting to coveting her lifestyle. 'She loved her husband,' my aunt said. 'But she envied our independence. She felt more attuned to us. I was quietly pleased. I thought, *Yeah, we are pretty good*.' Another of her married friends once attempted to pass herself off as a single parent. 'When I questioned her she said, "Sorry I'm not a member of that exclusive club."'

My aunt recalls one instance at the school gate of a mother 'manoeuvring' her out of the group, but it didn't faze her. 'I didn't feel hurt. I just thought, *How weird*.'

Perhaps most surprising, given the era, was how accepting Aunty Kate's staunchly Catholic parents – my grandparents – were of their daughter's 'position'. Her father, 'bewildered' at first, counselled her to marry her child's father. But, as time passed, he was respectful of her decision to raise her son on her own. Her mother, although 'sad because she would have expectations of what my life was going to be like', was more progressive and went to bat for Aunty Kate against the blatant judgement of their ultra-conservative relatives, including an 'incredibly religious' aunt who made her disapproval known. 'My mother got quite angry about my aunt's attitude, saying, "She's holier than thou"', recalled Aunty Kate. 'Fortunately my grandparents had passed away because I don't think they would've been able to accept my situation.'

Fallen Women

It wasn't so long ago that many 'unwed mothers', as they were known, a term designed to imbue shame, were forced to give up their babies for adoption, deemed unfit to raise them. In Australia, women who became pregnant 'out of wedlock' (more single mother lexicon) right up until the 1980s had few options: a shotgun wedding (so named because the father of the pregnant unwed woman would force the father-to-be to marry his daughter to prevent moral shame falling upon the family), or to be spirited off, out of sight, to a 'home for unwed mothers' to give birth, manipulated or forced into adoption and told to forget it ever happened.

'When these girls announced to their family that they wanted to keep the baby, they were often kicked out so as not to sully "the family name", explained Jenny Davidson, CEO of the Council of Single Mothers and their Children (CSMC). 'They were told if they love their child and want to do the right thing, they must give it up to be raised in a two-parent family. Post World War II, there was a social problem where you had these nice married couples that weren't able to have children – thus not a "complete family" – then you had women pregnant on their own, which was unacceptable. So this was considered to be a solution.'

Unwed mothers were treated differently in the hospitals where they gave birth, too, often not allowed to see their babies and some-times denied pain medication, the acronym BFA (Baby for Adoption) displayed unambiguously at the foot of their beds. Even those who desperately wanted to keep their babies were often forced to sign adoption forms and told that their babies had already been handed over to a more deserving – and intact – family.

Raising a child on your own was not only socially unacceptable and steeped in stigma, but was almost impossible to pull off given the social mores and the patriarchal system of the day, designed to benefit men and keep women in child care and homemaking roles. There were government benefits for widows and 'abandoned wives', but nothing for a woman leaving a marriage, or an unwed mother. 'They could go to a magistrate's court and try to sue the child's father for child support, and their sex life would be discussed by the judge,' Jenny said. 'She'd be asked how often she had sex and how many people she had sex with. They were painted with a moral brush as being loose, as fallen women and inadequate mothers.'

Unwed mothers, fallen women, loose, morally corrupt, unfit mothers, their children 'illegitimate'. This stigma persisted unchecked for decades. Divorce was similarly frowned upon, women often losing access to their children if they dared take this radical step. Their children were from 'broken' homes.

The CSMC was born from this prejudice. Adopting the term 'single mothers' instead of 'unwed mothers' (choosing to be defined by what they were, not what they weren't), this group of fiercely independent women banded together in 1969. They fought for the rights of women like themselves to keep their children, and also for the rights of their children, instigating a complete overhaul of the political and social landscape for single mothers.

But even these pioneers on the frontline had to hide in the shadows, often changing their names, wearing fake wedding rings or fabricating stories about dead husbands to avoid detection. 'Being an unwed mother could mean that you struggled to rent a house, or might be kicked out of your house,' Jenny explained. 'It was harder to keep a job or get one. It meant you weren't socially acceptable.'

Attitudes towards single mothers began a seismic shift with the securing of the Supporting Mothers' Benefit in 1973, at last allowing women access to welfare when raising a child on their own. The introduction of 'no-fault divorce' soon after, in 1975, set off a flurry of divorces as droves of abused or disgruntled wives leapt to their freedom, trailblazers like Selwa Anthony, who fled the family home with her two young daughters in 1976 to escape an emotionally abusive husband. 'I think about how women stay in relationships now where there's no real stigma,' she said. 'In the mid-seventies, that wasn't the case. It was "you're a married woman, how dare you leave". An uncle said to me, "You'll be a woman on your own now. Who's going to want to marry you with two children?" The attitude was you stay in the marriage for the children, not thinking of yourself and running away from your responsibilities. My decision to leave the marriage was the best decision I've ever made. I became an independent, successful businesswoman and met and married my soul mate."

Feminism helped change social attitudes, too, as more women started to claim their rightful place in the paid workforce, giving them economic and social independence (albeit earning significantly less than their male colleagues). More recently, in 2013, a long-overdue national apology for forced adoption in Australia by the country's first female Prime Minister, Julia Gillard, vindicated – but will never make up for – those women and children who were tragic victims of the misguided sentiment of the day.

The Stigma Persists

The sentiment that regarded women who raised babies without a man as inadequate, as 'less than' and unfit, sounds ludicrous to us now. However, the remnants linger. It's more insidious and less overt, but it's there. Many single mothers report feeling on the outer, of not being accepted. They're baffled by the reaction of others to their parenting status.

'There's something "yucky" about single mothers that makes people turn a blind eye,' said Lara. 'It's cognitive dissonance. I think women understand on a really deep level that there could be nothing worse than being cast out and having to raise children by yourself. Other people know how difficult it is but they don't want to acknowledge it. It's why you don't get praised, you don't get help. It's more comfortable for people to ignore you.'

'The whole world revolves around the union of a man and a woman. It's the foundation of our society. It's really hard being up against that,' said Sally.

'The ring was a real thing for me when I had to take it off,' said Zoe, a divorced mum to a young son. 'I never thought I would care about being a mum without anything on my hand but it really affected me. I felt like *OMG I'm a single mum!* I felt like I had a neon sign above my head saying, "Loser!"'

'One of the big drivers for me staying in my marriage was I had a lot of negative connotations in my head about being a single mum,' said Katrina. 'I felt like it was a failure. Like there was shame attached to it. But since I made the decision to leave my marriage, I've owned that decision and I've walked tall. I haven't allowed myself to feel other people's judgement.'

But acceptance is a big stretch for many single mothers attempting to slip under the radar, such as Joy, whose husband of seventeen years left, leaving her in denial. 'I didn't tell anybody about it for months. I only told a waiter, poor guy,' she laughed. This privacy gifted her a window to prepare for her new reality. 'You have to be quite careful about how you're perceived and what people are saying about you. My boy has broken his elbow twice. It's not a good look as a single mum, especially being black. I'm conscious of people thinking I'm not capable because my kids are from a split home. They're already mixed race; my ex is white. They're at home with a black single mum. I want to be perceived as being on top of my shit, we've got it handled.'

Since becoming a single mother, Joy said she's more aware of the pervasive racism that she's deflected her whole life. 'My kids had some time off school and the teacher flagged it with me, told me to keep an eye on it. And I thought, *Is that conversation the same with another family that isn't split? Is it the same with another single mum who's white, as opposed to me, who's black?'*

Joy has also become hyper-vigilant about her kids' school uniforms, making sure they're always pristine so it won't reflect badly on her. 'My perception is if I was still married I'd have the money for a new top, and they wouldn't be sent to school in an old one. I feel like it's a statement about us. So I spend my money on brand-new uniforms so my kids are always looking spot on.'

According to Jenny Davidson, CEO of the CSMC, this is quite a common scenario for single mums, who can feel 'out of step' with their school communities and, for those in financial hardship, their kids sometimes stand out for having the wrong uniform or equipment. 'Schools can be a very supportive environment, but often aren't,' she said. 'Single mothers can feel they are viewed differently at the school gate, "the late parent again". There's a lack of understanding that there's often no second parent to help with the juggle of family life.'

'The only time I felt a stigma was from a teacher at my daughter's school,' said Jane Marwick, a solo parent to a daughter. 'I was the only single mother and one of the few mums who worked and she made me feel like I was less of a parent. She told me no one played with my daughter and inferred she was behind in class. She knew I didn't have a husband to back me up.'

Like Joy, Jane admits that she 'overcompensated' with her daughter so she'd blend in. 'I was really tough on her. I didn't want to be the typical single mother, open to criticism. I wanted to prove I was as good as the married mothers. I wanted to raise her as a studious, well-dressed, good kid. I made sure she had impeccable manners.'

I'm similarly vigilant about my boys' manners, a bolt of panic shooting through me when they 'forget' them. While many parents let it slide, I drive it home – to the point of militance. 'Make sure you say thank you. Look them in the eye and use their name. Did I hear you say please?' I hear myself sometimes and I know I'm nitpicking, but I dare not ease off. It's partly me wanting to ensure I endow my boys with a comprehensive dossier of the basic rules of etiquette to give them a head start in life but, when I dig deeper, I'm aware it's also my fear of being judged. If my kids aren't perfectly polite, what will that say about me? I once noticed a single mum friend nudge her daughter firmly on the shoulder to 'say hello' when I ran into them at the mall. And I recognised that same irrational insistence.

We're on guard from other parents, too. They may carry the best of intentions, they might even think they're helping, but some coupled parents take the liberty of rebuking single mums and their kids for doing what kids do, not even trying to mask their disapproval. Would they do the same if we had backup?

'My kids were told off by their friend's mother for spraying water pistols outside on a hot summer day when they were all at it,' said Anika. 'When I called the mum to apologise, instead of letting me off the hook, I got a dressing down. I note none of the married mums got the same treatment. Like there's some inference that because I'm a single mother my kids are delinquents. I was shaking with rage.'

Eliza told of her daughter coming back sobbing from a pool party because another mum and dad had yelled at her for jumping on an inflatable flamingo, capsizing their son, who swam safely to the side of the pool. 'I texted the boy's mother to clear the air, and requested if she had any issues with my child to please come to me first instead of yelling at her,' said Eliza. 'She replied by sending a video another parent had taken of the flamingo "incident" as if to rub it in and I felt so shamed.'

I cried in front of Jasper's Year 2 teacher one morning when he had a gentle word with me about punctuality. We were late because I was trying to coerce two small kids to get ready and out the door on my own before the dreaded school bell, which, despite my best solo efforts, didn't always go smoothly. Simple as that. Consequences were not a motivator. Nor was the indignity of slinking into class after his classmates had already sat down, accompanying 'late note' in hand. 'Shoes', I once wrote in the 'reason' section of the Late Book and 'refused to get in car' more than once. Incidentally, I noticed another mother had written 'life' as her excuse for being late. I've been tempted to write 'single parent'. That alone ought to be grounds for dispensation.

My son's teacher was lovely about the lateness and suggested strategies: schedules in coloured textas stuck to the wall, 'incentives' (as opposed to 'bribes') such as iPad time. And he presented me with a prime motivator: that being late was hard on my boys. When they didn't have time to play with the other kids before class, they were behind the eight ball and it took them longer to settle into the day. I took it in but I also felt the hot rush of inadequacy that all mothers know too well, but which is exacerbated for those parenting solo because of the undue pressure we heap on ourselves to get it right, against great odds.

I couldn't blame my kids, not at their ages. The onus to get them to school on time rested on me. So now it goes like this: I make lunches, iron uniforms and pack bags the night before. There's no play in the morning until the boys have ticked off their to-do lists. It's not a bribe, it's an incentive. And here's the killer for me: I try to wake up half an hour earlier. Another sacrifice in the name of single motherhood.

Showing Up

It's not just showing up late that we've got to watch, but showing up to school at all. Many working single mothers report feeling stigmatised for not being 'around' as much as stay-at-home mothers.

'I'd turn up to the school yard and these women were so judgemental,' said Tory Archbold, a solo parent to a daughter and, at that time, the CEO of a global PR firm. 'They'd be like, "You're never available to read in the classroom"; "You missed assembly again." Of course I would love to be available, but my priority was putting a roof over our heads and ensuring the safety of my child. They judged me without understanding my circumstances.'

'When you have a baby, people make the assumption you're still with your partner,' said Shakti. 'A teacher at my son's preschool was trying to get him out of the sandpit and she said, "Don't you want to go home and see Dad?" I was the only single parent in the class, I was a bit of an anomaly. The teacher kindly said, "Wait another couple of years and you'll be the norm." Within a few months, another couple separated and now it's not as weird and I'm not as rare.'

The workplace is also lagging behind on its attitude to single mothers. Francesca recalled that a colleague once quipped, 'Keeping bankers' hours, are we?' when she was leaving work to pick up her child. 'I had negotiated those hours,' Francesca said. 'But, it triggered that part of me who feels inadequate. It gets to you because you're already having to do everything as a single mother, you're on the run and feeling guilty and this doesn't help.'

The media doesn't help, either. News stories will invariably high-light 'single mother' in the headline, as if that explains everything. Never do they specify 'married mother'.

As a producer in conservative AM radio, Jane Marwick was well versed in the entrenched stigma against single mothers that was fuelled on the airwaves. 'It was fodder for talkback radio,' she recalled. 'Bashing single mothers for "ripping off the system", being "a drain on the state", perpetuating the myth that some women have children just to get welfare. That was the environment I was working in. So it was firmly in my brain.'

A single mother herself and intent on 'proving them wrong' – the very beast she was inadvertently feeding – Jane said that she ran herself into the ground working to make a better life for her daughter, 'determined to not take welfare or child support'. As co-host of the number one FM breakfast show in her city at the time (incidentally, she was earning a fifth of the salary of one of her male co-hosts), she would sometimes take her infant daughter to work at 3.30 a.m. It meant leaving her child to sleep on the couch when Jane was on air, while simultaneously using her platform to smash the stereotype.

'It was part of my job to talk on air about my life, to be what's called "relatable"', said Jane. 'I talked about being a single mum, which helped break down the stigma. I would share snippets of my life, like "I fell asleep in my daughter's gymnastics – with dribble running out of my mouth – because I was so tired from coming in here." I hoped to normalise it. I was a trailblazer.' She would also take her daughter along to do promotions in shopping centres. 'My colleagues would roll their eyes. It was awkward. I felt complicated. But part of me was thinking, *Stuff you*.'

Despite Jane's efforts, the stereotype of the welfare-sapping single mum persists, especially in relation to young mums, who are often dismissed as not up for the job.

Jasmine was eighteen and single when she had her son, who is now almost two, a decision people around her branded as 'reckless'. 'People make comments like, "Did your parents teach him that?", assuming that, because I live at home, my parents are raising him when that's not the case. That really hurt. And it made me question myself as a mother. I didn't want my parents to do anything because I feel like, because I had him, I have to prove I can do it.'

From Jasmine's perspective, the cliché of the bludging young single mum is unmuted: 'That we sleep around, that we palm our kids off, that we're on Centrelink to spend the money on ourselves. None of it's true. I don't think I've met one young mum that's like that. And I've met a lot of young mums in the last two years.'

'There's not enough focus on single mothers who are success-fully navigating the system, showing a different side to being single mothers,' said divorce coach and family lawyer, Prudence Henschke. 'There's still a perception – all the negative connotations of being a single mother – that they're trying to get what they can out of the system and they're keeping fathers from spending time with their children. It's completely the opposite. Both in coaching and wearing my lawyer's hat, most women are focused on the children's best interests and, where possible, having a meaningful relationship with their other parent.'

Blessedly, the typecasting of the helpless single mother in popular culture is being phased out for heroines such as Erin Brockovich and Andy's mum in *Toy Story* (who appears to be raising Andy and his baby sister, Molly, on her own, their father inconsequential to the plot). A raft of contemporary TV shows star sassy, life-claiming single mothers, including Sarah Jessica Parker in *Divorce*, Christina Applegate as a widow in *Dead to Me*, Katherine Ryan in *The Duchess* (which she created, loosely based on her own life), and single-mum-by-choice Martha, played by Leah Vandenberg, in the Australian comedy series *The Letdown*.

With the number of single-parent families on the rise – the vast majority of these headed by women – the backstory to how a woman wound up as a single mother is becoming increasingly irrelevant. Single mothers are diverse – culturally, economically, by age, income level. No matter what their relationship status is, or whether they conceived their child via donor sperm, hook up, adoption or surrogate, or their partner has died, leaving them to raise their kids on their own, the sole thing that binds single mothers is not a chronicle of misfortune and lament, but of trying to do the best – and be the best – for our children. Whatever it takes.

SINGLE MOTHER WISDOM

- Even though the perception of single mothers has shifted somewhat in recent decades, a stigma still lingers. It's less overt, but it's there.

- People can be unduly harsh on single mothers, judging them on everything from their children's manners to the state of their school uniforms.

- Happily, the cliché of the lonely, struggling single mum is undergoing an overhaul that is reflected in popular culture, with women raising kids on their own depicted as empowered, capable and embracing their circumstances.

- Treat people the way we teach our kids to treat others: be inclusive, kind and non-judgemental. Women who are raising children on their own – whether by choice or circumstances beyond their control – don't need pity, but respect.

- With the number of single-parent families on the rise, the one binding theme is that these women are determined to create the best life for their kids.

CHAPTER 4

The Loneliness of Single Motherhood

On Sunday mornings when the boys are with their dad, the disquiet often sets in even before I wake up. Quite possibly it's what wakes me. *It's Sunday*, I realise as I come to. My mind then does a speedy inventory: *Are the boys here? No, that's right, it's a 'dad weekend'. So it's just me.* Well, that's something – as much as I miss them and would prefer they were around and I don't want my children away from me at all, at least I only have to think of me.

On 'mum weekends', I'm up and at 'em, all bouncy and exuberant, pancakes for breakfast, Spotify bopping in the background, games to play, places to be. The kid in me comes out: lighthearted, vibrant and creative with a ready laugh, seeking out the next impromptu adventure with my boys. But beneath the cheerleading bravado lurks another equally admissible part of me: my fear that I'm not enough for my kids. Because I'm not enough for myself. When it's just me, I don't have to pull myself together for anyone, so sometimes I don't. I'm no longer sure who I am when my kids aren't here to remind me.

Other single mum friends assured me at the start that I would come to relish this 'time to myself'. Coupled friends told me they were envious. But I'm still not sold. 'Me time' is overrated when it's enforced on you by circumstance. What I frequently feel is lonely. And it's exacerbated on Sundays.

Sunday is sold to us as 'family day', packed with barbecues and beach cricket and succulent roasts around jovial dining tables, which makes you feel like more of an anomaly when your own life doesn't in any way resemble the brochure. For single parents, Sunday can be the loneliest day of the week.

Monday to Friday can easily slip by unnoticed. It's the business end of the week with work to be done, a worthy excuse to account for our time. We're alone for legitimate reasons or with designated work colleagues who pass as company. Alone time is sanctioned, expected and rare. Saturdays are back-to-back with kids' sport, haircuts or grocery shopping – getting stuff done. But come Sunday, in the suburb where we live anyway, the trapdoors go up on the free-standing homes with garden frontages. Spinifex practically rolls down the street as two-parents-plus-kids households shut up shop, together, and single-parent families are left to fend for themselves.

When my boys aren't with me – when it's not a 'mum weekend' – I'm often at a loss. Most of my friends are with their own families. 'What I would give for a weekend to myself,' they say. Maybe they'd be up for just one weekend. But, I assure them, the novelty wears off when it's every second weekend for the rest of your life.

In her 'divorce memoir', *Falling Apart in One Piece*, Stacy Morrison said that she felt 'trapped by weekends' after she and her husband separated and she was at home with her toddler son. 'I dreaded Friday nights, which set me apart from the rest of the world,' she wrote, and she struggled to fill the single mother emptiness, to find who she was before she was married: 'On weeknights I was busy with work; on weekends I was busy with nothing.'

For the first few months of my daunting new reality of my kids out of the house every other weekend, I wandered aimlessly around our apartment, sitting on their bedroom floor and crying a bit. I left their toys where they were last discarded as if preserving my boys' playful presence, kidding myself they'd be bursting through that front door at any moment to pick up where they left off. I was glad I worked Saturday nights to give me something to look forward to.

Boredom is not the issue. There's always stuff to do. The issue is filling the days so that the subterranean layers of my fear don't have the capacity to rise up and confront me – the fear that I'm alone, that I'm all I've got. Given enough of a window, I will go there. I strive to ward off loneliness, to distract myself from its foreboding might.

This unease is not necessarily solved with company. Loneliness is different to being alone. Solitude can be a gift, but to be lonely is to be convinced of your disconnection to the world, so much so that it courses through your bloodstream, that rising panic of not matter-ing to anyone. It's an affliction not just reserved for the elderly or those living alone, it is also very much a single mother malady.

How Single Mothers Experience Loneliness

There's nothing formulaic about what might trigger loneliness for single mums. It can strike without warning or linger like a dense, impenetrable fog. There's the stark contrasting loneliness familiar to separated and divorced mothers who go from one extreme to the other – from being constantly needed to rattling around an empty house. Widows and single mothers by choice are affronted by a dis-tinct kind of loneliness: the burden of being the only grown-up in the family, without a minute to catch their breath.

'When my kids aren't with me, the loneliness is chronic, it knocks me for six,' said Lara. 'Days go past without speaking to another person. If something happened to me, no one would know until the kids came home on Sunday night. It messes with your head. You hear women say they're lonely in their marriage. Maybe so but at least there's another person in the house.'

'I thought I was lonely in my marriage, but being on your own is a different level of loneliness,' said Katia, a divorced mum of two. 'I feel it in my heart. It's triggered by being at a park and seeing a mum and dad with their child. I'm like, *Wouldn't that be nice to have a partner to do the mundane stuff with?* I did little things to heal the hurts like going to a park with a friend instead of on my own. I noticed what triggered the lonely feelings and I rectified it.'

'Any single mum who doesn't say they're lonely is full of shit,' said Skylar. 'You're on your own all the time. Even when you're looking after children there's no other adult to speak to.'

'Giving birth on your own is the most lonely thing a woman can do,' said Tina Clarke, who had both of her babies on her own to different donors. 'The first one was an emergency caesar after seventeen hours of labour, which was so tough without a partner there. When I held the girls for the first time I was deliriously happy but, still, I couldn't quite believe I was on my own.'

'It's hard to go out as a single parent when your child is small,' reflected Zoe. 'You don't have the money for a babysitter, nor do you necessarily want to get one, so it became Netflix and refill for me. It's very lonely.'

'I hate it when the kids aren't with me,' said Jo Abi. 'I think I want a break then they're gone and I feel so sad. It's like a rubber band between you and your kids. When they leave it's tense then when they come back, all that tension is gone. The early days I would smell their pillows until my mum told me I wasn't allowed to do that anymore. I go to my family for dinner or out with friends, but my heart's not in it. Getting out of the house is important. If you stay home, it's like you're in a place where the kids are meant to be and they're not.'

'It hits me when they first leave and the silence is deafening,' said Louisa, who only sees her boys intermittently. 'When they're with you there's this vibrant scene with sounds and motion, you're watching the clock, then it's silent. It rocks you. What gets me through is remembering it's not about quantity but quality. I think about my kids when they're with their other mother. And I look forward to having them back again and we can have fun and grow together.'

Other Lonely Moments

For many single mothers, the struggle isn't so much in the logistics. If we apply ourselves, we can all get dinner on the table by seven (or a bit after), school uniforms ironed (or not), spelling lists learned (or at least attempted). We find time to read a story, plan a birthday party, process our kids' worries, catch up on paid work after they're in bed and so on. Bring it on! But what we can't do is make up for what's missing: having no other witness to our children's lives. In an article for *The Guardian*, 'How hard is it to raise a kid on your own? Where do I begin . . .', British columnist Sophie Heawood expressed this perfectly. 'The hardest bit isn't having nobody to share the burden. It's having no one to share the love.'

That's when I feel it most, the strain of single motherhood. When Jasper, at eight, told me that 'endorphins are like a search and rescue mission to take me back to where I belong' and I wished I wasn't the only one to hear this profound piece of wisdom. When Otis sketched Van Gogh's *Man With a Pipe* and the attention to detail moved me to tears. When they stake out the apartment in full SWAT regalia and I can only laugh to myself. Or compose a rap song and I'm the only one in the audience. Merit awards at school, books coming to life as they learn to read, writing proof-of-life notes to Santa and the tooth fairy (aka 'Tooth Dude'). I'm the sole witness. But therein also lies the privilege of single motherhood: that we get to be in the box seat.

'I feel lonely when having to make important decisions myself, especially about the kids or household finances,' said Kelly, a widow with two young children. 'I feel lonely when I'm driving because Ant was the one who did all the driving with me in the passenger seat and the kids in the back. The sheer weight of responsibility makes me feel lonely, everything falling on my shoulders.'

'I feel it at night after I put my daughter to bed and there's no one to share a conversation with about the day, to celebrate her and share any concerns,' said Francesca. 'I also feel it on weekends when I might want time to myself for my mind to rest, but I can't because it's just me.'

'Loneliness for me is staying in with nothing to do, which is not my choice. I've been let down, stood up, disappointed by people,' said Lauren Miller, a divorced mother to a young son. 'My mind would go to, *Is anyone going to love me?* All that damaging, internal dialogue. But you're never really alone because you have a child who's dependent on you for their entire universe, in my case. Emotionally, morally, financially it's provided by me. Before I met my new partner, where I arrived at (with emotional breakdowns and heartbreaks in between) is that I can be alone, I might always be alone, and that's okay.'

Kylie Camps, a single mum of twins and founder of The Kind Parenting Company, said there's nothing like a sick child to make you realise you're alone. 'One of my boys was experiencing an asthma attack that resulted in an overnight stay in hospital,' she said. 'Not having another parent to look after my other son meant I had to take both boys with me. Being in the ER at midnight exhausted and waiting for beds, one unwell child and another just along for the ride, felt really lonely.' Kylie believes that, at the very least, we all need to feel 'seen'. 'Parenting can feel like a thankless task and having a partner among the chaos provides a sense of connection and camaraderie that you just can't create on your own,' she said.

'But there are ways to feel seen, like spending time with friends with kids to share the happy and hard times.'

Single mums often turn to their own mothers for companionship. I got chatting to a single mother with two kids under three at the park one day. 'I couldn't do it without my mum,' she told me as she breastfed her baby, while her mum wrangled a toddler.

'You will become married to your mother,' wrote Sophie Heawood. 'Your lack of interest in settling down young and making a marriage work like she did, in being normal in the suburbs, will lead, in the greatest irony of all, to you becoming dependent on the loving support you will find in her normal married life in the suburbs.'

Yael, a divorced mother of two, is aware of the tenuousness of this connection with her own mother: 'I worry I'm a little too invested in my mum. We're very close and I worry terribly about when she's not there anymore because without her, I'll feel very alone. It panics me, being an empty nester when the kids are older and move out, with no parents and no partner.'

'Loneliness is going to the supermarket and crying in the aisles because you don't have your kids,' said Inez. 'There's something about the supermarket. That family-size box of cereal, happy family on the front. I hated going to the shops. I'd sometimes go to my friend's house and cook dinner for her kids just to be around company. I'd call friends but everyone's busy with their own families and I'm crying on the phone. You've got to plan ahead so you're not at home going, *I'm missing the kids.*'

But Inez admits that being organised isn't easy when you're on a downward spiral. 'It's okay when you're in a good frame of mind, but it's really hard to plan things when you're depressed, then it keeps going because you haven't arranged anything. So you're sitting around feeling alone. You have to keep on top of it.'

Kylie Camps recommends scheduling 'coping strategies' for the times of the day you find the most difficult. 'I really struggled between

5 and 7 p.m. because for almost six years, this was the time when I was busy making dinner, overseeing baths and getting the kids sorted for bed,' she said. 'To not have that, the silence felt overwhelming and heartbreaking. I found it helpful to plan things for that time, like a long walk with a girlfriend or an audiobook or even doing the groceries or taking a book to a cafe, anything to make it more bearable. At first it was about surviving but I've come to look forward to these times.'

I, too, have learned from experience about the need to be prepared for my children's absences. The first few times my boys went away with their dad, I was bereft. I'm all for them going. It's imperative that kids have time with both parents and share experiences – in most cases, if that's the family set-up – but it doesn't mean it's not hard on the parent who's left behind. I would walk my boys to the car then go back inside to cry and it would take me a few hours to recover. It's about delineating between the two worlds you forever inhabit as a single co-parent: the one where you are constantly 'on' as a mother, and the one where you have to switch off to save your sanity.

Now I have a strategy. I arrange to see friends, go for bushwalks and do the occasional yoga class. I declutter, do my tax, meditate, read. I take my time. And, where possible, I get away.

One school holidays, I was presented with a golden opportunity for the ultimate distraction from my absent children: writing a story about the Kamalaya Wellness Sanctuary on the Thai island of Koh Samui. The world I momentarily inhabited on this rocky clifftop (meditating, yoga-ing and chanting), with its comforting blanket of humidity, was so at odds with the world I'd left behind (my empty apartment in the grip of a dull Sydney winter) that it was the optimum salve to any childless loneliness. This may have been a one-off, but it showed me that turning my attention inwards is the antidote to the perception that there's something missing. And I don't need to go to Thailand for that.

And . . . They're Back!

As soon as our kids are back with us, we're required to shift gears. I spend the time apart from my boys fortifying myself against longing, building defences, oscillating between keeping occupied and falling apart. I go about my days as if it's only me as that's more palatable than being aware that anything is amiss. When they come home, careering through the door, it takes me a moment to recalibrate. I have to brace myself for the dramatic change of pace. It's like living in a parallel universe. My inclination is to hold them tight, stroking their hair and kissing their faces, making up for lost time (my lost time, not theirs). But I'm careful not to smother them, to transfer my pining onto them, which is too big a burden for them to carry. It's a fine line to tread. As single mothers, we must be mindful not to lean on our kids for human interaction when there's no one else to fill the gap.

'In the back of your head you think you'll re-partner,' said Sally. 'Then weeks turn into months, and then years. You realise you fill a huge void in your life with your kids and what they're doing – sport, ballet, taking the dog for a walk. Even your mental space all day long is thinking about them.'

Sally admits that she has also relied on her kids for physical contact. 'When they're little you're getting a lot of that physicality and emotional connection,' she said. 'They invariably get into bed with you or you fall asleep in their bed reading a book. You've always got this little body next to you. As they get older, you're not getting that anymore and that's when the loneliness starts to kick in. My daughter has pulled back in puberty. She's awkward about cuddling. And you suddenly realise, *My God, the human touch. What am I going to do when they're not around?*'

Lonely but Not Alone

Even on a 'mum weekend', loneliness can linger. I feel like a cruise activities director, rolling out nonstop snacks, entertainment and emotional support, all without an assistant. The trepidation of a whole weekend stretches out before me, as well as the pressure to meet the persistent demands of 'What are we doing today?' with no other adult to help rally the troops. I must be resourceful, inventive and vigilant. The need to constantly occupy my kids can accentuate my latent unease of what's 'missing' in our lives, triggering my feelings of inadequacy for not being able to provide them with a solid family unit.

Of course, we could just hang out and not do much. But as my boys get older, their appetite for a packed itinerary sends me into overdrive. I scramble to fill our days, frantically working to come up with options, trying not to panic when there's a clean slate. Staying in isn't an option with two raucous young boys in a small apartment, worlds away from the home I walked out on with its rambling garden, slippery slide and trampoline. As the boys' child psychologist remarked when I shared my frustration at them playing soccer inside, the ball pinging off the couch, the lamp and sometimes the TV, 'Boys don't do walls.'

Against my own non-sporty inclination, I've enrolled my boys in soccer and rugby (they've tried both) in the winters. As well as giving them exercise and somewhere to kick a ball other than our lounge room, I appreciate the structure of having a place to be on a Saturday morning. But for many single mothers, Saturday sport is hard work.

'I'm bored of always being by myself at sport,' said Tina, a solo mum. 'Lots of married people are by themselves but they tag team. One comes one week, one the next. I'm the only one who's always there, week in, week out. It's relentless.'

Summer is easier, because we can go to the beach. It's got all the elements: sunshine, play and exercise. Still, it's confronting. It's not so much the worry of kids drowning (although that's always there with a one to two adult–child ratio) or the sand-filled car (although that's annoying). It's all the nuclear families who get to chill out and enjoy the day as one parent takes the kids boogie-boarding and the other sits on the beach with the young ones building sandcastles and splashing gaily about. I'm delighted for them all. And I realise that it's not always as it seems. But it's a reminder that I can't offer all that to my boys. I'm usually to be found at the shoreline, straining my neck to make out their bobbing heads to ensure they're still afloat. I'm the lone advocate for the non-negotiability of sunscreen and why they can't have yet another ice cream, coaxing them to help lug seaside paraphernalia to the car when the sun is high and I've said it's time to leave.

However, on the days when I get in the water myself, my boys swim towards me, and they latch on. They're lighter in water, the only place I can still lift them both, swinging them around like copter rotors. I teach them to duck waves and we ride them in together, skidding onto the wet sand and going again. It's impossible to be lonely with a set of waves barrelling towards you.

When Invitations Come

A good Sunday is one when we have a plan – perhaps an invitation to a barbecue or to swim in someone's pool, whiling away the day as it morphs into early dinner, feeling welcome and included, part of a bigger something.

In those moments, even though it's not our home we're in, I feel like I'm doing life right. I'm giving my boys access to fun and normalcy and, not lost on me, healthy interaction with coupled families. They get to experience what it's like to have more than one parent around, even if just for an afternoon. Not so they'll think it's a better way to be or wish this is how it was in their home, but so they get a taste of the relaxed vibe of multiple adults and a sea of kids. It's a contrast to the often-frazzled watchfulness of a solo parent who can never risk dropping the ball. It also takes the weight off me. For that one day, entertainment and company are taken care of, for me and my kids.

This is the perfect scenario for single mothers. Only we're often powerless to make it happen. For this to eventuate we're relying on the goodwill of others who might have the foresight to extend an invitation. When you live in a small apartment with no other adult, replicating such collective frivolity seems like an unobtainable dream.

Christmas, Easter and Other Significant Days

As single mothers, it's easy to feel that high-stakes festivities like Christmas and Easter are for other people. Whatever your religion or traditions, celebration days are generally geared towards families – the regular kind.

Spending Christmas apart from my kids was never part of the plan. But, as for many single parents, that's how it is every second year. It's only fair . . . on the kids. But it means one parent misses out. And it can be gut-wrenching. Billed as the happiest day of the year, for many single parents Christmas is anything but.

'There's a huge hole in your heart where your kids usually sit,' said Inez, who spends at least part of every Christmas alone, sharing custody of her two kids with their two dads. The one year she didn't have her children with her at all she spent with her mother. 'I was so out of sorts I spent the day in tears.'

'The first Christmas I had to give my kids away, I sat on the couch and bawled my eyes out,' said Sally. 'I organised for my family to come to my house, so I kept busy. But I felt so alone.'

'The thought of not having my son for a week over Christmas crushed me to my core,' said Lauren. 'It triggered a complete emotional meltdown, for me not him.'

The festive season tends to be just as demanding for solo mothers, having to deliver the Christmas cheer on their own. 'I find Christmas really stressful because I've got to buy all the presents and wrap them, I've got to drag the tree out and decorate it,' said Lara. 'I feel so much pressure to give the kids a good time. They're all excited and all I want to say is, "Can we just not do Christmas this year?" Christmas is like a work overload.'

Christmas can also be a stark reminder of the change in the family, as it is for Kelly, a widow. 'We've only had one Christmas without Ant and I really struggled through it,' she said. 'Everyone was sad and missing him while doing their best to be "up and about" for the kids. My kids are lucky to have several cousins they're very close to so they eased the pain a lot. But with Christmas and other special days, the pain is still very raw.'

'The thought of Christmas can hit single parents hard,' explained family mediator Gloria Hawke, who reports a noticeable spike in business at this time of year. 'Christmas represents family and togetherness. For most people, it's very sad to imagine not waking up with their children on Christmas morning.' I defer Christmas on my 'off years' and do a 'take two' on the whole affair when my boys get home. I'm selling it as one of the few perks of having two homes: two Christmases and double the presents.

While it's imperative to prioritise the kids, it's important for parents to be happy, too. Or at least appear to be. According to Gloria, as children get older they're often empathetic to their parents' feelings, adding pressure on the 'non-Christmas parent' to put on a happy face. 'You don't want them to feel responsible for your happiness,' she said. 'Reassure them you're okay so they don't feel guilty about being with the other parent. Be the adult.'

That part I can do. But as each 'off year' gets closer and I'm still not sure what to do with myself on Christmas Day, I get edgy. I'm grateful for the invitations from other families. But spending the day with other people's children and not your own can exacerbate your sense of displacement. I'm tempted to skip off to a meditation retreat to avoid the whole thing, but they're often booked out months in advance, presumably with others fleeing the feel-good pressure. One year I rostered myself on to serve Christmas breakfast to the homeless at the Wayside Chapel. Tellingly, there's a waitlist for that, too. I've worked out that the best thing we can do is to take a deep breath and treat Christmas Day like any other day, even though it's anything but.

Easter is traditionally a time for family, too. But, largely for the sake of self-preservation, I have found that it's easier to let it slip by without much fanfare. For kids, it's just about the chocolate, really. Stage a chocolate egg hunt and you're good to go.

The Gifts of Loneliness

Through occasional bouts of forlornness – chronic at times – and despite the outside 'evidence' of a roll call of friends and family, I have doubted my validity and considered if my existence is of any consequence to anyone but my children (until they eventually catch on, too). This train of thought seems highly rational when you're in the thick of it. Loneliness is not a head thing, it's visceral. When it takes hold, it's paralysing terror and dread, draining away any sense of purpose, and no manner of talking yourself around will stop it.

I was lonely because I had allowed myself to interpret the shift in my life – to being a single mother to two young children – as a deficiency. I viewed being without my boys, or even sometimes with them, through the lens of something missing. I was attempting to cancel out the gripping pain brought about by this seclusion and being unsure where I fit into the world. The impulse is to shun such discomfort, to distract ourselves however we can. I have come to learn that loneliness is not to be shied away from, but an invitation to see what matters beyond the confines of others' expectations.

'We give up believing that being able to escape our loneliness is going to bring any lasting happiness or joy or sense of wellbeing or courage or strength,' wrote Pema Chödrön in her seminal book, *When Things Fall Apart*, a book a friend gave me when things fell apart in my world. Chödrön advises that we make 'friends with our jumpiness and dread, doing the same old thing a billion times with awareness' and then, 'without our even noticing, something begins to shift. We can just be lonely with no alternatives, content to be right here with the mood and texture of what's happening.'

In the fifteen years since her marriage ended, and a decade since she ended the relationship with her second child's father, Katia has also come to see the benefit of time alone. 'I lost who I was in my relationships and gave up too much of myself, which made me lonely. I now embrace being alone. It gives you time to learn and grow. I've learned to honour myself. I focused on growing my business, I've done a lot of inner work. I've created a life that I love. It's only taken me ten years,' she laughed.

Julia Hasche, founder of the Single Mother Survival Guide website and podcast, teaches her followers that loneliness is a mindset that we have the power to change. 'I'm always trying to drum into women that loneliness is a feeling and feelings come from thoughts. So you have to try to rewire your thinking to, *I'm not lonely, I'm independent. I'm enjoying some time on my own to recoup, get my life back together, work on new goals.* Then you don't feel as lonely.'

Too much loneliness can be detrimental to your health and wellbeing. By giving into it I noticed I had become a little lost and a little less myself, disembodied from the extroverted, people-loving person I had thought myself to be. When I did get out among other people,

I forgot how to be, either talking way too much in an awkward attempt to not give the game away, or retreating – appearing otherwise occupied – in case I drew attention to myself or said the 'wrong' thing. For a time, I lost the knack of fitting in.

But loneliness can also do wonders, if we allow it. It's a chance to free ourselves from the old perceptions that brought us to where we are. I've been desperately lonely in relationships, but there it's easy to hide, attributing my pain to the person who's denying me their attention and care. As a single mother, there's nowhere else to look but within.

Loneliness has softened me, fuelling my empathy to the pain of others. It's sparked curiosity, sending me on a mission to uncap the deeper causes of my persistent narrative of rejection and abandonment. It's led me to rely on myself, to find out what I'm capable of. You have no choice in that when you think you're all there is.

'Loneliness is harrowing,' reflected Lara. 'But the only way through it is to feel it and when you come out the other side you've learned more about yourself and it's totally worth it.' If we can manage that, if we can embrace loneliness, we get better acquainted with ourselves and content with our own company. As spiritual teacher Eckhart Tolle put it, 'Through acceptance, one can say loneliness transforms into solitude. Solitude means being alone, and it's quite beautiful being alone.'

Being alone is worlds apart from being lonely. Gretchen Rubin, author of *The Happiness Project*, explained the distinction perfectly: 'Loneliness feels draining, distracting, and upsetting; desired solitude feels peaceful, creative, restorative.' Being a single parent gives us the perfect *excuse* to be alone, to gift ourselves solitude without feeling obligated or pressured to join in.

'I spent years before having my kid always feeling bad for saying no,' said Shakti. 'There's something liberating for me about not having to go to everything now.' Shakti said that her yoga practice helps, too.

'I get on the mat and I feel whole. I don't feel loneliness. I feel connected. I don't need anything from anyone else. That's a beautiful result of the practice.'

'Every night when I put the kids to bed, I lie there and ask myself, *Am I good?*' said Joy. '*I'm here on my own. Am I okay?* And so far I am. I never feel like I want someone else there with me. I don't want anybody else to talk to me once my kids have gone to bed. I'm good.'

I'm good, too. It doesn't mean I don't wish some things were different, that I hadn't had to scramble for connection or talk myself around into acceptance. But being alone no longer rattles my core like it used to. I have been brought to my knees by the fear that I'm of no consequence. Yet, I'm still here and I'm better than before because I now understand that loneliness, if welcomed, can be a conduit to expansion.

SINGLE MOTHER WISDOM

- Loneliness is unavoidable as a single mother, whether you're a co-parent or a solo parent. It can be confronting, but it can also be a gift.

- Although you may not have another adult to share things with – the highs, lows and burdens of raising children – it allows for a more intense relationship with your kids. You get to be a huge part of your children's lives, with no distractions.

- It helps to be proactive and plan ahead to mitigate loneliness when the kids are with their other parent. Have something lined up – a visit with a friend, a yoga class or arrange to work – so you're not at a loss.

- It can be just as lonely when the kids are with you, but loneliness is a mindset and it's up to you to shift your perspective.

- Christmas can be especially fraught for single mothers – all that pressure to be happy! It helps to focus on the kids – whatever brings them happiness and preserves their innocence is what matters most. Change the date, if you have to.

- If you can sink into loneliness instead of running away from it, it's an invitation for valuable self-reflection, an opportunity to go within and discover who you are beyond the confines of others' expectations.

CHAPTER 5

Keeping It Together (or Not)

The shower, I have found, is the best place to cry. It's a practical arrangement, the only opportunity for guaranteed solitude and taking advantage of a rare window to contemplate anything left undealt with after a day that's swallowed by the needs of others. It's safe in there where the kids can't hear.

I've always done my best to shield my children from my so-called negative emotions, worried it might unnerve them to see their mother, their touchstone of equilibrium and reassurance, undone. If I need to cry, and there has been need, I cry alone, swiftly eradicating all signs with a tissue and a ready smile. 'Show me your LEGO police car,' I trill as if nothing is amiss.

And yet I encourage my boys to cry. At seven, Jasper prided himself on never crying at school. 'Because I'm a big boy,' he said. I drew a breath when he told me this, sensing a pivotal point in the development of his child brain. 'Crying is good,' I insisted. 'It gets the sadness out. Never hold back tears.' While I do just that.

What might it do for them to see that I am not, after all, invincible? To see that this woman who looks like she's holding it together isn't really, not always? And if I'm losing the plot, what hope is there for my kids?

Then my father died. And there was no way I could schedule my grief. I got on with things, the way you do as a parent to a seven- and five-year-old: readers and homework, meltdowns and meals, reassurance and my attempts at a constant upbeat presence. But still it came, the tears forcing their way out, the realisation that one parent was actually gone hitting me like a fresh shock at unforeseen and inopportune moments, with an intensity impossible to stifle.

My boys, to my surprise, didn't seem too alarmed by my sorrow. They appeared by my side when I was hiding out in the bedroom, discreetly weeping. 'It's okay, mummies get sad, too, sometimes,' I reassured them, smiling through my tears, drawing them close.

'Don't be sad, Mummy, 'cause Grandad is coming back as a baby,' Jasper said, imparting wisdom of the ages, his tiny arm stretched around my shoulders. 'Think about love instead. Think about all the people who love you.' And he reeled off a heartening list.

And I realised that in censoring my grief for my young boys, not only had I underestimated them and their inordinate capacity for processing a gamut of emotions by presenting them with my one-dimensional self, I had been doing them a disservice. By airbrushing what it means to be human, I ran the risk of leading them to believe that unhappiness is a concept only. It's one thing to tell my children it's okay to cry. It's another to show them how it's done.

My mother was a tower of strength most of my childhood. With six kids to raise, she needed to be on her game. Given all she was dealing with, it's quite miraculous that she didn't lose it more often. I do vividly recall the few times I saw her shed tears as that's when I witnessed her vulnerability. When her own mother died when I was eleven, I came across Mum crying softly on the couch. I wasn't unnerved by that vision. Rather, I was moved. I nestled in behind her and brushed her hair and let her be sad. I was quite comfortable with my mother's raw emotion as that's when she felt most real.

Lara, whose kids have seen her cry exactly once, reasons she can't risk her children witnessing her distress. 'It was such a shock for them that they've never forgotten,' she said. 'It shakes the foundation of their world. Part of protecting your children is shielding them from your own problems. It makes them feel sad and insecure.' Lara's aware that she's repeating the pattern of her own childhood, as she was also raised by a stoic single mother. 'I only saw my own mother cry once, and god knows she had reason to. It absolutely devastated me. Now I know what she went through and I understand how unhappy she must have been. But my memory of her as a child is a fun, cheerful, loving mother who in my eyes was bulletproof.'

Author Suzanne Daniel, also raised by a single mother, found great comfort in her mother's ability to protect her and her siblings from 'adult concerns'. 'I never looked upon my mother as anything other than brimming with capability,' she said with clear adoration for her mum, Colleen, who died several years ago. 'She was so upbeat and positive. Somehow she managed to convey that the separation from our father was part of her story and it wasn't going to deny us of a loving home and secure childhood.'

But that was the seventies. The school of thought now is that parents are wise to let their children into their emotional complexities a little. If we present as indestructible, who will teach our kids about the capacity for struggle when their time inevitably comes?

Showing Emotion to Our Kids

In leaning into our own pain, we fuel our children's empathy to the pain of others. We encourage them to feel by feeling ourselves. Rather than keeping a lid on our sadness, we teach them how to lean into it and emerge unscathed. We owe that to our children, says social researcher Brené Brown, whose groundbreaking work on vulnerability and shame is shifting the way we view these 'less desirable' states. In her famous TED Talk, 'The Power of Vulnerability', Brown said it's imperative that we 'let ourselves be seen, deeply seen, vulnerably seen'. She said that our job is not to protect our children or to keep them perfect. 'Our job is to look and say, "You know what? You're imperfect, and you're wired for struggle, but you are worthy of love and belonging."'

'We need to show emotions in front of our children,' parenting educator Maggie Dent told me. 'By being authentic with our emotions, it's the only way to learn how to manage them, and it's how our children learn that it's a normal part of being human. Emotions aren't good or bad, they just are.'

Maggie also believes that what we model can have a profound impact. 'Sometimes I would cry in front of my boys, and sometimes I would cry at night because I thought there could be too many tears. There's grief 'cause your world is reshaping. Then when my dad died, my boys saw me experience a different form of grief. They would make me cups of tea and give me hugs and just let me be, but they were also getting comfortable around sadness. When we're honest and real about emotions, we're letting them be honest and real with emotions, too, which will serve them in their own relationships.'

'There was one time after separation where I'd found out a heap of things. I was just devastated by it and I cried in front of my son,' said Lauren. 'I said, "Mummy's just a bit upset." I'm not afraid to cry in front of him because he's autistic so he needs to learn appropriate reactions. He needs to learn that everybody goes through emotions, then you come out the other side.'

'I didn't try and hide my suffering, but I also didn't want to frighten them,' said Neve, a mother of three sons who also lost her young daughter. 'Children get worried if they see their grown-up unhinged. That's terrifying. So I didn't try to hide my pain but I'd do my howling in the car or I'd go bushwalking or in bed after they were asleep. One night, I didn't think I was being noisy but, one by one, they ended up coming in and it was so sad. When your children are comforting you, that's heartbreaking.'

Neve said she could see that her family's collective grief at the breakdown of the family unit was a vital – if completely unwelcome – life lesson in resilience. 'I didn't pretend everything was fine, that I was fine,' she said. 'I said to them, "We're in the shit. I'm not going to pretend we're not. We're up to our neck in it. But we're not going to lie down and roll around in it. We're going to keep moving forward because one day we'll realise that we've been moving through the shit and it's down to our armpits then it's down to our hips then it'll just be lapping around our ankles." A bit later when I was much stronger one of my boys said, "You're further ahead than me." And I said, "Yeah, I am. I'm not gonna leave you behind, but I'm not gonna lie down with you." I want them to see that you don't have to stay stuck. It might take a while but you have to keep trying.'

'I could have fallen apart but I didn't,' said Jess about the time when she first separated from her husband and she was raising their eighteen-month-old son on her own. 'The only thing that kept me going sometimes was looking at him and thinking, "It's not about me." That gives you strength. The resulting person I am when I don't let negative stuff affect me is a much better example to my son. I want him to not worry about me but admire me.'

Neen, a single mother of three after her husband's suicide, tried to keep her emotions in check for her children's sake. 'I had to put on a brave face and keep it together until the kids were in bed, then I'd shut the door and spend a lot of the night crying. Or when they left for school I could fall apart. But I showed no signs of it to my children because if I went down, they went down.'

Kelly, also a widow, said she doesn't try to conceal her deep grief: 'I'm conscious of the effect my mood has on the mood and wellbeing of the kids, so I try to shield them a little, but not too much. I want to encourage them to know it's okay to be sad. We work hard to keep moving forward through life and to take the sadness with us. We don't need to get rid of it or run away from it.'

Controlling the Narrative

It's not just our emotions we have to manage in front of our kids as a single parent, but also our narrative – the inevitable inquiries they raise about everything from their living arrangements to why their family looks this way. Along with the emotionally charged and complex litany of issues we're already dealing with, it's a lot to take on.

'My youngest used to say, "When I'm with you, I miss Dad, and when I'm with Dad, I miss you,"' said Stella. 'To me, that's the most heartbreaking part of single parenting. My kids used to worry that I'm lonely. I'd say, "I'm not lonely. I've got the cat."' When she told her kids that she and their father were separating, one ran for the hills and didn't return for several hours. 'Mostly they were embarrassed,' Stella said. 'They were worried what their friends would think. There's no right way to handle it.'

Maybe Stella has a point. But writer Jo Abi believes there's certainly a *wrong* way to handle it, as she did when she left home with her three kids, informing them after the ship had already sailed. 'I couldn't have made a bigger mess of telling my children their dad and I were getting divorced if I'd tried,' she wrote in an article for *9Honey*, one that was shared thousands of times (suggesting her botched job is all too familiar). 'I told them in the car, all of them huddled together, just blurting it out with little thought for their individual needs. It was so, so bad . . . I said something along the lines of, "Mummy is going to live in a different place to Daddy from now on. I'm so sorry ... This is where we are going to live now. It has a pool! Wanna see?"

'It was like a bad movie with no soundtrack,' Jo told me, three years on. 'My daughter was hysterical because she thought it meant she'd never see her dad again. Once I'd answered all their questions about pets and wi-fi and said they'd be seeing their dad every week, it was like someone flicked a switch. They ran inside to check out our new place. I look back and go, "How badly did I stuff that up?" But we laugh about it now because the kids realise how much better our lives are, and I hold out hope they won't show any permanent damage from my decision.'

Women who have babies on their own, like Bek, get to decide how to narrate the story of how their family came to be. 'From when he was about three, I have explained to my son, "I wanted a baby and to make a baby, you need a girl part and a boy part. As I only had the girl part, the doctor found a really nice man to provide the boy part and the doctor then put the boy part and the girl part together to make you." I know he'll want to know more as he gets older and I'll elaborate then, but I'm being honest and upfront from the beginning and starting to sow the seeds in a simple way he will understand.'

My desire to 'write' the story for my boys is one of the reasons I was keen to leave home before they were old enough to remember – that us three, together in a new house, and them returning to their dad in their old house every second weekend might be all they've ever known, their new world order. When they started asking questions (exactly what I'd dreaded), I would stick to the script from the separated parents' playbook: that Mum and Dad get on better when they're not living together. Two happy homes are better than one unhappy home. And, bonus, you get two Christmases!

'You've got one job,' I say to my boys. 'It's to be a kid.' It's a line their child psychologist suggested I say to them and I roll it out often. When they come to me angry and confused about being pulled between two houses, I kneel before them and look them in the eyes so they won't miss this. 'What's your job?' I ask. 'To be a kid,' they chorus. And I watch their shoulders drop in relief, with the 'permission' to sink into their innocence and the reassurance that I'm the one in charge, and I've got this. My intention is to model strength. It's vital that they see this in me, too – steadfastness and constancy – aside from the occasional overwhelm and just getting by.

One day, five-year-old Otis presented to me with a swollen eye, blackening already despite its freshness, the result of an accidental collision with a cousin while chasing a ball. Yet, to my dismay, he didn't shed a single tear. He told me later that he cried out of sight, hiding in the bushes, because 'big boys don't cry'. I took him in both arms and insisted that they do. That the best men cry. So do women, just like his mummy is doing right now, for the little boy who equates greatness with stoicism, not helped by me crying in the shower.

SINGLE MOTHER WISDOM

- It's important to show a range of emotions in front of our kids because that's how they learn that all emotions are valid.

- Parenting educator Maggie Dent says that striking a balance is important – too much sadness from a parent might be overwhelming for kids, but it's healthy for us to model vulnerability. Children learn empathy that way and understand that being vulnerable is part of being human.

- By being open with our kids about the way we're feeling, we're giving them permission to be authentic with their own emotions.

- As single mothers, it often falls on us to control the narrative around our circumstances to help our children come to terms with it. It's a lot of pressure, but the more content we are with the life we're leading, the more we will pass that on to our kids.

CHAPTER 6

Learning to Suffer Properly

I was sitting cross-legged before a monk in a room carved out of a cave, offloading my woes. There was more than enough time. I had signed up for the 'Embracing Change' program at the Kamalaya Wellness Sanctuary in Koh Samui, Thailand, for the purposes of a story, and hopefully to find more purpose for myself. I was there for five whole days without children, work or any distraction. Even mobile phones were contraband.

My monk, Rajesh (who's technically no longer a monk, but a Life Enhancement Mentor assigned to guide me through whatever change I was attempting to embrace), told me that the trick to ease suffering is to suffer. The only way out is through: this is the path to rapid renewal. 'If you're going to suffer, suffer properly,' he told me. I started to wish I'd chosen the detox program instead.

Rajesh went on to teach me 'the art of suffering properly'. I took notes. I needed to, because this concept was new to me. Like most of us, I was, in Rajesh's words, 'adept at the game of avoidance of pain and suffering'. But to run, he warned, keeps us stuck in spiralling patterns of desperation and hopelessness.

In short, the art is this: when emotional pain arises, go within. Stay in the discomfort and wait for it to dissolve. Which, I'm assured, it will. If we allow ourselves to really feel it, the bodily sensation, at least, will dissipate rapidly – 90 seconds, tops. It doesn't mean the pain won't resurface – always driven by our thoughts – but the 'energy' passes through quicker when we don't resist.

'You may not be responsible for causing the pain,' Rajesh said soothingly. 'But be responsible for ending it.'

Although this was a novelty to me, it's a movement, of sorts. Leaning into pain is something wise people have practised for eons, while the rest of us have been too busy avoiding pain to notice. We're taught these days to think positively, to haul ourselves out of darkness before it takes hold, to sweep it under the carpet, distract and deflect, anything to make it go away. But most spiritual masters prescribe a healthy dose of wallowing (that's my word – they tend to call it 'awareness' or 'presence') to get to the other side.

No matter which guru you turn to, there's no escaping this central theme of struggle as a gateway to personal growth. In *A New Earth*, spiritual teacher Eckhart Tolle writes, 'The truth is that you need to say yes to suffering before you can transcend it.'

'One of the essential requirements for true spiritual growth and deep personal transformation is coming to peace with pain,' writes Michael A. Singer in *The Untethered Soul*.

'To stay with that shakiness – to stay with a broken heart, with a rumbling stomach, with the feeling of hopelessness and wanting to get revenge – that is the path of true awakening,' writes Pema Chödrön in *When Things Fall Apart*.

In her book *A Return to Love*, Marianne Williamson writes, in a chapter fittingly titled 'Hell', 'A certain amount of desperation is usually necessary before we're ready for God.'

Another master sufferer is author Glennon Doyle, who has mined deep despair for personal elevation, urging her readers to welcome doom as their greatest teacher. 'Pain knocks on everyone's door. If we are wise, we will greet it and say, *Come in, sit down, and don't leave until you've taught me what I need to know*,' she wrote in 'The Important Lesson You Can Learn from Heartbreak', an article that featured in Oprah's *O Magazine*. 'I've learned that when I run from pain, I bypass transformation,' she concluded.

Only, transformation is the last thing on our minds when we're in survival mode, the default setting for many single parents. We usually got here in the first place following the calamitous life upheaval that is separation, divorce or death of a spouse. Those who have had children without a partner invariably face their own unique challenges. Many – but not all, of course – have arrived at the place of acceptance of having a child on their own after letting go of the ideal of doing so with someone else.

Suffering, according to Rajesh, comes in many forms: emotional pain, struggle, overwhelm, hopelessness, envy, vengefulness, grief. No one can escape suffering. It sweeps in, often in tiny, barely there but consistent ripples, and then, without warning, gargantuan waves that threaten to knock you over, despite your toes gripping on to the shifting sand. Left unattended, suffering will send you tumbling.

Suffering as a Single Mum

There are endless occasions for freaking out when you're raising kids on your own. Aside from the day-to-day pressure of managing it all – getting nutritious food on the table every night, bolting to Officeworks before closing time with kids in tow to print pictures of Uluru for the project that your seven-year-old just informed you was due yesterday, mediating disputes over LEGO while mopping the kitchen floor, cleaning calcified toothpaste off the bathroom sink, responding to birthday party invitations, sending invitations for birthday parties, organising birthday parties, piling the kids in the car to head to the service station for milk for breakfast, rehearsing 'Macavity: The Mystery Cat' poem several times the night before the recital, and making crucial daily decisions that fall solely on your head, all while doing your own paid work (often late at night) – there are the constant curve balls.

The pressure can get way more intense than that, of course. These are real-life examples of situations faced by single mothers I've met:

- Not having enough money for rent due the next day and no idea how to get it
- Legal bills coming in for tens of thousands of dollars when she can't even afford a washing machine
- Trying to compensate for the dad who took his life
- Being dragged through the Family Court for years with no end in sight; if she walks away, she walks away with nothing – except legal bills
- Kids caught in the crossfire of their parents' dysfunction
- A child unable to sleep at night because she's miserable at school but her mother doesn't have autonomy to move her
- Spending all day in a soulless courtroom trying to get a fair deal for her kids, then racing straight off to school pick-up with open arms and a ready smile as if nothing is amiss
- Unable to work because she has a child with autism, whose father won't allow her to visit because it doesn't suit his new girlfriend
- Hiding out in a women's shelter with her two kids under two with no idea where she'll go the next week, let alone for the rest of their lives.

In my role as an ambassador for the Barnardo's Mother of the Year campaign, I met some of the most phenomenal mothers in the country. It's hardly a coincidence that a great bulk of the finalists were single mothers being applauded for their heroic efforts raising children by themselves – their own kids and, in many cases, foster kids as well – in the face of extreme adversity. Karina Elliot is a single mother of three who's been deaf since she was a toddler; not only does she homeschool her kids, but she has also taught them Auslan so they can communicate with her. As if she didn't have enough on her plate, she also welcomed a deaf foster child into the family. She told me, with a wry smile, that being deaf gives her a stronger connection with her kids as 'they're forced to look me in the eye'.

Noelene Lever was widowed at 37. She raised her five kids as a single mother and fostered more than 50 others, sleeping on the couch to give them all a bed and working three jobs to make ends meet. 'To give love costs nothing,' she told me. At 79, when she was nominated for Mother of the Year, she said she still sleeps with the phone by her bed in case any of her 'babies' need her.

On top of all that there are the more existential crises of dreams veering off course, heartbreak, loneliness and fear of the future, and it's one punishing road ahead. No wonder that, for single mothers, meltdowns are par for the course.

'I learned to cry in the car,' said Zoe, speaking of when she first separated from her husband. 'I'd use the time from leaving work to picking my son up from school to do my crying. You'd hold it together at work – totally fine, "See ya, guys" – then get in the car and cry. I'd put my son to bed then I'd slide down the wall. You learn to cry quietly.'

'At my worst, I was absolutely paralysed, crying every day,' said Inez. 'Not just over the breakup, but a protracted argument about money and custody. You're crying uncontrollably and your toddler is getting you tissues. I wasn't able to cook dinner, going into my bedroom and closing the door at five o'clock 'cause I couldn't cope. I didn't attempt suicide, but one day I was like, *I just want to jump off the cliff.*

Or driving along the highway and seeing a truck come towards you and closing your eyes and wanting to swerve into it. That thought crossed my mind so many times when I was at my worst.'

Neen said that she did her best to keep things tracking normally for her three children after their father took his own life. 'I wanted them to see that I could drive a car again, make a meal again, that I could take them on holiday and I could do everything that Dad did. That I was okay and had both roles covered.' But eighteen months later, Neen said she 'broke apart'. 'I got in my car and I was looking for a way to drive into Sydney Harbour because I knew in my current shape I was incapable of solo parenting three children who themselves were in a lot of pain. Then I pulled off the side of the road and had that moment of clarity. I asked myself, *What's the choice?* And the choice was I've got to rebuild me so I can do this. I had to go deep. I had to face the pain.'

'I don't think it serves anyone to dodge pain. It has to be gone through,' said Neve, a single mother to three boys, who is all too familiar with suffering after her three-year-old daughter died suddenly. Several years later she was blindsided when her husband called from a 'becoming your authentic self' weekend to confess he'd been unfaithful for a good part of their marriage. 'That's profound trauma,' she said. 'The truth is that the shock, trauma and grief of it outstripped that of losing a child. Losing a child is deep grief, but it's pretty straightforward grief. It's not crazy making. It's just sad. There's a big hole but eventually you figure out a way to live with a hole. They've gone, but there's no doubt that there was so much love, and the love never goes. But betrayal is mind fuckery of the highest order. It turns reality on its head. You come adrift from your moorings. There's wave after wave of fresh shock. As you begin to realise the length and breadth of the lies, memories are poisoned and your self-esteem is shredded. It's death of a thousand cuts.'

Facing the Pain

I had endured nothing like the pain that many women had been through. But I was suffering in my own way. Just not properly, it turns out.

My suffering was erratic and immature. I was adept at hiding it – mostly behind closed doors – but it was pointless and undirected, the kind that perpetuates, rather than airlifting me out. I cried, I journalled, I ranted to friends. Occasionally, when alone, I slammed a door or stamped my feet like a four-year-old, gripping my hair, cursing the turn of events that had brought me here. I lamented, I blamed, I looked outward, attempting to distract myself from my anguish but really just keeping myself stuck. I cried out for it to stop. 'I can't take this anymore!' I wailed at the moon. Yes, I did. I was caught in a circle of pain that had no outlet, so it kept dishing itself up as if I'd asked for more. I wasn't going *through* it. I was lodged firmly in it.

My torment was nothing to do with the demise of the relationship. I had ended that for good reason and grieved the vision of a united family long before that. Any despondency was largely driven by the overwhelm of being so responsible for two precious lives. Of having to make so many decisions alone, leaving me feeling constantly exposed and vulnerable, perpetually at risk of getting it wrong. It's hard to be a parent by yourself, appeasing one child over a disappointment with a friend while the other one's demanding snacks and the house looks like a bomb's gone off, or helping one with his reader while the other one needs his hair de-liced and the pasta sauce needs stirring.

In the early days after leaving home, I had gently explained the lay of the land to my boys: it's not possible for me to do everything at once and they'd have to cut me some slack. But, by their very nature, kids struggle to comprehend anything other than the immediate meeting of their needs. I tried to schedule 'special time' with each of them. But even that brought fallout, with the other one left to his own devices. 'You've forgotten about me,' said one of my boys after I spent time chatting with his brother one afternoon after school. 'You think I'm strong but I'm not really.'

One night, when my youngest was seven, I left him in the bathroom to dry himself so I could bolt to the kitchen to whip the lasagne out of the oven before it burned. I came back to find him standing there, wrapped in his towel. I knelt on the tiles and took him in my arms. 'What is it, my darling?' I asked.

'You don't dry my hair anymore because you have too much to do,' he said softly, burying his head on my shoulder. I vowed to myself that I would dry my boys' hair until the day they no longer wanted me to.

That's what causes me to suffer – that I can't be all things for my boys. And the guilt of being the one who brought this upon us all.

My suffering was taking up just as much time and energy as my to-do list and it was impinging on my ability to be fully present with my children. I was up for learning how to find a way out. Rajesh – the Indian ex-banker ex-monk turned spiritual mentor – might have the map.

The Art of Suffering

On day four of Embracing Change, it was time to learn to suffer. I sat on the floor opposite Rajesh in the cave room at Kamalaya, cross-legged and all ears.

'So,' he smiled knowingly, a twinkle in his eye, 'I will now tell you the art of suffering properly.'

Rajesh took me through five simple steps. I diligently logged them in my notebook, giving me easy accessibility for future use.

1. Recognise that you are suffering. This isn't as easy as it sounds. If we live our lives in denial, as so many of us do, we may not actually notice anything is amiss. The misaligned state we're in has become habitual.

2. Turn your attention inwards to the place of silence where there are no thoughts. This is also not easy because the overwhelming pull at this point is to go anywhere but within. We're tempted to blame others, berate ourselves or spiral down into the past for which we attribute our current malaise. When thoughts arise, return to the inner stillness instead.

3. Catch your 'escape routes' – those things we do to distract ourselves, such as scrolling Facebook, bingeing Netflix, offloading to friends, drinking. Notice the temptation to go down those paths and resist them all.

4. When you can sit with your pain without adding meaning to it, observe that it dissolves automatically. If the discomfort persists (if it's 'too heavy'), take some deep breaths to help it pass through your body.

5. At the end of this current round of suffering, ask what meaning you gave to that incident. Under no circumstances should you pose that question earlier or it becomes another 'escape route'. It's not the circumstance itself that causes our suffering but our thoughts about it. When we ruminate and analyse through the prism of our layered perspective (which is never objective), it keeps us wedged in a perpetual cycle of drama and misery. 'Analysis is paralysis,' Rajesh cautioned.

Taking this route removes the 'emotional charge' of the incident without dragging in the thick layers of other past hurts as fuel for the never-ending story.

'When you're in pain, please be in pain,' Rajesh said. 'Focus on the pain and try to heal it instead of blaming others. The other person is not relevant. If you do this for six months,' Rajesh assured me, 'the whole focus of your life will change.'

How to Embrace Pain

I've since tried Rajesh's technique many times – there are plenty of 'opportunities' with all that comes at you as a single parent – and it's not easy. But, in a way it actually is.

A few months after my lesson in suffering, I received an upsetting phone call. I was pulled straight out of the present as if by centrifugal force and thrown into a spin. My heart started racing, my hands actually shook and I was tempted to roll onto the floor, sink into child's pose and sob. And stay there. Instead, I remembered Rajesh and I whipped out my notebook to remind myself how to suffer properly.

Step one, note that I'm suffering. I could do that one. I stayed put, sitting on my bed, closed my eyes and breathed. 'This is pain,' I said to myself. I wasn't sure if I was doing it quite right but it was all I had. I figured it would get me further than my default position of rage and recrimination.

I turned my attention inwards – step two. I located the discomfort in my body (solar plexus) and focused on that instead. And I took deep breaths. It took all my might – as if I was about to scale a sheer cliff face. I was tempted to give up. I'd have preferred to get straight on the phone to a friend to reel in support, sympathy and validation for my righteousness.

That was me looking for an 'escape route'. At least I was aware of it – step three. Okay, so I wasn't going to call anyone (big step) but I itched to check Instagram (another escape route). If the phone was out, then at least I could look to the past, scouring the recesses of my mind for evidence of all the times in my life when I had felt this way: powerless and victimised. Instead, I forced myself to stay the course.

Back to the pain. *It's not working*, I thought. Undeniable suffering was still reigning supreme. I kept breathing, slowly and deliberately, just for the exercise. And then, ever so gradually, I felt lighter. The intensity had eased. Dare I say that was step four – pain dissolving?

I no longer felt tempted to call anyone, which not only saved me (and them) time and energy, it proved to me that I had improved my state. The charge has dissipated. It didn't change my circumstances – no miracles there. But there was less chance of me being heavily laden with a thorny, epic, tangential storyline that would divert my attention from the ultimate task at hand: to alleviate my suffering. And ultimately to break a pattern.

Only then did I risk attempting step five, to circle back and look at the meaning I gave the incident: that nothing good was happening in my life. That I was doing it all wrong. Had I indulged that old story at the time, it would have sent me under.

'One of the essential requirements for true spiritual growth and deep personal transformation is coming to peace with pain,' writes Michael A. Singer in *The Untethered Soul*. 'Even though you may not actually like the feelings of inner disturbance, you must be able to sit quietly inside and face them if you want to see where they come from.'

It's not the thing itself that 'disturbs' us, but rather our reaction to it. We get to decide whether we experience fear or freedom. That's almost impossible to understand when we're in the throes of it. But having followed Rajesh's process a few times now – having successfully embraced pain – I know I can do it again. I suspect it'll be my life's work.

How to Compartmentalise

We run from pain because we fear it will take over. When I feel rocked, everything else comes to a standstill as I dedicate all my energy to crashing. My mind is a blank, reserved only for obsessing over whatever is causing my distress, angling for a way to make it go away, or to make it not my fault.

But it's possible to suffer and also to live well. I have watched other women deal with calamitous life events while still managing to focus on other things, and I've seen how it's done. They don't let the calamity be the only thing. They compartmentalise.

Lisa and her husband separated after sixteen years together and nine years of marriage. A few months later he was dead. While processing her own profound shock and grief, Lisa was forced to 'go into mum mode' and break the news to her three children one Sunday morning. They were due to fly to Bali two days later for Lisa's fortieth birthday, the kids' first overseas holiday. Despite the turmoil she and her family were in – suffering greatly – she decided to press ahead to, as she put it, 'go somewhere and just be'.

'The gift of that holiday was that my kids and I learned that grief and joy can coexist,' Lisa said. 'We could go to a water park and have cheeks that hurt from laughing so much. And their dad died. I was so present with my children. Sometimes I'd sit on the sun lounge and cry. Sometimes they cried, too. Kids are really good at feeling their feelings, being in it then moving on. Adults can learn a lot from that.'

Kelly, whose beloved husband, Ant, died suddenly in a road accident, has also leaned into her suffering. 'I haven't shied away from the pain,' she said. 'I've encouraged myself to really be in the moment with it and accept that it's part of the process, rather than trying to squash it or put it in a box in my brain. I also welcome it as it shows that what we had was special and irreplaceable and I often remind myself that it's better to have loved and lost than never loved at all. I draw a lot on gratitude to buffer the pain.'

'We're not taught that suffering is okay,' said Eloise King, who, since becoming a solo parent to a son, has trained as a psychotherapist. 'We're not taught that weakness or negative emotions are okay. We want to bypass them. Don't talk about it, get on with it, put a brave face on. But all we're doing is creating more defences and trapping that suffering in our body. We need to get better at being able to say, "I'm in a lot of pain" or "I'm not coping". We need to reduce the stigma around vulnerability.'

Suffering Is an Opportunity

The gift in suffering properly – in moving towards the pain and not away from it – is that there's an end to it. There's also growth. If we allow ourselves to suffer, that's where we learn who we are. Hardship is often the incentive that we need to delve into the depths of our being, beyond our own PR spin – to stare down those long-buried, darker aspects of ourselves so we can bring them out into the light and move on.

'Numbing is idiotic and doesn't do you any favours in the long run,' said Neve, who has clearly suffered greatly. 'Don't numb, go head on, go through it because if you don't go through it, you're not going to get out the other side. Grief or pain if you actually give yourself to it is a way to learn about yourself and the human experience. It's invaluable.'

Neve's deep dive has included regular counselling and a transformative 'heal your life' retreat. 'It was a temporary step out of my life and the responsibility of being a mother, which operated as a reset button,' she said. 'It was a powerful experience to have with other people all in a terrible place for different reasons. I also put in a lot of hard work reading, listening to podcasts, reflecting. I did the work. It doesn't do itself.'

Neve doesn't recognise herself from the woman she used to be. 'I actually like myself a lot more now. I was quite a diminished person in my marriage, always being knocked off balance. I wasn't surefooted. I have done the most phenomenal amount of growing up between 50 and 53. My mum likes to remind me that after my daughter died, I used to say, "Don't do the what ifs and if onlys." It's achieving the goal of contentment right in the moment, not grieving too much over the past or wishing that the present were different or dwelling on a future you thought you might have.'

Fiona said that her Buddhist practice helped her deal with the overwhelm she once felt as a single mother. 'The first noble truth of Buddhism is that we all suffer,' she explained. 'It helps to recognise that everyone's suffering, including people who seem to have their lives totally together. All of that suffering is created by us wanting things and grasping and having expectations of the way things should be.'

Staring Down Fear

One afternoon after a meditation session at the Kamalaya retreat, I had an experience that was like a heaven-sent metaphor for how to respond in the face of fear. I took myself off for a sunset stroll on the beach. I was feeling quite elated and light in the spirit of all the evolving I'd been doing over the previous few days, ambling without destination or agenda across the white sand into a hot pink striped sky. Suddenly, a rabid pack of dogs came out of nowhere, piercing my solitude. I heard their barking first – incessant and ferocious yapping – then I was surrounded. There were at least five of them, angry and menacing and utterly fearsome, baring their jagged yellow teeth, their eyes as black as the stones on the shoreline. They were so close that their frothy, churned-up saliva was landing in droplets on my bare legs.

Assuming I must have been in their territory, I circled ever so slowly, pivoting gently with my feet on the sand, to make my way back to the safety of the retreat, which now seemed a world away. The dogs pursued stealthily, keeping me circled on all fronts, back along the beach, up a pile of rocks and down the other side, even through shallow water. I knew not to run. If I took off, the dogs would chase me and I would be a goner, torn to shreds on a foreign island, my children left without a mother. Yet to stay might lead to the same outcome.

'What have I ever done to you?' I wanted to shout at them. I saw in them a metaphor for all the people in my past who had ever tried to tear me down. I also saw them as a symbol of my own inner critic, attacking without any cause or justification. Flight, fight or freeze. They were my only choices, but none of the options would actually save me.

Don't look them in the eye, I thought. That handy little survival tip came to me from deep within my memory bank. Or was it look them in the eye? On instinct I went with the first one. I noticed there was a ringleader. He came closest, leading the charge, his teeth centimetres from my thigh. None of my usual reserves – calling a friend or breaking down and crying – could help me here. So, I did the only other thing: I went within. I closed my eyes and stood utterly still.

'God, please help me. What is required of me in this moment?' I asked in my mind. I have often asked that question of God or the universe, but not when it's been life or death. Life or death seemed like the only possible scenarios here. I was in deadset fear, quivering all over. But I knew that if I could override my fear, I could be free. It felt like a test. If I could master this here, I could master it in my actual life.

Then I spoke. Out loud but in a sort of whisper. The words tumbled out of me. 'I'm not afraid of you. I'm here in peace. You cannot hurt me. You cannot stop me. I will keep going no matter what.'

I looked fear in the face (although not literally because I was avoiding eye contact!) and I stared it down. I stared down these rabid mutts – without engaging. And I kept moving forward, tentatively but with obvious intent and quiet determination. One foot in front of the other, not too fast to become a run but fast enough to gain momentum. I didn't try to appease or reason with this barking mad lot. I didn't beg or scream or panic. I simply walked on. I stayed the course.

I chanted as I walked, I prayed, I stayed completely present. And eventually, with the welcoming shores of Kamalaya in sight, I was saved. A man appeared out of the scrub, shouting loudly in Thai and gesticulating at the dogs and, just like that, they retreated, skulking back from the direction they came, resigned and defeated. He was gone, too, and I wondered if he was real. Or if he was the part of my subconscious that knows deep down it's okay – necessary sometimes – to accept help from others. I don't have to handle this on my own.

I know why this encounter happened – I knew even as it happened. It was to demonstrate to me this very timely lesson that when faced with fear, which we are every day to some degree, the only thing to do is to stare it down. To keep going in spite of it. Running or standing still are deathly choices.

When I told Rajesh about the dogs the next day, he smiled, perceptively. Like me, he was wise to the profound lesson in it. 'Self-knowledge is your saviour,' he said. 'You can't expect the world to change or get others to see your perspective. That's outside your circle of influence. But you can be aware of how you react and choose differently. That is where growth happens.'

The Victim Archetype

While I was learning to suffer and face my fears, the next step in my transformation was to pay heed to my role in things. I needed to watch my 'victim archetype'.

Many spiritual teachers – from as far back as Plato and further refined by Swiss psychologist Carl Jung – have believed that we each 'inherit' traits aligned with a series of archetypes. Renowned medical intuitive and author Caroline Myss prescribes that there are four universal archetypes with which we've all been encoded. When we lack self-awareness, our archetype is free to run our lives, commandeering our beliefs, reactions, motivations and perceptions. But when we *suffer properly* and accept the invitation to get real with ourselves, we have the chance to see our archetypes in the cold hard light of day and take back control.

I hated to admit it, but after my children and I moved out of home (and for most of my adult life, really) I had adopted the narrative of the victim archetype. It became my default, perpetuating the story of the 'things people have done to me' and how hard done by I'd been, taken advantage of, bullied at times. Yes, that might have been the case – those things had gone down. And I had a long list of examples to cite to anyone who might listen. But if I was going to give myself any chance of elevating beyond this suffering, I had to own my part in it. I wasn't sure who I would be without a sorry tale to tell. I was subconsciously perpetuating this litany of evidence to keep me stuck in the victim archetype where I had made myself a home, albeit not a very comfortable one.

I sometimes catch myself mid-sentence, spinning a yarn that stars me as the hapless loser, and, in those moments of awareness, I have a choice. I can stop right there and re-tell the story with a more empowering ending. Or I can stop altogether and talk about something else.

There are payoffs in being a victim: you elicit sympathy, support and attention from others. You get to be the centre of attention with a ripper yarn to tell. But at what price? This victim narrative was condemning me to a life of powerlessness, self-pity and defeat. A life of suffering. And I was done.

'Do you want to be right or free?' Rajesh asked me on my last day at the retreat as I sat back in the cave. I had to think about that for a moment. 'To be free you must let go of being right,' he continued.

'There's being right and there's love,' my meditation teacher, Tim Brown, often reminds me. 'Once the elephant has been in the tent, the tent is never the same,' he once told me. By this he meant that when we become aware that there's a choice between being right or love – to suffer or not – we can't go back.

If I can't grasp this concept of how we get to choose our reactions to suffering from the monk or the meditation teacher, my son Otis has me covered. I took him to see *Operation Ouch Live* at the Sydney Opera House – two doctors, who happen to be twin brothers, explain biology and the human body as kids' entertainment. They did a skit demonstrating how the 'reptilian brain' (amygdala) snaps into fear when it perceives a threat, and how the 'thinking brain' (frontal lobe) can override it with reason and a calm mind. Ever since, when Otis sees me freaking out – about anything from trying to get dinner on the table in time or attempting (and failing) to assemble an IKEA table – he says, 'Mummy, remember your frontal lobe.'

It's my call.

Handing It Over

I may not always have suffered properly, but I have suffered. I have spent many nights lying face down on the floor of my bedroom, crying it out. I may not have known it at the time but I was close – oh, so close – to surrender. The line between suffering and surrendering is a fine one.

'Hand it over,' said Wendy, my kinesiologist at the time. She demonstrated for me: elbows bent, arms outstretched in a low 'W', palms turned up to the ceiling, her eyes closed and reverent. 'You have to surrender.'

Wendy has been where I have been. In her early forties, her husband up and left overnight and she found herself a single mother with three teenage kids, a dog and a cat, no access to money and very little hope. 'I lay in bed with the doona over my head for two weeks,' she recalled. 'One night I'd had enough. I sat up, tears streaming down my face, and I said out loud, "Whoever or whatever you are, this is too big for me. I have no idea what to do. Please guide me. Show me how to get through this. Lead the way and I'll follow." I was completely broken. I was also completely open.' There was no great epiphany that night, but Wendy said that from that point on 'life flowed'.

I started doing sessions with Wendy back when I was still in the family home, trying to muster the courage to end that ill-fated arrangement. By helping me tap into my authentic self and peeling back the thick layers of fortification I had piled on over my lifetime, I soon found the fortitude to leave.

Wendy called me one day not long after we had moved into our rental. My boys were running amok, playing soccer indoors, the ball pinging off cupboards and walls, toppling jars of textas and knocking pictures off shelves. It was hot and I was bothered. Wendy didn't often call me. She's a practitioner and we have a professional relationship, but she said she'd been thinking of me and was wondering how we were getting on. I told her I wasn't sure how I'd get through this long summer with all the pressure I was under. 'Hand it over,' she reminded me. 'Right where you are. Just surrender.'

I made a cursory attempt right there and then and I didn't notice a major difference, but I did feel lighter. I decided to keep at it.

Surrendering works best, I find, in the middle of the night. I've had my share of bleak, dark nights of the soul, when the pain is so overwhelming that embracing it isn't an option, the dread so all encompassing that my harried mind can't cut a path through to any semblance of salvation. It's then that I've tried my hand (upturned and elevated) at surrender.

The fear that I might be left destitute with two young children (or, worse, with my two young children only part of the time) and nowhere to live was a general theme even before I left our family home. That daunting scenario hovers sporadically but I'm usually able to bat it away with a meditation and a reality check: I'm okay for money (for now), and have friends and some family who surely wouldn't let it come to that. The very real panic for me lies in being destitute of connection and inclusion, not without a place but without a *sense* of place. It appeared to me – in the distorted reality that is the dead of night – that this was shaping up to be less of a delusion than a 'quite likely' scenario.

My worst night – my absolute rock bottom – was when we had nowhere to go one Easter. It's hard enough for anyone feeling on the outer at the best of times, but it's undeniably exacerbated as a single parent when you already feel like a piece of you is missing.

I got through the day – a friend invited us to the beach with her family – and we had fish and chips while the kids played in the sand and I tried to keep it together, craftily and subtly crying behind my oversized sunglasses. But once we were home and the boys were showered and in bed and their breathing took on the heavy rhythm of child sleep, my reinforcements fell away. I really had no say in it. I climbed into bed despite understanding that sleep was futile. The tears wouldn't stop, cascading down my cheeks and pooling in my ears. I clutched my aching stomach, pinching at it as if that might deflect the deep emotional pain that ripped at my sides and coursed through my whole being, my limbs quivering. Somewhere before dawn, after several hours of this torment and not one ounce of sleep, I wondered if this was what death felt like.

I slid onto the carpet, seeking solace on lower ground. I'm not sure why I went there. It was a gravitational pull, as if my anguish was too heavy for the bed. I started on my knees, an almost subliminal pose from childhood prayers by the side of my bed. But, when I could no longer sustain my own weight, I slumped flat onto the floor, knuckles in a grip, weeping and pummelling the carpet. 'I can't take this, I can't take this,' I cried out loud – I think. Or maybe it was within. It was all a bit of a blur. I was not quite myself, yet I was lucid enough to notice that, this close up, my bedroom was in need of a vacuum and there was a LEGO fireman under the bed.

I wanted to live, that much I knew. My two beautiful boys needed me and that was enough at this point, a pinhole of light in the literal darkness. But in my sleep-deprived, emotionally depleted state of delirious hopelessness, I did contemplate whether checking out might be best for all concerned. I didn't want to die, not at all. But at one point while lying on the floor, gripped by fear and the disorienting disconnect with the primal need of belonging and being wanted, I wasn't so convinced of the point of going on.

Then I remembered Wendy and her upturned palms. With nothing to lose, nowhere further to fall, I decided to give surrendering a whirl. I felt pretty silly at first. Self-conscious, even though there was no earthly witness, beside myself. But I had to do something, and reasoning with myself, trying to talk myself off the precipice, was not doing the trick.

I ceased sobbing just for a minute, unfurled my clenched fists and splayed out my hands. 'Please, God. Please,' I whispered hoarsely. 'This is too big for me. I don't know what to do. I don't know how to feel okay again. Please help me.' I was begging. I'm not sure that was the intended spirit of this exercise, but I was going in hard. Giving it all I had.

I was in full submission, capitulating to whatever guiding force might have the clout to release me from this unbearable turmoil. It wasn't just Easter. It was all the things. The terror that I was untethered to anyone, the fathomless responsibility of raising two children on my own. The frustrating wait to be free of my past, fed up with living in limbo. Admonishing myself for getting into this mess, but not quite regretting it because I have my boys to show for it. The frustration of not having the life I dreamed of or being able to provide a better life for my boys, instead bunkering down in a place outgrown by the three of us, with no discernible way out.

At some point – I don't know what time it was, but there was birdsong – I gave up trying to work it out. I gave up 'efforting'. And I gave in. Nothing obvious happened. No voice from above or angel at my shoulder. But what did happen was that I stopped feeling so desperate. My shaking body settled. My breathing returned to equilibrium and I noticed I was no longer crying. 'Now what?' I asked the ether. No response. All I knew was that I needed to sleep and I understood that I already had the answers. Maybe not at hand, but somewhere deep within. I clambered back up to my bed and fell asleep and that was the greatest – and most-needed – miracle of all.

When I awoke later that morning, I was no more okay about my life, but I wasn't felled by it, either. I hadn't gone over the pain or under it, I had gone through it. I had *suffered properly*. I was woken by one son leaping onto my bed, the other flying into the room wearing a chicken hat and asking if they could have chocolate Easter eggs for breakfast. And, why not? I'd made it through the night and I still had them. I still had love, and wasn't that all I needed?

Making Surrendering a Habit

Since that raw, pivotal night, I've become *au fait* with 'handing it over'. Surrendering has become my superpower.

I used to surrender as a last resort. There's plenty of that when you're a single mother, whether you are your children's only parent or not. There were times when I felt like I'd toppled into Alice's topsy-turvy Wonderland where everything I knew to be true was thrown under scrutiny. I had two choices: crumble or surrender. I crumbled at first. Properly crumbled. I scanned for escape routes and took them: ringing friends, self-flagellating, railing against what is, bingeing *Schitt's Creek*, scoffing Maltesers share packs in one go.

When none of that got me anywhere, I settled for option B: I raised my hands and surrendered. 'God? Are you there?' I whispered, because in those moments, I'm highly doubtful that he/she is. 'I don't know what to do. Please take this from me.'

Sometimes I feel like I'm cheating the system, like I'm meant to suffer (properly) through all this and wear the harsh repercussions for bringing it on via my own poor decisions and unlovableness. To surrender seems to be taking the easy way out, like ducking out a side door before the show's over, before I've paid my dues. But I've come to see – to *know* – that surrender, when I think to attempt it, is a fast track to evolution.

'Surrender is often seen as giving up, as if we've failed,' Wendy said. 'We've got this view that there's this perfect life that you're given if you've done everything right, been good enough or grateful enough. When we don't get it we think we've been denied it so we come at life from a place of lack and unfulfilled desire. The only way back is to surrender our desire and our fear. It takes more effort to hang on than to let go. Just let it go.'

I'm working on it.

Get On the Floor

There's good reason why I'm drawn to the floor on those desolate nights when I can find no earthly solution to the overwhelm. The inclination is to slide off my bed onto the carpet and 'give up'. It's an innate instinct that's not at all considered.

When you're on the floor, you can't go any lower. It's the ultimate act of submissiveness, yielding to a higher power, putting our life in the hands of a force far greater than us, which usually happens when we're backed into a corner and finally face that there's no other option for a reprieve. There's a physiological aspect to prostration, too: lying low places the heart above the head, and it's the heart (not the head) that we need to defer to when all hope seems lost. No wonder so many religions and spiritual traditions have followers on the floor, or on their knees at least.

'Until your knees finally hit the floor, you're just playing at life,' wrote Marianne Williamson in *A Return To Love*. 'The moment of surrender is not when life is over. It's when it begins.'

Elizabeth Gilbert wrote of surrendering on her bathroom floor over the unravelling of her marriage in *Eat, Pray, Love*. 'In times of incredible trial, of eternal darkness, pull out the rug from under you then the floor out from under you and now you're getting close,' she said during a talk to hundreds of women in Sydney. 'It's dark, cold, abandoned fear, until you surrender. That's the paradox of surrender: you've never been so relaxed.'

The Art of Surrender

I surrender often now, no longer saving it for the times when I'm buckled under. Letting go has become part of my daily practice. After my morning meditation, I bow forward and say a little invocation I came up with: 'I surrender to the beauty of this day and all the gifts within.'

I've also written out a surrender prayer written by spiritual teacher and author Gabrielle Bernstein and stuck it on my wardrobe: 'I trust there is a plan far greater than mine.'

You can surrender on the very micro level by letting go of the day-to-day issues that arise and cause you 'suffering': health and car insurance are due at the same time, how to occupy the kids in the school holidays, trying to find a babysitter for Saturday night so you can get to work.

And you can surrender on the macro level – on big stuff such as court cases determining the living arrangements of your kids, or the existential dread of feeling like you've lost your place in the world.

When so much is beyond our control in separation and divorce or the death of a spouse and the general raising of kids on our own, which we're not primed to do, it tends to feel bigger than us. To surrender is to go with the flow. Take the path of least resistance. Put one foot in front of the other. Accept what we can control and let go of what we can't, as prescribed in the oft-quoted Serenity Prayer, a recurring theme on single mothers' online forums, for obvious reasons:

> *God, grant me the serenity to accept the things I cannot change, courage to change the things I can, and wisdom to know the difference.*

Joy believes that surrendering is a strength. 'There's the cliché of being a strong, black woman,' she said. 'But what people perceive as strong is not what actual strength is. My strongest days are when I've been in tears on the floor, not when I'm holding it together. People say, "She's so strong, she'll be fine." No, I'm not. I'm strong because I was on the floor and I'm still here. It's when my kids are in tears and it's just me carrying it all. I fall into bed feeling like I've been battered for the last two hours. That's strength.'

For Shakti, a single mum and yoga teacher, surrendering has become second nature. 'Fear is something to get very comfortable with because it always points me towards things I need to look at,' she said. 'I ask, *What can I control? And what do I have to just frickin' let go of?* That's the dance. At the end of my yoga practice, I go, *Let me feel what surrender is. Let me feel what trust is.* It's like a game. If you surrender little things in a playful way, you've flexed the muscle then, when the terror arises in those big moments I go, *Dude, you've got to surrender.*'

Bronte, a divorced mum to three boys, has formed a lifelong habit of praying 'for everything'. 'The prayer I often say is simple.

"God, this problem is too difficult for me. Can you please handle it? You've gotta take over." That saying, "Let go and let God", that's really helped me.'

'As a Muslim we have a saying, "Let God be the manager of your affairs" because God is the best manager,' said Aisha. 'Islam as a word is derived from Arabic letters "aslama", which means "surrender". Finding peace through surrendering your will to the higher will of the creator of the universe. Putting complete trust in something outside of myself has helped me deal with divorce and the struggle of raising my boys on my own. It's made me who I am today.'

The peace that's left in the backwash of my long nights of reckoning rests, paradoxically, in the realisation that no one is going to rescue me. My suffering can be largely attributed to my incessant scramble for the love and approval of others, for non-conditional inclusion. When I accept that it's just me and only me, I relieve myself of the burden of such unrealistic expectations, and I'm free. To just be.

Trying to make things happen is the hustle of scarcity. My new understanding of the way life works comes at me in a staccato formation of interlinked thoughts: *There's nothing to fear. Love wins. This is an unravelling. I need to dismantle to create. Be grateful for all of it. Be grateful for my boys and their getting of wisdom. I'm breaking the cycle. For me and for them. Be excited.*

If I needed any proof of my own growth, it's in my boys, my ever-evolving consciousness rubbing off on them. 'Three is a triangle. A triangle is the strongest shape, you know,' said Jasper, apropos of nothing, from the back seat of the car one afternoon. It's exactly what I needed to hear.

SINGLE MOTHER WISDOM

- Suffering is unavoidable. But it is possible to *suffer properly.*

- Most of us see emotional pain as a bad thing and attempt to avoid it or distract ourselves from it, but this only creates more of the same. If we can learn to sit with emotional pain, it will eventually dissipate.

- Suffering is a gateway to personal growth, if we allow it.

- It's not circumstances that cause us pain but rather our reaction to them; we get to choose our reaction.

- Instead of suffering, we can surrender. Rather than swimming upstream, we can go with the flow.

- In letting go of what we can't control, the pressure valve is released and we're free to just be.

- Surrendering is a superpower for single mothers.

Part Two:
RESET

'When there's something for you to do
you'll be notified; until then, do nothing.'

ELIZABETH GILBERT,
Business Chicks talk, Sydney, 10 March 2020

CHAPTER 7

The In-between

Almost three years after leaving my home with my two young boys for a better life, I was still stuck in the same 'temporary' apartment and entrenched in a painstakingly drawn-out separation and, from where I sat, there was no end in sight.

'You're in the in-between,' Wendy, my kinesiologist, said to me. She said it like it was a good thing. I didn't see it that way. I called it limbo. Wendy called it a time for growth. 'It's a necessary pause,' she said. 'Unless you pause and be still, you can't see what you're doing or where you're going. You could look at it like it's disastrous, or as an opportunity to return to yourself. It's a choice.'

I felt like I had no choice whatsoever. I was champing at the bit. I wanted to get on with my life, for the sake of my boys if not for myself. As much as I tried to carry on as if we were playing out our actual life, it was all pretend. This didn't feel like the real deal at all. Yet, like many women attempting to extricate themselves from a traditional family structure, I was hampered by forces that were completely beyond my control and I had no idea what it would take to release me from this stranglehold.

I was in reset mode. My meditation teacher, Tim Brown, calls it 'maintenance'. It was a chance to collect my thoughts and recover after the inevitable 'destruction' of the old and before rebuilding and moving into a phase of 'creation'. All phases were as indispensable as each other.

The in-between did serve me. It was a vital lull between the mad rushing, hyper-alertness and dread I'd been living in. Here, there were no major decisions to be made – oh, blessed relief! All that was required of me was to stay still. Not to put my feet up, mind, but to rest in 'awakened awareness', to get comfortable in 'that which is', taking advantage of this rare opportunity to realign, to regain my strength. To grow up.

Most realisations emerge when we're not looking, when we're not obstructing insight with busyness, trying to fill up the space by distracting ourselves. It's why we have epiphanies in the shower. The in-between is a chance for us to contemplate, to integrate all of the knowledge that we've acquired along the way, to breathe and stop trying so hard.

Still, limbo is disconcerting. And our living situation certainly wasn't helping matters. Our move was only ever meant to be a stop-gap, a small rental apartment to catch our breath before shifting to a more fixed address. I had lobbied for a six-month lease. Luckily, I didn't get one.

Our New Home

There was nothing wrong with the new place. In fact, it was quite lovely – freshly renovated with just-laid carpet, egg-white paint barely dry and brand-spanking-new appliances, the plastic film still on the stovetop when we moved in. It had, as they say, a pleasant outlook. You could make out the sea from the balcony over the roof-tops of the grand homes in between.

Yet I had baulked. After applying and being rejected for five apartments (one real estate agent admitting, when pressed, that it was because I was a single mum), you'd think I would have settled for anything. But my resistance had nothing to do with the layout or whether it was close to shops. It was that this was not how the story was supposed to go. To settle in and make this place home felt like a betrayal of my vision. Family breakdown is discombobulating enough without having to deal with starting again. I couldn't quite face the pressure of permanence.

My boys took their cues from me. Jasper made a 'reception' sign for the front door, under the impression that our apartment was a short-stay hotel. He wondered when we were checking out.

It might not have been what I imagined for my life, but it dawned on me that maybe it was what was *required*: the three of us together in one room where we could hear each other breathing while we slept, where my little boys could reach out their still-chubby limbs and feel me to be reassured I was right there, defying the turmoil of their existence. To know that while everything else they'd ever known was pulled out from under them, I'm a constant.

It didn't yet look like an ordinary home with their own beds (although I had paid a deposit on a cool set of bunks) or any of the trappings such as a couch, but none of that mattered because all that mattered was it kept us close. Like we needed to be – me just as much as them.

'I love that when I call you can hear me,' Jasper said. 'When I build LEGO I don't have to look for you to show you.' Yes, that was handy. I was never too far away, providing reassurance not just of proximity but of presence. My job was to draw my boys in close to prove to them that while everything else around them might seem out of whack, I was as solid as a rock.

Setting the Tone

For the first time in too long, I had dominion (as much as you can ever have) over my own territory. Nothing could disturb us there between those four small walls. The one thing I could guarantee was that there would be peace. My boys may not have known that was something they needed. But I knew it for them. That four-roomed apartment was our safe haven. It was also a demarcation, a clear parameter between our old life and the new.

I got to determine the vibe of the place. I set the tone, the emotional temperament, as I might a thermostat. As a single parent, I got to call the shots. I could make promises and keep them – promises of civility, harmony and stability, of a grown-up in charge. I started with the front door. This wasn't just any door, it was a 'magic archway'.

'Our front door is like a portal,' I announced to the boys a few days after we moved in. 'When you walk through it you enter a world where you are safe and loved unconditionally, where people speak kindly to each other ... and if they don't, because sometimes they forget or lose their temper – and that includes (okay, maybe most often *is*) Mummy – we say sorry and start again. Beyond this magic archway we respect each other and look out for each other. I have your back. Always.'

This was the only place in the world where I could promise all that. I couldn't preside over preschool or school or anywhere else. But behind this door, it was on me.

To drive it home, we made a list. It wasn't spontaneous. I had thought about this list even before we moved in, another distinct marker of our new beginning. It would be a set of 'rules', a constitution of sorts, for our reconfigured family. It was imperative that the boys help write it to give them a stake in our collaborative code of conduct – a guiding set of tenets, fundamental yet basic principles on how we were all to behave in this home. In this life.

Here's the list that we came up with together, handwritten by me on a piece of paper:

Be kind to each other.
Look after each other.
Ask about each other's day.
Use nice words.
Do what Mummy asks.
Hands off, feet off, no kicking. (This was inspired by a school rule.)
Take plates into the kitchen after meals.
Pack toys away when you're finished playing.
Put dirty clothes in the laundry basket.

The three of us signed it, even Otis, who had just learned to write his name. Then we stuck it with a magnet on the new stainless steel fridge so we would be reminded every time we got milk.

These were big words. They might seem obvious, standard pre-requisites for any family, but coming from the unpredictability of our previous existence, this simple list signified the heralding in of a new order, one of consistency and intent.

As a single mother I could pretty much ensure that any guiding principles I set could be followed through without interference. I had autonomy over my little family, at least while we were together, one of the great upsides of single parenting.

I had no intention to rule with an iron fist, although gentle discipline was most certainly required and craved. But in creating a framework for mutual regard and responsibility for my boys, it would not only help our household run more smoothly, but also hopefully set them up for life. When they detract from the fridge list, when I remember (and can be bothered), I insist that they walk out that front door – that 'magic archway' – and only come back in when they're back with the program.

They appeared to catch on. When he was in Year 2, Jasper made his own sign for the door. It was an acrostic play on the word 'think', as in 'think before you speak', something he'd learned at school:

Is it true?
Is it helpful?
Is it inspiring?
Is it necessary?
Is it kind?

It became another checklist, one we couldn't miss on our way out every morning.

The Upside of Being in Limbo

It's hard to know what to do with yourself during a hiatus that's not of your choosing. There's no direction or clarity at the crossroads, and you're not sure which way to turn. You're often tormented by uncertainty and ambiguity.

Single mothers often find themselves in this no-man's-land (pun intended) by default, especially when going through divorce or separation. There's interminable waiting while the legal process runs its course or a financial settlement is reached that will afford these women the freedom to move on with their lives.

Single mother support groups on Facebook are full of women crying out for resolution and finality, frustrated to the extreme at being stuck in a perpetual vacuum.

'How do you cope with having to sell the family home and go back to renting? It breaks my heart to think my kids won't have a home to go back to. And to have to rent for the rest of my life.'

'How long does it take to receive the Single Parent Payment? I can't afford the rent and the bills are stacking up.'

'Please tell me things get easier. It's been twelve months since separation. I have the kids one hundred per cent of the time. I feel like I'm hanging by a thread. I just want to enjoy my life but everything is a massive struggle.'

'Back to court again tomorrow. Four years and still going. Wish me luck.'

Widows are waiting, too, for the grief to lift and the overwhelm to subside. 'I love being a mum but I've been feeling lost ever since my child's father died. Time is slipping away,' wrote one mum.

Similarly, single mothers who've had babies on their own rarely skip this mandatory transition period between their old life and the new. There's a sense of waiting for life to begin. Of living for the day 'when . . .'.

What we don't realise is that this deferment is valuable. When we resent it, willing it to be over, we miss it. In that we miss a unique window to disentangle from our old ways and start again, a chance you rarely get when you're on the go. We get to greet the unknown, an uncertain future stretching out before us, by tuning into our innate wisdom because when life's on hold, that can be all we've got left. We get to be in the 'now'.

One day about two years in, frustrated with living in the in-between, I resurrected my yellowed copy of Eckhart Tolle's *The Power of Now*. I had attempted to read it a good decade earlier, but it was lost on me. The very concept of being in the present seemed like some sort of esoteric in-joke I didn't get. Now the underlined passages sank in. When the student is ready, the teacher appears.

'As soon as you honor the present moment, all happiness and struggle dissolve, and life begins to flow with joy and ease,' Tolle wrote. 'When you act out of present-moment awareness, whatever you do becomes imbued with a sense of quality, care, and love – even the most simple action.' When we stop relying on what the future might bring to fulfil us and make us feel whole, we can turn our attention to what is, to what Eckhart calls 'the life underneath your life situation'.

Being in present-moment awareness is a powerful place to be, if we use it gainfully. From the unique vantage point of perspective, we can be fully aware of what brought us to where we are in the first place, so we have less chance of replicating it. We are free to toy with our unmapped futures.

What to Do in the In-Between

When you're living in the in-between, try not to freak out. Trust that this is a vital part of the process of adapting to your new role as a single mother. Here are some of the habits and mindsets I found most useful for mining the 'gifts' of this time.

Journal

Whether it's every day or only when you get to it, offloading pages of unfiltered thoughts is a safe way to process your assumptions and purge your laments, regrets and self-recrimination. Allow it to all spill out of you. If you stick with it, journalling can bring peace of mind and clarity, giving an outlet to the maze of clanging thoughts that swirl around your frenzied mind. Answers begin to emerge on the page as if by magic. When I started journalling during this period, I broke out in a rash on my décolletage, the anger that I had repressed for years seeping out of me. (But don't let that stop you!)

Meditate

I meditated twice a day, without fail. It has been my salve and my salvation. Meditation keeps you present and positive, tapping into the stillness and inner wisdom that lies dormant in all of us. Whether you do a meditation course (like I did) or use a meditation app, it's an imperative tool for times of flux.

Sometimes, although not often enough, I did nothing. I just sat still. That's also essential.

Make Vision Boards

The premise of vision boards is that by focusing on what we desire, it's more likely to come into our orbit. We're drawn to what we think about most (or the theory is that it's drawn to us), so it's in our interests to be specific. And to dream big.

I made vision boards for myself and for my boys, with their input. We sifted through piles of old magazines, ripping out images of things we wanted to attract into our lives, then gluing them onto cardboard. The first thing Otis chose was a bath. It was symbolic. Our home that we left had a bath, our rental apartment didn't. He spent every shower for a good year begging, 'I want a bath.' It wasn't about a bath at all, but was a metaphor for his longing for things to be as they were and it broke my heart that I couldn't deliver – on the bath or the nuclear family. He also chose a ferris wheel and a family huddled around a firepit. Jasper cut out a cruise ship, a ski lift and a house with a pool. And a kitten.

We took the activity lightly, filling a rainy Sunday afternoon. I told my boys that it was all about imagining experiences we'd like to have in our lives, while making the most of the ones we already had – like a wish list. But I knew the power in this exercise, too.

I recently unearthed an old faded vision board that I had made several years earlier, before I became a mother. And there it was – everything had come to be: children (two of them), another book published, fulfilling work and, yes, even the tropical island (not owned, just visited). The house – mid-century – is uncannily like the family home we used to live in. I had been in a relationship (I forgot to specify 'forever'), I had learned to meditate, and forged more enriching friendships.

Now it's back to the drawing board.

Do the Work

When life is at an impasse, it's an ideal time to go within. To 'do the work' to determine what role we have played in bringing us to this point, and bring lifelong patterns and entrenched, limiting beliefs into the light of day. We can do this work ourselves, but it's not easy to see our own blindspots. I recommend therapy and kinesiology as powerful modalities to help you to see yourself.

Be Present

The in-between kept me present with my boys. There was nowhere else to be, so I figured I might as well be here.

I heard other mums talking about their renovations (a rite of passage in our suburb) – passing on recommendations for architects and landscape gardeners, choosing splashbacks and flooring – and entertaining in their shiny refurbished homes. While I would have loved that, too, I consoled myself with thinking of all the time I had to spend with my boys instead of being caught up with tile selection.

We play loads of games. Charades, Monopoly, Cluedo, Battleship, Trouble and there is a deck of Uno cards always at the ready for when we are waiting – for one of the boys to finish their shower, for the rain to stop, for the roast to cook. No matter what is going on outside or how up in the air our future is, nothing can take away from the meaningful moments that we three share on the lounge-room floor.

Children are masters at present-moment awareness. They only know one time and that's right now. It was my boys who taught me how to stay in the now. There is no choice in the matter, really, when I am so needed.

Read

Finding the time to read is a luxury as a single mother (any mother of young kids, for that matter) but, when you do, read books that inspire and uplift and help you to feel seen. I devoured divorce memoirs, mainly, by women who had grown from the ordeal (in no coincidence gifted to me by women who had similarly grown from the ordeal): *Falling Apart in One Piece* by Stacy Morrison, *How to Sleep Alone in a King-Size Bed* by Theo Pauline Nestor, *Split* by Suzanne Finnamore, and *Aftermath* by Rachel Cusk.

Not long after leaving home, I happened across a copy of *Spiritual Divorce* by Debbie Ford, about how to transform the devastation of divorce into an 'enlightenting experience', which turned everything on its head.

Learning to Embrace the In-between

Still now, at nine and ten, the boys splay on the rug with their 'army guys' waging 'war' for hours, or tip out the LEGO boxes and play uninterrupted (apart from regular requests for food) constructing coastguard ships, a TV station with a satellite dish, a hovercraft with Spiderman at the helm. They dress up as policemen and send their remote-control cars hurtling around the apartment, crashing into walls, the more prangs the better.

As my kids get older and more self-reliant, the temptation is there to leave them to it. *Oh good, they're occupied. I can check emails/ mop the kitchen floor/meditate.* And I do all that. But, sometimes, when I 'remember to remember', I remind myself that I'll want this time back one day – that I would do anything to have my little boys at my feet muttering to themselves as they invent stuff – so I get down there with them and I join in. That's how I find myself wearing a 'police' helmet and playing 'air hockey' with a stick (retrieved from a trip to the park) or crouching in my wardrobe while they scatter off to find me in a spirited session of hide-and-seek, or embroiled in an intense foosball tournament, where I'm assigned the team that has the player with the broken leg. I do this because I'm conscious of the speediness of time. And I do it because I want to model for them that life is now, not someday when. Although I'm the one who needs the most reminding.

While my boys are far better at being in the now than I am, it does sometimes fall to me to bring us all back. They ask when we can get a 'real' home, or a cat, or a bath, and it jars with me because this is our home (for now) and I think, *Did I teach them that? That we're in limbo?* I go out of my way to shield them from what's going on. For all intents and purposes, this is our life. So what gives them the idea that we're waiting it out?

Perhaps they've read it in my actions. Perhaps they've noticed that I'm not rebuilding my own life. I've been so caught up raising my boys and protecting their emotional wellbeing, which takes time and energy, recovering from the mammoth change we've all been through, while trying to work and keep house and solve problems, I haven't been all that focused on planning ahead. They'd be right in sensing there might be something else beyond this.

I was existing to 'get out the other side'. But what's the marker of that? And is it possible to move on while in the in-between? I needed to hurry it along.

I turned up to an appointment with Wendy, sighing at the laboriousness of the limbo in which I was stuck. I couldn't get traction. I was in a ceaseless holding pattern and I didn't know how much more I could take. She told me to go into nature and breathe in the green (plenty of it there). And pray. Ask the universe to remove the blocks that were holding me back. Something about staying in one place was working for me, even if I wasn't sure how.

I discovered that I was 'afraid' to move forward because I had a subconscious belief that I wasn't lovable unless I was struggling. Being 'stuck' gave me an excuse for not progressing. I had been invested in keeping this storyline running for fear of who I would be without it.

I told myself I had no choice in the matter, and by the looks of things I didn't. There were forces beyond my control that were holding me back and I was powerless to act. But, if you subscribe to the premise that our thoughts create our reality, as I do, then I had a part to play, too. I needed to address my line of thinking before anything would change.

The in-between might be where we need to be for a spell to catch our breath. But there also comes a time to move on. The wisdom is in being able to tell the difference. And being prepared for change when it comes.

SINGLE MOTHER WISDOM

- Living in the in-between can be frustrating, but it's also necessary to recover and reset, especially after a period of upheaval and change.

- Shift your thinking from being stuck and powerless to seeing the benefits of being in limbo. The in-between is an offering to live in the moment and be present with your kids.

- Try making the most of this time by journalling, meditating regularly, making vision boards (to get specific about your dreams for your life), doing the emotional work that will help bring clarity to your situation, and reading inspirational books and stories about women who have been where you are and have come out the other side.

- Take time to explore the deeper reasons that are keeping you stuck. No matter what our circumstances are, we are always playing a part.

CHAPTER 8

The New Normal

I have never pined for a normal life. In all my imaginings of what life might look like, back when life itself seemed a long way off, it was not domestic bliss I yearned for. The bundled package deal of husband, house and kids wasn't on my wish list. I equated all that with selling out. For me the goal was about broadening my horizons, testing my limits and making my mark. It didn't occur to me that these weren't mutually exclusive. That it was possible to be tethered while keeping things interesting.

Until well into my thirties, I harboured a latent disdain for a conventional existence. Yet, like some ironic told-you-so outcome, I have wound up in a family-friendly suburb where neighbours host barbecues and get the kids together and ambition ends at a happy home, and I catch myself thinking I would quite like that, too.

Most of the coupled mothers I know – including the mums of my children's friends – seem to have it all together. Whether they have demanding careers or are stay-at-home mums running around after a pile of kids, they appear to be governed by the customary compulsions of family life (albeit ones of privilege). They discuss renovations and recipes, have kids for sleepovers and give to chosen charities. They plan ahead for holidays, go on group camping weekends and have guests to stay in designated guestrooms. They're in book clubs, own several handbags and pets, and host lunches with matching cutlery, entertaining other families by their backyard pools. They have, for the most part, intact families. I love them and I admire them but I have trouble comprehending their realities, as if they come from a foreign land where their daily happenings and their air of contentment are completely removed from my own mundane preoccupations.

'I sometimes see myself self-pityingly as the lone divorcee among the snug little familial knots of three and four playing frisbee in every park and heading up to the ski slopes in their Subarus,' wrote author Theo Pauline Nestor in her memoir, *How to Sleep Alone in a King-Size Bed*. I can relate to that. And to author Sophie Heawood, who wrote in her memoir of single motherhood, *The Hungover Games*: 'I began to feel what it is to sit outside the narrative, trying to fit yourself into a fairytale with some of the pages missing.'

I also feel outside the narrative at times. I'm well aware that these suburban tableaux are not standard, nor the ideal, for many families. And that beneath it all things are rarely as enchanting as they seem. But when it's played out in front of the backdrop of these conventional green-lawn surrounds, it fuels my long-held suspicion that I'm not doing life right.

We may start out with alternate intentions but it's near impossible not to be swept along in a linear trajectory of sorts, a preordained pattern of career, partner, house, kids, puppy and regular family holidays. To divert from that path, whether by choice or circumstance, can be disconcerting.

Not being able to offer my kids a traditional family unit heightens the fringe-dweller status I have long held. It's like looking on as the grown-ups keep it together.

I don't covet their lives. I don't regret any of the decisions I've made that have brought me here. But I would like to sail through some more, to not question so much how life works. To not default to the internal assertion that I've got it all wrong. I'd like to be one of those easygoing types that author Sarah Wilson calls 'Life Naturals' in her book, *First, We Make the Beast Beautiful*. Life Naturals are more centred and laidback and don't stop to question everything.

I do question everything, forever seeking. It's exhausting and disconcerting. Yet, as time goes on and I'm now responsible for my two young sons as a single mother, what I'm really searching for are confines, anchor points for my life. In the absence of traditional foundations, we create our own. There is freedom in that, in not being tied to a sanctioned storyline.

Children crave love, stability, time and structure, say the experts. Those I can give. I cast ahead and work backwards, using values as my benchmark, doing my best to embed the lessons I want my boys to learn, their moral compass taking shape before my eyes.

I model habits such as 'thank you' notes, compassion and allowing both perspectives in their daily disputes over who has freehold over the LEGO. I try to show them that we have independence in our own lives. When parameters are hazy, we get to write the script, making it up as we go.

When he was little, Jasper was given a wooden star as a gift from my sister-in-law Lucy. One night before bed, he pulled the star out of its box and made a wish (what's become a loose ritual). 'I wish life was normal,' he said.

'What does a normal life look like?' I asked, my heart ripped inside.

'Like the other kids', with a mum and dad in one house,' he replied without missing a beat.

His brother says it, too. 'I wish life was better,' he once wrote on a sticky note, and he stuck it on the wall above my bed. I didn't sleep well that night.

All I can hope is that my boys will come to see, as I have, that to be 'normal' is not the be all and end all. It's not the only way.

Loving Where We're At

Since becoming a single mother, I've gone out of my way to show my kids that there are many other workable family templates. I bought a copy of author Jessica Shirvington's book, *Just the Way We Are* as soon as we left home and read it to the boys regularly. It features varying family representations including gay dads, foster kids, a single mother by choice and, of course, divorced parents living in two separate homes. Each scenario concludes with the line that our family is perfect, 'just the way we are'.

My boys spotted themselves straight away. 'Hey, that's like us,' they said about Henry and his brother, who live with their mum and spend alternate weekends and part holidays at their dad's place. 'At first I didn't like living in different houses. But now I prefer it this way, because everyone is happy,' says Henry. Several years on, my boys are way past picture books, but they still occasionally pull that book off the shelf and flip to Henry's story. Seeing it on the page validates their own storyline, which they don't see reflected so much in their actual lives.

I need this reminder, too, especially in the ultra-conservative suburb where we live, because 'normality' is in our faces. I sometimes feel like I'm on the outside looking in at perfectly symmetrical family dioramas behind all those picture windows that we drive past on our daily route to school. It's hard not to get swept up in longing for that alternate reality when it's all you see. It's hard not to convince ourselves it's the preferred way to be and that we are somehow missing out. No wonder my kids are wishing on stars.

It rests on me not to try to change anything, because I can't, but to not want to, either. To understand that the life I have created for my two kids and me is not sub-par. We're not 'making do' or pining for something else. Things wouldn't necessarily be better if we were like all those families we know with two parents and puppies and backyards, but we are content 'just the way we are'. I had to get this straight in my own head first because the way I handle it will set the tone for my boys. They will be guided by me.

It was another invitation from my single motherhood journey to grow – to love where we're at instead of acting like something's missing, like we are deficient. It was an invitation for acceptance.

Just because there's no other parent in our house doesn't mean we three are not a family. This is our new normal.

Living with the New Normal

Single mothers may relate to this sense of not doing life the way we're expected to, as we're bombarded with images and examples of what families 'should' look like. But this is just a mindset. It may take some adjusting to living with your 'new normal', depending on how long you've been a single mother and whether or not it was your 'choice'. Other single mothers have boundless wisdom to share about acceptance and not settling for 'ordinary'. Here's how some of them described it to me.

'My daughter found a picture on the internet of three kids, a husband and wife, all smiling and wearing matching white linen shirts,' said Annabel Horsley, a solo mother to three kids. 'She wrote underneath, "This is a proper family. I approve of this image." and stuck it on her bedroom wall. It was confronting for me because I knew I couldn't give her what she wanted. But now she's done a complete 360. Over time she's come to see there are so many definitions of family – through friends she's met at school and what she sees online. She's really proud of me being a single mum and working and doing it on my own.'

'The only thing that makes a family is love,' said Tina. 'I've drilled that into my kids. The other line I say to them is, "Some people have one mum, some have two dads and occasionally some people have a mum and a dad." In our world, that's true.'

'If my kids are having issues with their friends I'll say to them, "Be compassionate because they're at home with a married couple and that's hard work,"' laughed Joy.

'I don't want an ordinary life, I want an extraordinary life, a life less ordinary,' said Danielle Colley, a divorced mum of two. 'I want adventure and passion, I want the marrow of life. Longing for something that was never going to be in the circumstances creates discomfort. You're scared that what you dreamed of is dying, but perhaps something better is waiting for you that you haven't considered yet. Life might not look how we expected but it can look so much better.'

'I sometimes feel left out when school holidays roll around and people are going on family holidays and camping and you're like, *I wouldn't mind being a part of that,*' said Inez. 'Friends are having their twentieth wedding anniversaries and you think, *I'm never going to experience that with either of the fathers of my children.* But you have to change that stereotype of the traditional family. All that stuff you see on Facebook, you have to keep it in perspective. It's never what it seems. I feel pretty balanced. I've got my two kids, and that's our family.'

'Our suburb is nuclear-family central so when my marriage broke up, we were like the freak show because my family looks different to everybody else's,' said Michelle. 'My youngest child was upset because she wanted a "normal family" like her friends. People found our situation confronting because on the outside we looked like the perfect family with a beautiful house and they were shocked it didn't last. I felt like we were characters in a TV show except it was actually our life. But I have lived that fairytale where it all looks fabulous on the outside and I was in despair. That normal life just doesn't exist.'

A high-profile journalist, influencer and single mother to two young children, Phoebe Burgess makes single motherhood look utterly carefree and idyllic in her frequent Instagram posts. But, as she admitted in a profile interview with journalist Angela Mollard for *Stellar* magazine, these images are not reality. Nor is it the life she expected. 'I had an idea about how I wanted them [my children] to grow up and that's not going to happen now,' she confessed. 'But I'm adjusting and I embrace being their mum every day. And if that's being a single mum, then I'll embrace that as well. I'm just trying to make sure they're surrounded by love, regardless of how that family looks.'

Learning to Be Adaptable

Raising kids alone (or at least partially) requires not only a mindset shift but also a total realignment of the family dynamic. You have to be adaptable and bring your children along for the ride. What you soon realise is that, far from this being to their detriment, being raised by a single mother can be the making of them.

'I'm a social person and go out a lot so I would take my daughter with me when she was little,' said Fiona. 'She'd be under the table in her baby capsule, or get passed around. She would come to parties with me and I'd put her to sleep in the bedroom. She became very flexible. She talks to adults, she's very easygoing. This unconventional life has made her who she is.'

Parenting educator Maggie Dent, who was once a single mother to four young boys, said that it's up to us as parents to define what's normal and help our kids adapt. 'One of my sons said, "I did some research in my class and there are more kids who live in two homes than one, so we're actually the normal." I said to my boys, "Your dad will always be your dad. We're just living in two different houses. That's the only shift that's going on." They were very pragmatic and used it to their advantage. They said, "It's really cool. We get two Christmases, two birthdays, two lots of holidays." In their eyes, they doubled up on the good stuff. We have to adapt to our new normals and whatever our new reality is.'

Our kids might not realise it yet, but what they really want is for their parents, single or not, to be happy. They're also benefiting from being raised by one parent. As the constitution of families is ever evolving and single-parent families are becoming unexceptional, they're getting a crash course in invaluable life lessons.

Maggie Dent agrees that being raised by a single mother can do wonders for children. 'Any life experience that's outside of what's considered normal has the opportunity to teach our kids. When I became a solo mum, my boys stepped up and helped out more than they'd done when there were two parents in the house. They'd do the dishwasher or they'd feed the dog without being asked. They grew into an awareness that they were part of this system and they could influence the outcomes of that collective by the choices they made. It gave them a nudge to being more responsible. It wasn't what I had planned for my life, but now that my boys are co-parents, partners and husbands, I see four emotionally healthy men. It certainly hasn't diminished who they are.'

My boys have had to step up, too. I give them a bag each at the supermarket and they call out the items on our list, then – now that they're old enough – they help carry the shopping up the three flights of stairs to our apartment. One packs the dishwasher, the other unpacks (in theory). Some nights, when we're not rushed, I get them to choose a meal for dinner and help me cook. Otis was given a Donna Hay cookbook for his eighth birthday and the boys are working their way through it. They made Chinese dumplings one rainy Saturday night, folding wonton envelopes for the steamer.

They're not quite doing chores without being asked (or being bribed with iPad time), but the awareness is there. I wonder if I would expect this of them if there was another adult around.

'You've been through a lot more than most kids your age,' I remind them when they lament the difficulties of being push-pulled between two homes and all the rest. 'But it's giving you a head start. When you face struggles in life, which you inevitably will, you've already had practice at being strong and resilient and knowing you will come out the other side.'

That's better than any normal.

SINGLE MOTHER WISDOM

- Single mothers are bombarded with images of what a 'normal' family is supposed to look like: two parents and a happy home. But that's just one version, it doesn't mean it's better.

- It's up to us to adjust to our 'new normal'. It's a mindset.

- You get to define your family story; there's freedom in living outside the box.

- The onus is on us to set the tone for our kids, imparting to them the 'gifts' of our family template, including resilience, wisdom and the freedom to create.

- Being raised by a single mother might well be the making of our kids. It will help shape them in ways they would never have experienced if all had gone to plan.

CHAPTER 9

Adventures as a Single Mother

If the hire car had sat nav, I might have been all right. But trying to find my way on the 'wrong' side of the road using the US customary system of intersecting multi-lane freeways in downtown Los Angeles, the only grown-up in the car, without directions or any sense of direction, was no fun at all. I exited several times, taking a punt that it would take us into a friendly neighbourhood, with night falling and two hungry kids in the back, to ask directions. The hand-drawn scrawls I left with from obliging locals in various gas stations only got me so far until I had to go through the whole process again.

I ended up being guided to our hotel over speakerphone by my mate, Wazza, who was in Sydney but lives part time in Los Angeles. He insisted on staying on the line until we made it onto the correct freeway. We eventually pulled into our hotel a good three hours behind schedule. It wasn't quite how I'd imagined our first trip to Disneyland, but when it comes to navigation, one head is not better than two.

I'm an old hand at holidaying alone with my kids. The three of us have been on countless road trips together, including one twelve-hour trip to Byron Bay. I've taken them to Fiji, the Grand Canyon and on the Polar Express near Flagstaff, Arizona, all in the name of travel stories. There have been many adventures closer to home as well. We've been camping just up the road in Pittwater – I erected my first-ever tent by myself after picking it up at Aldi and thinking I had best put it to good use.

I've taken my boys skiing almost every winter since they could walk, which means me lugging three sets of skis to the mountain while negotiating requisite meltdowns over clunky boots and cumbersome helmets. But it's worth it for this: schussing down the slopes together, the boys' arms outstretched like mini aeroplanes as they squeal with the thrill of it.

One summer, I hiked Mount Kosciuszko with a seven- and nine-year-old. I was unprepared, only taking two mini boxes of Smarties to 'bribe' the boys to go the distance. Thirteen kilometres and some six-and-a-half hours later, we made it back down, exhausted and in need of a takeaway pizza. They might have resisted at points – taking it in turns to down tools, slumping on the side of the alpine walkway in protest – but we did it. We climbed the highest mountain in Australia together. We will always have that.

'I don't know how you do it,' people say to me. My answer is simple: 'If I didn't, we wouldn't go.'

Holidaying with children is tricky at the best of times, but the complexities are magnified as a single mother where you're required to be both parents at once: fun mum and disciplinarian, while bearing the huge weight of responsibility for planning, the kids' wellbeing and a truckload of luggage. Travel companies act like we don't exist, the glossy brochures showcasing gleaming nuclear families and proffering neat little packages designed just for them. But we plough on, refusing to let circumstance stifle adventure.

Barbara Bryan is one of those leading the way in solo parent travel. Single mum and founder of Australia's largest single-parent network, Single Parent Australia, and website letsgomum.com.au, Barbara has been travelling alone with her two daughters since they were babies. She admits that it hasn't been without its challenges – negotiating toddler tantrums at boarding gates, ferrying kids up a cliff to catch a Kakadu sunset – but she believes it's worth forging on: 'If you go into a holding pattern of *I'm a single parent, I can't do that anymore*, life will pass you by. You have to push yourself. I would love another pair of hands or another adult to chat to but sitting at home won't improve matters. I used to travel solo before I had kids. It's better than that. It's like having little mates with you.'

Evie Farrell is another single mum who hasn't let her situation hinder her love of travelling. Using money she'd originally saved to renovate her kitchen, Evie and her young daughter Emmie headed off with no fixed destination and no return date. Four years on, they're still on the road. 'There's a certain strength and determination you draw from when travelling as a single parent because you're the only one,' Evie said. 'Everything rests on you. That's the adventure of it. I feel proud of making it happen, doing it together. It's the best thing I've ever done.'

Evie advises taking it slowly, starting with small trips to build your confidence. 'It's worth all the effort,' she said. 'The benefits of travelling and spending blocks of time with your children far outweigh any obstacles or fears about making it happen. I feel like I was just existing before and now I'm really living.'

Regrettably, we can't all take off indefinitely with our kids. And travelling as a single parent isn't always fun and games. Many find it too daunting to be the only grown-up on holiday, preferring to hold off until their kids are older.

'I found it really lonely and hard,' said Lara, who once bailed on a beach holiday early because it all got too much. 'I decided that, while they were young, I wasn't going on another miserable single mother holiday in a strange place with no other adult when I still had to do everything. It added another layer of difficulty and it was so exhausting!'

Lara said things changed when her children became teenagers. 'Now it's heaps of fun. We can have a conversation, listen to music, go to restaurants. We really bond and enjoy each other's company. There's no school or work. We're all available to have fun.'

Of course, we don't have to travel to create fun. It's all about building connections with our children away from the day-to-day demands and distractions, which isn't easy to do when raising kids on your own.

Holidaying with Others

Well-meaning people sometimes suggest you holiday with other families. However, note that they're not offering, and finding people to go with is not as easy as it sounds. Single parents feel like outsiders enough without going in for confirmation and risking rejection.

In her memoir, *Falling Apart in One Piece*, Stacy Morrison described the time she went on a beach vacation 'near friends'. 'I was starved for adult company in a way that my friends weren't,' she wrote. She tried to recruit other friends to join her and her son in their empty beach house to 'buffer myself from that awful feeling of lonely panic'.

I know that feeling. Holidays with other people around are the best – not just company for me, but for the kids. There's something comforting about staying with other families as my boys are absorbed into the happy commotion that they rarely get when it's just us three. Like the times we've stayed at my friend Jade's farm, where there are three kids around the same age as mine. There are fresh eggs to collect, paddocks to roam free in and a mini tractor to ride.

Jade's farmer husband, James, takes my boys for real tractor rides, and all the kids pile into one room for a 'sleepover'. At my friends Marie and Chris's farm, there are poddy lambs, stick forts and leaping into the pool after sundown, the only water as far as the eye can see. Here my kids were educated in the realities of the relentless drought sucking the country dry, leaning on the fence at sunrise and scouring the brooding sky for rain clouds. On one stay with my sister Cait's family in the Southern Highlands, my boys spent hours shovelling dirt for a new vegetable garden, a novelty when you live in the city. My Aunt 'Nanine' and Uncle David had us to stay at their beach house in Western Australia one summer, taking my boys on their first fishing expedition and treating them like they were grandchildren. I felt held as much as my kids did. We have been enveloped into each of these families, and many others, like it was no trouble at all.

One of the best holidays we've had was a ski trip with other friends and their kids. We put the little ones in ski school while the grown-ups headed off to higher climbs. One of the dads carried my boys' skis back to the lodge after we left the slopes, and other mums got them showered (while I was doing an interview for a story). These little things help so much. It makes me think, *Ah, so this is what it's like for regular families who vacation in packs.* By comparison, on another ski trip the previous winter – when I was the sole adult – I had to edge my way down the mountain at a snail's pace with Otis wedged between my knees and Jasper lodged behind me to prevent him picking up pace and losing control. What I would have given for some help on that hill!

We once went 'glamping' (more like camping except with the tent already up) with a bunch of families. A friend pulled it together, commandeering everything from which beach to visit to designated dinners and corralling the kids for roasted s'mores around the campfire. With all the pesky logistics taken care of and no decisions to be made, I could relax and enjoy myself – and my kids. It makes for a different kind of holiday when there are other people around. One you rarely get as a single parent.

As my boys get older, I've pretty much given up seeking out other people to go away with and have come to value instead the scope for unfiltered and uninterrupted time with them that only getting away from it all can bring. Or maybe I'm just over hustling for company.

Rather than waiting around for invitations that may never come, Fiona said that she makes it happen. 'I was always trying to create opportunities to go away with friends when my daughter was younger. I'd keep chipping away 'cause I'd be too lonely otherwise. You have to do that as a single mum. You've got to be proactive but not pushy and not feel hurt that you're making the effort more than the other way around because sometimes people just don't have the bandwidth.'

Ana, a solo parent via a known donor, goes on lots of trips away with her daughter, but admits she prefers to go with someone else – not just for companionship, but for safety. 'I wouldn't travel around with just me and my child,' she said. 'I might go to a hotel and we did go skiing together once when another friend cancelled, but I draw the line at camping. I feel too vulnerable as a woman to take off to some camp site. When someone else is there, if something were to happen to me, there's someone there for my daughter.'

When it comes to finding friends to holiday with, Ana said that you only need one. 'It helps if the kids get on well and you get on with the mother and you like doing the same things. It's like a formula.'

Jess, who has also travelled a lot with her son, advises going on organised tours. 'It can be more expensive but it's safer and you've got instant company – other kids to play with and other adults to talk to,' she said. 'You don't have to stress about anything. Just turn up at the airport and let someone else take care of the rest.'

After countless trips on her own with her three kids, Annabel has found it takes the pressure off not to plan ahead too much, preferring to 'wing it' and let the adventure unfold. 'It can be daunting when you're doing all the planning on your own,' she said. 'I panic if I think too far ahead about logistics. It becomes overwhelming and we'd never go anywhere. So long as I have a basic framework about where we're going then I can let the details fall into place. We just get up and go and once we get there, I'm fine and the kids always have a great time.'

Making Memories

It's not just trip coordination that single parents are forced to negotiate on their own, it's also heightened emotions. And that includes the grown-ups, especially those who are still dealing with the pain of separation or loss of a spouse. Holidays, with all the weight of expectations of unbounded glee and freedom, often exacerbate unresolved grief.

When Neen went on her first trip with her three children after her husband died, she felt responsible for setting the emotional tone, all of them rolling in grief. 'As the only adult, I knew I had to keep it together,' she said. 'It was very emotional. At least one of them was falling apart at any time. I had to stay calm to defuse the situation.'

As demanding as it can be, Neen said that she's determined to keep travelling as a family and 'making memories' while her children still want to. 'I'm showing them that we can do this without their dad. We're one man down but mum's got it covered.'

I know the feeling. I remember driving into a hot pink dawn outside Flagstaff, Arizona, saguaro cactus silhouettes framing our route, my two boys singing in the back as we barrelled into a new day. *I've got this*, I thought. And I do.

Go on Local Adventures

Holidays can be expensive and they're not always easy to pull off. It's not so much the time away that's important, it's venturing beyond the day to day, and there's nothing to stop us doing that in our own backyards. Or beyond.

Before my boys started school, we had Adventure Tuesday once a week. We frequented Taronga Zoo, the Art Gallery of New South Wales, Sydney Aquarium and Banksia Buddies at the Royal Botanic Garden, and we also sought out different scooter parks all over the city. When Jasper started school, Otis and I would have picnics on the 'island' off our local beach. He staked out a special spot and to this day he calls it 'The Mummy and Otis Rock'.

I would have taken my kids on adventures regardless of whether I was alone or not; I see these escapades as one of the points – and the privileges – of childhood. But I wonder how much of my enthusiasm has to do with me as a single mother trying to overcompensate, to pack my boys' lives with colour and distraction. And meaning. Many single mothers feel the same, working overtime to make each day count.

'Just because they don't have a dad, I don't want them to feel like they never do anything,' said Tina. 'I try to give them memorable experiences. I'm conscious of staying present with them and putting the phone down. My youngest daughter and I are big on morning swims. We'll walk down to the beach at 6 a.m. in the middle of winter and swim. I hope she always remembers that.'

'I don't want my kids' lives to be adversely impacted by my life choices and how things played out in my marriage,' said Melissa. 'That's why I try and go above and beyond to make sure we're still doing fun things – all the things we would have done if we'd stayed as a family of four. Sometimes I look around and see other families and I'd get that resentment and think, *Everything I do is so hard.*

I wish I had a supportive partner who wanted to spend time with us. But as my kids get older, I'm enjoying their company a lot more.'

Melissa believes that the trick is to 'have things on'. She tries to have at least one adventure on the weekends her kids are with her, taking them ice-skating, to the water park, the zoo, the beach and, almost without fail, to the local pub for dinner on a Friday night. 'A whole weekend stretching out in front of me makes me feel anxious, lonely and resentful,' she said. 'If I have things planned I feel like I'm living my life. People would comment on social media, "How did you take a five-year-old to the aquarium by yourself?" You just have to because if I didn't make things happen, we'd be stuck at home and that's not good for your mental health. I'm not going to stop living just because my marriage ended.'

'Mum gave us as many wonderful experiences as she could on her budget,' said Suzanne. 'We'd go apple picking, horseriding, bushwalking. She was always up for an excursion. In the school holidays she'd get us to write down what we wanted to do and we'd plan ahead. Whatever we were into, she would embrace. My brothers got into the speedway so Mum would take us. When they'd go surfing she'd sit on the point and wave. She'd take me to the theatre. She wasn't just an observer, she was a participant. I got the impression she really loved hanging out with us.'

I write lists, too. When I run out of my own ideas, I google 'things to do in school holidays' and ask my boys what piques their interest. That's how we've wound up at the convict barracks in the city, the Maritime Museum, the Archibald Prize at the art gallery (okay, maybe I pulled some sway there) and taking the remote-control boat for a spin in the pond.

I don't go to cafes or restaurants very often with my kids. There's the expense, but it's also tedious as they get bored and edgy as soon as they've polished off their chocolate milkshakes. I occasionally forget this and give it another shot, convincing myself it will be special. It rarely is. The trick is to get in and out, quick sticks. And to take a book each (for the kids, not me).

Bek lets her son take an iPad (and headphones) when they go out for dinner. 'It buys me some peace so I can finish my meal,' she said.

It's about prioritising time and money on what you and your kids genuinely get a kick out of doing together, not what you *think* you should enjoy.

Plays are our thing. They can be expensive, but I treat us on special occasions and book ahead to get good deals. Babies Proms at the Sydney Opera House became a Christmas tradition when the boys were little. We saw other plays there, too, including *The Incredible Book Eating Boy* and *Possum Magic*. We'd catch the ferry into the city and the boys would scooter around from Circular Quay, beating me to the box office and the free entertainment in the foyer. *Pete the Sheep* at Monkey Baa Theatre was one of the first plays my kids saw.

'Staying a night in a hotel is an adventure ritual for us,' said Lauren. 'We get room service and watch a movie in bed. It's fun, it's a treat, it's a bit decadent. We pull the shutters down and say, "Goodbye, world. I've got everybody I'm responsible for right here." The reason why our relationship is so connected is because I've spent this intense time with him.'

Free Adventures

There are plenty of adventures that don't cost anything. My kids jump off the jetty in the summer after school and I have to drag them out of the water past sunset. They ride scooters and bikes on the oval, climb rocks and collect sticks (the larger the better!), which they insist on bringing home with us. We explore rock pools and beach caves, climb trees and we take a ball or two wherever we go. When I can, I drag them on a bushwalk. We go to the library and they walk out with twenty books – each. I cook lamb chops at home and take them down to the jetty for a sunset picnic dinner. It's more of a novelty than eating at the table, and it also saves cleaning up.

I take my kids to Sydney's Vivid light festival every winter, making our way into the city on the ferry just as the sun throws a ribbon of pure gold before it dips out of view. It's packed in the city for the light spectacular. It would be easy to lose a child, especially when you're outnumbered, as I always am. Parents say they wouldn't dare go to Vivid without at least two adults and I think what a luxury it would be to make such caveats. If I put conditions on adventures, we'd miss everything.

Jess recalls taking her son to play beach tennis after school and handball in their courtyard. When the novelty of that wore off, they played ping-pong and pool. On weekends she would take him to the driving range to hit golf balls. 'I have no doubt all those years just playing together strengthened our relationship,' she said. 'We banter all the time and get on so well. Like good mates, except he respects me as his mum.'

Admittedly, regular outings that couples with kids take for granted can be a logistical nightmare for single mothers.

As much as Melissa loves taking her young children to the beach, she finds it incredibly stressful on her own. 'My daughter loves the water but my son gets cold and wants to get out,' she explained. 'So I have to stand right where the water meets the sand, close enough to get in the water if my daughter needs me and close enough to keep an eye on my son in case he wanders off. I'm trying to keep both kids safe but it's not easy.'

And that's just a day at the beach, something heralded as a carefree pastime. But there's always a way. When my boys were younger, I would recruit a kind-looking stranger to keep an eye on one on the shore while I swam out with the other. I had a hack for going under water: I would hold Otis aloft (all 20 kilograms of him) while I swiftly ducked my head beneath the surface.

When friends ask you to join them on outings, it takes the pressure off and can make it so much more enjoyable. But in lieu of an invitation, you have to be proactive. We don't need to let our single motherhood-ness hold us back. It's more than possible to do most things with our kids, without thinking about something 'missing'.

A Lesson from Buddha

One school holidays, we were lucky enough to go to Bali where I was commissioned to write a story on Green Camp, the abridged version of the famous Green School in Ubud. The camp was all about connection (and disconnection from the demands of our daily routines). We were challenged to build a raft from a stack of bamboo and old bicycle tyres, then steer our rickety vessel down a rushing stream. We climbed a 14-metre coconut tree (3 metres was my limit), practised Balinese martial arts in a muddy rice paddy in homage to the soil that sustains us and slept in our own dirt-floored yurt. This was a golden opportunity for us three to make memories, while learning about sustainability.

But the bigger learning actually came the night before Green Camp, when we stayed in a humble bamboo villa that I found on Stayz. We wheeled our suitcases down a scraggly dirt path beside a patchwork of rice paddies to find that the villa had a pool. Pay dirt! Within minutes I was lounging by the side of said pool, watching the boys larking about. It was the perfect set-up and I couldn't have been happier. Until I heard an almighty splash, clearly distinguishable from the splash of a child, and I looked up to see that one of the stone Buddha statues adorning the side of the pool had gone in, too. It transpired that my oldest had put his arm around Buddha (as you do), and the statue's foundations weren't strong enough for them both, so in Buddha went. Blessedly, the statue was of Buddha in his skinny phase.

Still, I freaked right out. I blamed my boy for hugging Buddha, I blamed myself for being a single mother and daring to take time out to read instead of hover, and I blamed our circumstances. Who was I to possibly think we could live a normal life and do what regular people do with only one grown-up in the mix – like mucking around in a pool? When I had calmed down (and after two young Balinese men with snorkels had come to the rescue, fishing broken Buddha out of his watery tomb), I saw that this could have happened to anyone. Me having the audacity to carry on with life as if nothing was amiss was not the reason that Buddha lost his footing. It was not retribution. And it was not going to hamper my resolve to live fully. In fact, nothing would.

It sounds like the sort of thing Buddha might have told me himself, if only he wasn't in pieces.

SINGLE MOTHER WISDOM

- Travelling alone as a single mother with kids is not without its challenges, but it's absolutely worthwhile. It's unfiltered and uninterrupted time with your children away from all the day-to-day distractions.

- It's fun to travel with other families, but it's usually up to you to be proactive and invite others to join you (and don't take it personally if they decline).

- You don't have to go away to share experiences with your kids. Set aside time for local adventures – get out of the house and make it happen! Adventures don't have to cost much, and many are free – such as climbing trees, beach days, jumping off the jetty and sunset picnics.

- The goal is making memories with our kids, slowing time. You don't need another parent to create that.

CHAPTER 10

Single Mothers' Network

Not long after leaving our family home, it became apparent that I needed new friends. I loved the friends I had – many of my friendships went back decades and I cherished them. I didn't want to lose a single one of them, not if I could help it. But since becoming a single mother, my life had spun off on such a divergent trajectory that I needed to add new friends to the mix – ones who understood the place I was in, whose current life experience mirrored my own. I certainly didn't realise until the day I moved out that you can't possibly know what it's like to raise children on your own – to be there day and night, responsible (solely, in many cases) for their emotional, financial and everything wellbeing – unless, God forbid, you've been there. Or are there.

Many of my old friends – my pre-separation friends – haven't been there. They were thoughtful and inclusive, reaching out when they thought of it. They were remarkably patient with my unavoidable lack of flexibility with my time, with my intermittent falling apart and the never-ending saga I seemed to be embroiled in. They forgave me for the often-stark imbalance of my incessant offloading.

As Rachel Cusk wrote in *Aftermath*, her memoir on marriage and separation: 'The drama of my life dominates, uses up the fuel of conversation like an ugly army tank guzzling petrol. This is not equality.'

Even when I could manage to keep it together and act like myself – the myself before all of this – it was hard to keep up with my coupled friends. It was impossible to entertain, for starters. Our rental apartment is way too small to have people over. I didn't get out much, either. And I still don't. I hardly ever go to the 'mums' dinners' through my boys' school, for example. I would love to. But it means hiring a babysitter, which isn't just an extra expense – another $80 on top of the tab – it's also less time with my kids.

Since becoming a single mother, I've formed a loose protocol around my social life: aside from a few exceptions for special circumstances or when I really feel like it, I only go out on nights when the boys are with their dad. It means that I miss out on things. But my single-mother-enforced agenda has made me more discerning about how I spend my time.

Shakti feels the same. 'I used to try and make it work and pay for a babysitter or drag my son to my mum's house,' she said. 'But I was spending a hundred dollars to go to dinner before I even went to dinner. It got to a point where I had to say I'm not free Monday to Friday. That works better for everyone else because they want weekends with their families, but not for me. I bow out of social occasions if my son isn't with his dad. I got a bit rigid in my social life. Either people get it or they don't. The friends who've stuck around try to make it work for me.'

Rejection Hurts

Women who have left relationships (or have been left) talk of the sting of losing friends to 'the other side', inevitable collateral damage of the fallout. 'We had mutual couple friends who we'd go on holidays with,' said Katrina. 'I heard from my children that the invitations were still coming – they were still going for barbecues and on camping trips with those same families – but I was no longer invited.'

This 'natural attrition' forced Katrina to reassess who was important in her life: 'At the beginning I felt like a pariah and it was a huge blow to my self-worth because I thought, *What's wrong with me?* It was tough. They say you're the sum total of the people you surround yourself with. I realised these people were relevant to my old life, but now that I've experienced so much growth, I've got new people around me that are reflective of where I'm at now.'

Zoe had a similar wake-up call when she split with her husband. 'What I found difficult was the disappointment that some people were really just around because of my husband,' she said. 'I actually thought the wives were my friends but there's that moment where you go, *Oh, okay, you've gone to that side of the room not my side of the room.* We'd split briefly a few years prior so I'd already seen the people that were going to be 'team my ex' and 'team Zoe' and it really broke me. But I didn't rush to try and get my side of the story across because what they think about me is not my business. It's funny because most of them come back eventually and then you get to choose whether they're in your life or not.'

Anika said that it hurt her deeply when a family at her children's school continued to invite her ex-husband and the kids over for barbecues. 'The kids would tell me they'd been to this family's home and I'd have to go to another room to take deep breaths because I was so hurt. I'm genuinely happy that my kids have had a good time. But it was pretty blatant that they never once invited me when my children were with me. They had chosen their side.'

For other women, it's not about losing friends to the other side but about losing family – like Eliza, whose husband's family haven't spoken with her since she ended their marriage. 'I was really close to his sisters and mother,' she said. 'They had even advised me to end the relationship for the sake of my children. But as soon as I left they acted like I didn't exist. It's as if I'm dead to them. I've come to terms with it but it saddens me for my kids because I don't know how to explain it to them. I tried to keep the lines of communication open but my ex deleted his family's numbers from my phone.'

My waning social life wasn't helped by the invitations inexplicably drying up. It's one of the binding themes of single motherhood. Despite the myriad circumstances that led us here – our divergent backgrounds, socio-economic status, lifestyles and proclivities – one overriding shared experience seems to be the perplexing propensity to be overlooked (deliberately or not) for social gatherings.

As soon as you start raising children by yourself – with only one adult in the mix – you're dropped from the guest list for get-togethers with coupled families. Not always, of course, but often enough for it to be a thing. It can be as devastating as the separation or loss itself, perpetuating the sense of dislocation so many are already grappling with.

'We lived in a street with lots of young families and we socialised a lot,' said Lara. 'The kids used to run between each other's houses and we'd have barbecues together. Then as soon as I was on my own, the invitations pretty much stopped straight away. I'd sit on the front porch and watch the kids running into each other's yards but no one came to our house anymore. It was so blatant. I was devastated.'

Lara choked up when she recalled running into these families at the beach one Sunday after her separation and realising that she was on the outer. 'It was really crowded and the kids and I managed to get the last shady spot under a tree. I saw a group of our neighbours wandering around with their picnic baskets and I said, "Come join us." They came over and set down their things, and then they formed a circle and turned their backs to me. They were chatting and pouring wine for each other and no one even talked to me. It was the worst thing. I thought, *I've become invisible because it's too uncomfortable for them to look at me.* I was somehow shameful. That was a really low point.'

Tellingly, Lara noted that as soon as she met her new partner a year later, the tide turned. 'Since I've re-partnered, it's like, "Baboom, party time!"' she said. 'Couples are in hot demand, single mothers are not. People want to hang out with people who are like them, and our society is built on intact marriages.'

Tina had the same experience when she re-partnered. 'You don't get invited to dinner parties when you're single,' she said. 'I only had one friend who invited me the whole time. But it changed when I started dating. Another friend who hadn't included me in anything for ten years invited us for dinner. I was like, *Why am I suddenly good enough?* You get excluded all the time. People don't like loose ends.'

Gigi felt the isolation of being the only single mum in her mothers' group. 'The couples were getting together on weekends and I wasn't included,' she said. 'There was no malice in it but there was a distinct difference in the way I was treated. It felt like I was being left out of that social arena because I didn't have a partner. It's kind of natural to want to create relationships with other couples so that there's an even energy of male and female. But it's a different reality for single parents. It felt like a stigma. It was quite hurtful.'

'I think couples feel awkward when they invite one,' said Lara. 'Couples have couple topics that singles can't relate to. Who knows why they do it? It's partly subconscious and partly conscious. But the reality is we single parents have to deal.'

Only, the exclusion isn't just confined to couple events. Milly's daughter received an invitation to attend a *Frozen* birthday party one Saturday afternoon. But when she arrived to collect her daughter, it was evident the other parents weren't going anywhere. 'All these other mothers started arriving, fully dressed up and carrying bottles of champagne,' she said. 'I passed them at the door as we were heading out. No one asked me to stay. I felt so ashamed, like I wasn't good enough. On the way home my daughter was asking why we couldn't stay. I didn't want her to think there was anything wrong with us, so I said, "Some people are just really rude.'"

Maggie Dent also experienced this when she became a single mum. 'Any time we're excluded from anything where we felt we belonged, it hurts because we're social beings,' she said. 'I stopped being invited to gatherings after my divorce. I think part of it's because women are constantly assessing their relationships, wondering, *Is this going to last?* When a marriage ends, it triggers others. *Stay away because it might be contagious. Let's pretend it's not really happening and keep our nice little world as it is.*'

'Married people with kids default to other married people with kids,' said Fiona. 'They don't know what our lives are like. They also don't realise that if they cancel on you how much we've had to juggle to go out with them. They're like, "I'm tired, I can't make it." That can crush you and make you feel rejected and alone. Even though that's not what they intended.'

I, too, have felt the admittedly disproportionate let-down of a blasé cancellation. Those with family to keep them company, no matter what, often have no concept of how an afternoon kicking the ball at the oval with the kids might have been the social highlight of our weekend. When they pull the plug at the last minute, for whatever reason, it leaves us with a gaping hole to fill, triggering the ever-persistent, not-so-dormant fear that we're in this alone.

Of course, there's always the possibility that we're left out because we're not great company. Neen says she was forced to consider that when many of her friends 'vanished into thin air' after her husband's funeral. 'When I look back I can see that it was pretty hard to be around my grief,' she conceded. While that's understandable in Neen's case, I know I haven't always been much fun to be around either. Single parenthood can make you think your problems are bigger than anyone else's, and that's hard to be around.

Create Your Own Community

One of the many freedoms of being a single parent not beholden to the confines of a traditional family unit is that we get to create our own. We can seek out new connections and friendships and forge a 'family' of our choosing, surrounding ourselves with like-minded people who pique our interest. If that concept seems too daunting – the cringe-worthy awkwardness of making new friends as an adult – life will often force our hand as many connections from our previous lives fall away.

Creating a community is usually organic – people find us. But it serves us to be up for it. And to see the gift in it, of forming enriching, high-grade relationships with people we may never have met or certainly wouldn't have bonded with were we not raising children by ourselves. We lean on others more and share a unique dynamic, distinct from parents with ready-made families.

Fiona came to find it was worth the effort of being vulnerable and putting herself out there. 'It's hard work and you feel rejected a lot and a bit bruised and like, *Why do I have to work so hard? If people really liked me wouldn't they just want to do things with me and come to me?* But it doesn't work that way.'

Speaking from experience, constantly inviting yourself along and putting yourself on the line to face rejection (which comes often) from distracted people who have no idea what it's like to have to hustle for human connection can be energy sapping, time consuming and demoralising. I do it for a bit, then I go through phases where I relish the fact that it's just us – me and my two boys – and make the most of that. It's a relief and slightly liberating. Until we're at a park some Sunday and we're surrounded by carefree gatherings who have multiple kids and grown-ups to talk to, and I think, *Wouldn't that be nice?*

Friends as Family

For many single mothers, friends become family. They come to mean much more to us than people whose company we enjoy and might see sporadically. With no other adult in the family to defer to, or even talk to, our friends take on a more intense role – as confidantes, advisers and support crew – sharing meals, weekends and occasional holidays. Where coupled families go home to each other, we go home to no one. We migrate to our friends instead – especially other single-parent friends – falling into an easy familiarity and filling a void that you don't realise is there unless you're in it.

I talk to my friends exponentially more since I became a single mum. They're the ones I'll call to share when one of my boys gets a merit award at school, say, or to ask their advice on what sort of birthday party to throw, or what car they think I should buy. They'll call to check how I am, too, and how the boys are doing, roles ordinarily fulfilled by the other parent.

'I'm lucky that one of my best girlfriends has got two kids who are the same age as mine, she also split from her partner, and the kids adore each other,' said Sally. 'When I go away for work she takes my kids and each kid's got a mate. She's also the sort of friend who'll tell me to pull my head in if I'm feeling too sorry for myself. She's the real deal. She's family. The kids know who we can count on.'

'I don't have family in this city so my friends are my family,' said Melissa. 'I'm surrounded by other women who are like-minded and supportive and kind. Like attracts like. As a single parent working full time, I only have time for people who make me feel good and supported and without drama. You're left with the friends who are there for you.'

'I have a very strong tribe of women friends,' said Francesca. 'These friendships have sustained every part of my life, and I wouldn't have made it through motherhood and now single motherhood without them. Our home is filled with female energy and it's a beautiful environment for my daughter to be encouraged to own her womanhood – to be fierce and feminist and fantastic.'

Single Mothers 'Get It'

As enriching and precious as old friendships are, single parents tend to stick together, sharing an inherent appreciation of each other's unique circumstances. They're often the first to reach out because they 'get it'. Try as you might – and bless those who do try – you can't comprehend the reality of being a single parent unless you are one.

'When I had an emotional breakdown, the two core people who supported me were single mothers,' said Lauren. 'They were my support network. Also my mother is my hero. She was a single mother herself. I don't know who her village was. How did she do it?'

'The only time I've been away with other families is when a friend who's also a single mum rented a house at the beach one Easter and invited other families,' said Tina. 'That was one of the best holidays I've ever had in my life. I finally felt like I was included. Being a single mum, she knows what it's like.'

Alice considers herself 'lucky' that a few of her friends separated from their husbands around the same time. They get together often with and without the kids, bonding over their shared experiences. They call themselves, aptly, 'The First Wives Club'.

Delilah, who was only eighteen when she had her son, is part of a 'young mums' group called Bump. She said that those mums are her support crew: 'We meet every week and have a group chat going all the time. They're always there to support me and my son with no judgement. It's awesome.'

A close friend went through a horror divorce a few years ago and has raised her two children on her own since they were little. I called her often to lend my support and was always on the end of the line, but I could never really have any semblance of understanding of what life was like for her. She had walked the formidable steps of the Family Court on her own and sat in a disheartening, windowless courtroom, the fate of her family in the hands of the law, all alone. Court aside, I didn't fully grasp the enormity of her ordeal of being with her kids, day in and day out, with no other adult to talk to. The early dinners and school projects, soccer training and birthday cakes. Just you and only you. I'm wise to that now. Being a single parent increases your empathy, not just for other single parents – it gives you a general empathy injection. I note that I'm more thoughtful, more inclusive and acutely more aware.

'I feel like I have a deeper understanding of the loneliness in the world,' reflected Karen. 'I've realised how important it is to maintain your friendships and check up on each other and to make each other laugh. It's soothing and it creates a deeper connection.'

'Whenever I organise anything I always invite single friends,' said Tina. 'I make an effort to include them because I know what it's like to be left out.'

'When I split up, most of the people in my world were couples so I felt very alone,' said Zoe. 'I've got friends who are going through what I went through and I'm checking in because you know what they need, especially on a weekend if it's just them and the kids, because I've lived it. You need people that have your back.'

Zoe is also an advocate for virtual friends. 'I have a wonderful connection with people through Instagram,' she laughed. 'Some of them I've never met but for years we've commented, reached out, connected. They come on the journey with you. It's important especially if you're a single mum and you're stuck at home on the sofa with a young child. They become your tribe. It can lift your day.'

Social media is a salve for many single mothers, providing a ready-made coterie of women in the same boat. Groups such as Single Mums Support Group Australia; Australian Separated, Single

& Divorced Mums; and Beanstalk Single Mums offer resources and advice on everything a single mother needs to know, from child support to finding love. The Facebook forums are a safe and supportive hub for single mothers to commune with women who know exactly what they're going through. They're like virtual mothers' groups, with tens of thousands of members.

'Hey single mums, how do you deal with the loneliness?' posted one woman late at night. The respondents suggested podcasts, books and how to meet other mums, one offering the sound advice to 'love yourself every second of every day'.

'Ladies, how do you co-parent with a narcissist?' asked another mum after she'd dropped the kids to preschool.

'Anyone got any advice on mediation? We're on tomorrow and I'm scared.'

'I'm feeling like a bit of a failure tonight. Just wanted to vent.'

Julia Hasche originally started up the popular Single Mother Survival Guide as a Facebook group in her local area after she separated from her baby's father, in an attempt to meet other single mothers like herself. 'The women in my mothers' group would often complain about their husbands and I felt like our challenges were so different,' said Julia. 'It was only when I started my Facebook group that I met single mums that had babies my daughter's age, and it was so much better. We can all talk about the same things. Like, "It's so hard when your baby won't stop screaming and there's no one there to back you up." Having people that understand that, it's really valuable.'

Julia has now parked her career as an engineer to host a website and podcast bringing single mothers together, inspiring them to embrace this time of their lives. 'One of the best things to come out of that group was it helped me to see that being a single mum isn't shameful, it's normal,' said Julia. 'There were all these amazing women around me who were going through the same thing.

Beautiful, educated, smart, intelligent women. As I healed myself, I was able to help support other single mums. It's a huge source of connection for other women, feeling like they're not alone.'

Champagne Cartel is another online community created to support single mothers, specifically those going through separation and divorce. Best friends Gillian Moody and Carolyn Tate bonded over their own separation woes within a year of each other and started a blog to help other women in the same boat, a blog that soon became a paid membership business with some 30,000 subscribers. 'There were days binge-watching *30 Rock*, tears, laughter and, of course, drinking champagne,' Gillian told me. 'We also gave practical help like creating budgets, applying for Centrelink, connecting each other with lawyers and financial planners and minding each other's children.'

This grew into the Champagne Divorce Club – an 'expert hub' of resources encompassing everything from dealing with grief to family law and dating again. 'It's everything we wish we had access to when we were going through it,' Carolyn said. 'Our mission is to help women turn their divorce into the best thing that's ever happened to them. Even on the darkest day, there's always something to laugh about.'

There's also an explosion of women joining online support forums for single mothers by choice, including the Australia Solo Mothers by Choice Facebook group. Its followers are women who've conceived a child – or are thinking of doing so – with the help of a donor ('known' or anonymous) or via surrogacy, or who have adopted.

Becoming a single mother can be daunting at first. The idea of starting again is often overwhelming. No matter what your backstory, single mothers have all, at some point, had to start again.

But that's what makes them who they are – the kind of women you'd want to be friends with.

How to Help Single Mothers

Since becoming a single mother, this is what I have learned: that soul-searching, centredness and forgiveness are vital healing procedures, but the graciousness of others will pull you through. If friends ask how they can support you (or other single mums), here are some simple ideas:

- Show up. Don't say 'call if you need me' because they probably won't. Single mothers are unlikely to reach out, but will gratefully take help if it turns up.
- Invite them over with the kids; invite them over without the kids.
- Cut them some slack. Let them be sad and self-pitying for a bit. Let them be boring. Sometimes it's too hard to fake it.
- Be there. 'The most precious gift we can offer others is our presence,' said Buddhist monk Thich Nhat Hanh.
- Don't ask what happened. It's completely irrelevant to their current situation.
- Don't ask, 'Have you met someone yet?'; you'll hear when they do. And don't ask, 'Has your ex met someone yet?' Who cares?
- Don't assume single motherhood is a negative. 'The horrified looks on people's faces when I mentioned I was separated!' recalled a friend. 'It didn't occur to them that having the courage and strength to leave a destructive relationship is a good thing.'

SINGLE MOTHER WISDOM

- It falls to us to be proactive in forging new friendships with people who understand our circumstances. We have to put ourselves out there and risk rejection to make it happen.

- We get to create our own community with like-minded people; friends become 'family'.

- The benefits of having single mum friends is that they 'get it'. We can support each other and be there for each other without the need for explanation.

- Here are some simple ways to support single mum friends (whether you're single or coupled):

  » Be inclusive. Single mothers are often left out because they no longer fit the mould. Be mindful of the upheaval they have gone through and cut them some slack.

  » Get on the front foot with invitations and opportunities to make them feel a part of things.

  » Don't cancel! But if you absolutely have to, make it up to them because they've likely gone to great lengths (and had high hopes) to make it possible to get out the door.

CHAPTER 11

Asking for Help

The prospect of having a skin cancer dug out of my nose, followed by plastic surgery that would require fifty-plus stitches and a month off work, didn't really faze me. I was just happy that I'd found it in time and put my faith in the doctors to take care of the rest.

What threw me was when the nurse rang a few days before my operation to ask who'd be picking me up as I wouldn't be in any state to drive. 'Who is your person?' she asked expectantly.

I paused. 'I was planning on getting an Uber,' I said.

'You don't have a person who could get you?' she prodded. Mild shame crept over me. *No, I don't have a person.* Did this make me a lesser person? I have lots of 'people'. I have many friends – rock-solid friends – and some family. My friends are always there for me in a crisis and there's rarely a shortage of people to catch up with and workshop life with. I have people who care about me and understand me and want the best for me.

But a 'person' is a different thing altogether. And in a moment of sobering clarity on the other end of the phone, it hit me that I was starkly devoid of one of those. It's got nothing to do with being single, mind. I've been in some relationships where I still didn't have a 'person'. It's a harsh reality for many single parents – that it all falls on us.

Until the nurse asked me, I'd barely noticed my lack of a person. I was getting by okay raising my two young children mostly on my own, making tough calls every day for their best interests – the greatest responsibility of all – with no one to bounce them off. I had long branded myself by my independence, wearing it as a sort of badge of honour, a sign of my enduring strength and capability. I prided myself on being able to manage just fine on my own. I didn't need a person. Unless, as it turned out, I was being collected from day surgery.

Asking for help has never been my strong suit. I know why. It's because potential rejection is one of my most potent triggers – a portal to my vulnerable self – so I avoid it at all costs. And there are costs. I fortify myself against the likelihood of it by getting the job done myself, or paying for it if it comes to that.

We might be more connected than ever before, but the dread of not really mattering to anyone is our collective suffering, which is why a rebuff – even an unanswered text – can feel like a calamitous desertion, a threat to our very existence, especially for single mothers. Coupled families would have no idea of the impact if they decline a request to mind our kids, for example, no matter how legitimate the excuse. Unless you've been on the receiving end, you can't imagine how that lands. I try to avoid putting myself in situations where being knocked back is even an option because it's hard to handle the emotional fallout when it comes.

Yet, by necessity of my impending operation, I had to find a person. I bypassed my friends with school pick-up duties and paid work, asking only those who were more likely to be around. I got a couple of 'nos' and I was still standing. Then a friend who lived on the other side of town, who is raising three kids on her own (one in hospital at the time), stepped up. 'I've got you covered,' she texted.

I might have cried. She delivered me home afterwards with sushi and Panadol and the guts to ask again.

It's on Us

As single mothers, it serves us to get good at asking for help because we can't really get by without it. We were not designed to raise children on our own, yet here we are. As Danielle put it, 'It's the relentlessness of the Groundhog Day. There's that knowing that there's no cavalry coming home at six o'clock to help with the load, the bedtime routine, the cooking and the cleaning.'

'Those moments like when my daughter wouldn't get ready for school, I was running late for work – and that utter panic of trying to do it all yourself,' said Fiona. 'I'd have a critical presentation that my career depended on and I'd get the call from daycare that she was sick. I'd ring around in a state trying to find someone to step in. I didn't like it but I didn't have a choice.'

The idea of being the only one there for your children is a particular concern for solo parents with no one to fall back on. 'What if something happened to me? What if I got sick? What would I do?' asked Francesca. 'I have an incredible tribe of women around me but I don't have a co-parent to step in if I'm unable to be there. If something goes wrong, and I can't get to my daughter, I have no one. My daughter has no one. That's a really lonely place to be, to think that it all lands on my shoulders. As organised and as philosophical as I try to be, in the end it all comes down to me. It's an enormous weight to carry. That's the truth about being a solo parent.'

'Whenever I've had health concerns, it's like, *Fuck, if I'm not around, what happens to him?*' said Soraya, also a solo parent, who almost died when her son was a toddler. 'When you carry the whole weight yourself, it's something extra you've got to think about. That you're it. As a solo parent it's always in the back of your mind, and if you've been confronted with it as I have, then it becomes very real. You're very conscious of your reach and you have to be there for your kid until they're self-sufficient and can survive in the wild on their own.'

Sally admits that she 'welcomed' getting sick so her ex-husband would step in. 'I've got Crohn's disease so I get hospitalised quite a lot,' she said. 'I would sometimes will myself to get sick so I could have a break. Going to hospital was my release. I'd go "Awesome, I can sleep."'

Hospitalisation might seem like desperate lengths to go to in order to get a breather, but that's how difficult many women find it to ask for help. I've learned to adapt over the years to my self-imposed aversion to assistance, expecting nothing, preferring to settle for struggle over ministrations. I'm far more comfortable with doing everything solo than the only other option – a far less desirable one – of laying myself on the line and requesting help. I'd rather be pulled in all directions (as is my default state); I'd rather make do, than put out a hand. Because with that comes the ever-present risk (too daunting to even contemplate) that it might not be met, and then what might that say about me?

Learning to Receive

'It isn't so much the act of asking that paralyses us,' wrote musician Amanda Palmer in her book *The Art of Asking*. 'It's what lies beneath: the fear of being vulnerable, the fear of rejection, the fear of looking needy or weak.'

Yet when we do ask for help and allow ourselves to receive it, there's a payoff. The exchange brings people closer. There's as much in it for the giver as the receiver. As Amanda said in her TED Talk, 'The Art of Asking', tears welling in her black-kohled eyes, 'When we really see each other, we want to help each other.'

It's the seeing each other part that scares most of us off, the fear that we'll expose our vulnerability, that it will be regarded as a deficiency instead of being appreciated for what social scientist Brené Brown calls the 'courage and daring' behind it. Single mothers come to fiercely guard that vulnerability – our deep wounds and hurts – reserving all our energy (well, any that's left over after tending to our kids and all the rest) for holding it together. We can't risk letting our guard down because giving up isn't an option when you're the sole adult in the house.

'That fierce independence, the desire to keep your shit tidy, runs deep,' said Danielle. 'We have this need to look like we can do it all. You don't want to appear unable to manage your lot. There's shame attached to needing help, which is completely illogical. It actually gives everyone great satisfaction and feelings of connection, security and joy, which are basic human needs.'

For Aisha, support is always on offer in her Muslim community, but she still finds it difficult to accept. 'My father died when I was four and my mother was hospitalised so I learned to be incredibly self-sufficient. That's not always a good thing 'cause it blocks you from receiving. There were times when I had to move house and I didn't have money and I had people saying, "Why didn't you call me?" I'm the worst, I swear.'

Delilah admits that being a teenage mum makes her think she doesn't deserve extra help: 'I don't ask anyone for anything. I don't want to be a burden. It's like, I put myself in this situation, I chose to keep my baby, so I need to pick up my game and do everything and be the mum and the dad.'

Asking takes not only courage, but also time. When I'm stuck and need someone to mind my boys, I weigh up the effort of texting friends or school parents or my brother and sometimes I decide it's easier to pay for a babysitter. That way I'm not having to hold out for a response or feeling guilty for potentially causing inconvenience.

When friends look after my kids, I try to even up the ledger. I tally up the help and make sure I return the favour. Not that anyone's asking – it's my hang-up, not theirs. But as much as I love having my boys' friends over and wish I could do it more often, it's not easy without a backyard. I come up with other offerings: taking other kids to the beach after school or to soccer training, drama classes or after the game on Saturday mornings. There are always a few extras in the back of our car.

Zoe says that she often defaulted to paying for help when her son was younger so she wasn't beholden to anyone. 'I found it hard asking others to take him because I didn't have the capacity to have the play dates back when I was working. That quid pro quo thing. So you end up either not going or paying for a babysitter.'

'I've had to lean on people for school pick-ups and to take pictures when my son was getting an award and I couldn't be there,' said Soraya. 'People know as a single mum you don't have the capacity to do it all but I still find it awkward to ask for help, especially when you feel like it's a one-way street.'

I watch mum friends rally around women whose husbands are away on business, offering to pick up the kids and drop around meals and I think, *Welcome to my world.*

'I felt exhausted for years, going back and forth to my son's school,' said Karen. 'Because his father lives interstate I do everything on my own. The schooling, every soccer game, everything. If I was a single dad, everyone would be falling over themselves to take my son after school and help out. But a single mum, not so much.'

When Help Is Offered

When I'm asking people to mind my boys, I work up to it. I put it off for days. I consider the wording, give them an out – 'no problem if not'. I review and edit the text. Sometimes my hand shakes while

I press send. Then I flip the phone over, too scared to read the response in case it's a 'no', which is less crushing for the inconvenience and much more for the way I might choose to interpret it. I take it as a reflection of my lack of deservedness.

That's why I'm so grateful for friends on the front foot, who offer without being asked, as if reading my mind. I hold in high esteem those who step in off their own bat with unsolicited assistance – such as Lisa, a school-mum friend, a mother of four herself, who offers to take my boys when I'm tied up. She gets in early before I've even got around to contemplating the week ahead. I turn up to her house harrowed and she hands my boys back, fed and spent from the afternoon trampolining. She texts reminders that it's mufti day or a project is due or asks if we want to meet for trick or treating at Halloween.

Another school mum, Carolyn, is on it, too, taking my boys for sleepovers when I worked nights, or dropping them to school if I have to be somewhere before the bell, and inviting us for pizza on a Saturday night more times than I can count.

School mums often get it best because they see our lives up close, day in, day out. They see the pressure for us to be on top of everything – logistical, financial, emotional – for our kids and ourselves. They witness, to a degree, what's involved, close enough to understand that it's superhuman.

Another friend, Sophie, who has three kids and a husband of her own, had my boys to stay one weekend when I was working and was in the lurch. She had repeatedly insisted she would be there for me if I needed her and, when the time came, she was true to her word. I let myself in a side door at 2 a.m. after my newsreading shift to find her asleep in the bed beside my boys. 'Just in case they woke up and missed you,' she whispered, as she stumbled sleepily back to her own bed. (Incidentally, one Mother's Day, Sophie sent me flowers. 'For all the boys know that you do for them and all that they don't,' the card read. I cried, of course.)

When assistance is proffered, it's a godsend. We get the help we need, bypassing the utter discomfort of having to request it. But in the ease of that exchange, we do miss something. We miss the growth that comes with asking. And the connection. Those who ask are expressing a kind of faith in humankind, viewing themselves, as Amanda Palmer put it, 'in collaboration' with the world, which loops us into it instead of keeping us separate. When making gentle requests of others, we are in the flow of life.

I experienced that when my hand was forced on the weekend I went skiing for my birthday. It was a rare treat and one of the few times I'd been away sans kids since leaving our family home some four years earlier. The plans I had in place to look after my boys fell through at the last minute. I had two choices: work the phones and call in favours or not go. Such is my reticence to ask for help that I briefly contemplated the latter. But there were friends standing by and a massive cold front coming, and I'd been so looking forward to it, so I decided to press on. I needed to become a master asker.

I took a deep breath. Then I lost my nerve. I put the phone down. I chastised myself for allowing myself to be exposed in this way, as if there was a gaping hole in my fortifications that I'd forgotten to seal. I'd always been there for my boys the whole way through, all bases covered. How had I not seen this one coming? I needed to give up my own wants in retribution, get back in the trenches where I belonged, not go swanning off on ski weekends.

But then I stopped myself. This spiralling thought pattern wasn't helping me. This wasn't growth. It was stagnation.

Also, I reasoned, wasn't it good for my children to witness me asking for help? To model to them the art of reaching out to others so they didn't end up with such a chronic aversion to it as I had? To show them that I was not just their mum doing the cooking ('Your favourite room is the kitchen,' Jasper said to me recently; no, it's not at all, but I can see why he might think that), drumming in times tables, doing never-ending loads of washing, but that I liked to have fun with my friends, too.

I picked up the phone again as if it were a dangerous weapon and I got on with it. Several calls and texts later, I had my boys accounted for every minute of my four days away. I drew up a roster system of other parents, my brother and sister-in-law, Ticka and Lucy, and Jasper's 21-year-old trumpet teacher, Miles, ferrying them around from school and soccer and birthday parties and each other's homes. A quick call each morning from the mountains to cross-check the day's timetable and all went smoothly. I returned home Sunday night to two soundly sleeping boys in their bunks, and Miles propped up on the couch waiting for me, the dining table decorated with dusky pink roses and fairy lights left by Otis' friends' mums, Alison and Mel, who'd kindly delivered my boys home earlier on. Mission complete.

I had done it. *We* had done it.

The exercise not only proved to me that when I seek help, I'll be supported. It also changed me slightly. I felt held, swept up in a movement of reciprocity where people are there for each other, just because. I was a part of the way of the world, a state that had become almost outlandish to me in my persistent solo striving – what I had come to believe was my only option – to get stuff done on my own. I felt in alignment. Just for four days, but still . . .

The next day I was felled by a headache so severe that I was forced to take to my bed. The pressure of remotely coordinating my kids for my long weekend in the Alps had clearly taken its toll. The shift might have happened on the surface – the child-minding roster group texted to the relevant parties perfectly executed – but the deeper shift of accepting that I, too, am worthy of support was still in need of refinement. That might take a little more work.

SINGLE MOTHER WISDOM

- Asking for help is one of the hardest things; it requires us to be vulnerable and risk rejection, which might feel like more than we can take. As single mothers, we have to put ourselves on the line and get over it because we need help – we're not designed to raise kids on our own.

- Asking for help is like flexing a muscle – you get better at it with practice.

- Helping others is just as beneficial to the giver as the receiver. Most people love helping others – it makes them feel more connected and purposeful. They just don't always think to offer. So, make it easy for them and ask.

- Some tips for asking for help:

  » Texting is easier because you can take time to think about how to word the request, and it gives the other party time to consider before responding (and if it's a 'no', it's less awkward).

  » Give plenty of notice – I sometimes sabotage my request by asking for help at the last minute and taking it personally when it's declined.

  » Think of ways to reciprocate when help comes your way – you may not be able to have kids over for play dates, but there are many other ways to do your bit like driving other kids to weekend sport or taking them on an outing.

- Get good at receiving help, too. It doesn't make you weak or mean that you're not coping. To ask for help or to accept it when it's offered – especially in raising our children – places us at the heart of the cycle of human connection, being there for each other and being truly seen.

CHAPTER 12

Money Matters

If I hadn't had a job, I could well have ended up homeless. When I made the tough decision to move out of the family home, my part-time job – a deceivingly flimsy premise with no guarantees of longevity – was the only thing standing between myself and having nowhere to go. I googled women's refuges, hardly believing it had come to this. Not only are refuges short term, but I also felt guilty taking the place of a woman who might need it more than me. A woman without a job, for instance. For the first time in my life, I was given a glimpse into just how fine the line is between security and destitution.

It's no surprise that women over 55 are the fastest-growing group of homeless in Australia. This can be the most crucial time for women who are separated or divorced (which is the case for the majority of homeless women). They often have no access to their ex-partner's earnings, if indeed there are any, there may be limited or no child support (which can also take months to kick in, is hardly enough to cover rent and is difficult to enforce if the other parent refuses to pay), and financial settlements can be delayed for years on end in the Family Court. In the meantime, many women are not just in limbo, they're in chronic financial panic.

The determining factor to the degree of difficulty for most single mothers is predominantly financial. Despite having no support from her ex-husband, Lara believes she's much better off than many single parents, and many partnered ones, too. 'I have a good job and a high income. If I wasn't in that position, we'd be living in poverty because my kids' father makes zero financial contribution. I have the kids 24/7 and no family help.'

According to Jenny Davidson, CEO of the Council of Single Mothers and their Children, the financial hardship experienced by the great majority of single mothers is what sets them apart most from other family groups, creating an interminable cycle of socio-economic disparity. 'Women often end up with more of the caring responsibilities so they're working less, have less income, less super, not able to own a home,' she said. 'They raise their children in financial duress, if not poverty. Many others experience financial hardship or money is tight. In many cases these women end up in poverty and even homeless.'

'My biggest stress was that I wouldn't have enough money to provide for the children,' said Danielle. 'Even though I always had enough money, I was always fine, it raised my adrenaline and cortisol to a point where I lived in a constant roller-coaster of fear.'

'I'd only just started my business when my marriage broke down, so I wasn't earning much money, which was very scary,' said Michelle. 'I'd be sitting on the lounge at night eating Twisties, drinking wine, and looking at jobs on Seek. I had to sell my house to survive.'

'I could be a single mother easily if I had loads of cash,' said Eva. 'It's the money that's the problem, not the single mothering. It was when I ran out of money that everything became really traumatic.'

'Everything's on you, whether it's school fees or day-to-day costs, there are no maintenance payments or support,' said Soraya, a solo parent. 'There were periods where it was hugely challenging. I was lucky that I had a history of work and investment so I was in a position to support us even when things were tight. I could liquidate assets and keep us going. When you don't have money, you don't have choices.'

As a journalist, Rita Panahi has written often on the topic of women 'missing out' on motherhood. She believes financial disadvantage for single mothers is the greatest deterrent to many women having children on their own, like she did: 'If it wasn't for the financial concerns, I think so many women who want to have children, but aren't in a relationship, would be utilising IVF or whatever means they want to have kids while they still can. If you've got financial security and you're in a position to have a child on your own, I would encourage any woman to look into that rather than forego their chance of motherhood, because that's a huge price to pay.'

It's not easy juggling work and kids at the best of times. This stretch is often magnified for single mothers when there's no one else to share the load. Child care costs money and in some cases it's hardly worth your while going to work. It's often impossible to get help minding the kids – paid or otherwise. I had to take my boys into the studio with me many times while reading the news. I was tempted to give up because it seemed impossible to make it work. But I hung in there, not just because I needed the money to support my family, but because I feared losing the career that I had invested so much in.

Career fulfilment is a bonus, no longer the prime motivator, when you're a single mother. When the buck stops with you, there's no scope for 'off-ramping', taking leave from your career while the kids are young and later attempting to pick up where you left off. The economic benefits of staying in the workforce are cumulative. Your career stays on an uninterrupted upward trajectory and, crucially, your superannuation top-ups go along for the ride.

Shakti works hard to maintain her career as a yoga teacher, writer and actor, while raising her young son, mostly on her own. 'I could have gone down a more stable career path,' she said. 'But I lost so much of me in the process of becoming a single parent that I wanted to retain the bits of me that made me "me" and that I relished in being. I felt like, if I lose this last part of me, I've lost me.' She spent a 'large chunk' of her earnings on babysitters to care for her son while she was performing. 'I was very clear that these are not my years for making money. These are my years of surviving and keeping a foot in the door, while also doing what I love, what I'm good at and brings me joy, and allows me to contribute to the world.'

Being Financially Savvy

I have always been 'good with money' – a good saver. I bought my first apartment at 29, a cool little one-bedder in a converted flour mill in a gentrifying suburb. It was my aim to be in the real estate market by 30 and I just scraped in. I had reserved enough money for the deposit despite having recently returned from an overseas trip, scrupulously saving from my job as a TV reporter to head to Canada and London on a working holiday. I snapped up another apartment a few years later. By my mid-thirties, these two units – albeit modest in size and value – were my very pragmatic and sensible nest eggs in case I found myself alone and, heaven forbid, even a single mother. I rented out one of the apartments and lived in the other until I gave birth (as in, days before), renting that one out, too, and moving into a larger rental home to start life as a family. Eventually they were both sold to help purchase the family home in which I no longer lived.

I'm financially savvy in other ways, too. I don't drink alcohol or coffee (I just don't like them, but it does help save money!). I don't covet designer handbags (buying a bag for the cost of an overseas holiday makes no sense to me). I wouldn't dream of buying myself a facial or real jewellery, going out for dinner was a rarity (still is), and I've had the same pair of sunglasses since 2015. I rarely splurge.

And yet I found myself living on my own with two little kids, renting a small apartment that cut into most of my earnings, with barely any money in the bank and living payday to payday, direct debits bouncing all over the place. All my life savings were funnelled into the house I had just left. After all the limitless expenses and sundries that come with raising young children, the ledger just didn't weigh up. For the first time ever, I was in a state of near terror about how I would make ends meet.

I got a call from my son's teacher one day. When the school number came up on my phone, my heart skipped a beat. No need – she was ringing to tell me that Jasper said in class, 'My mum is too poor to afford apples.' She thought I'd like to know. I assured her that we could indeed afford apples and that my boys were well and truly well fed.

That afternoon on the way home from school, I inquired about the apples. 'I told the boys that because my mum's a single mum, sometimes we can't afford apples,' Jasper innocently recounted from the front seat as he munched on a Bakers Delight finger bun, a regular after-school treat that cost the same as a couple of apples.

'We can always buy apples,' I reassured him calmly, a little perplexed. My boys ate an apple a day pretty much all year round.

'But you say we have to get the ones on special,' he said. He had me there. If my kids equated sensible shopping as near poverty, I had work to do.

'Are we poor?' my son asked me another night, sliding in beside me in the kitchen as I was cooking spaghetti bolognaise again (their favourite and the best way to stretch mince).

'Of course not,' I said nonchalantly, but really I was spinning. Where was this coming from? Was it all because of the apples? I suspected not. It was from living in this affluent suburb where some of his school friends' homes were the size of our whole apartment block. 'Where's the rest of your house?' one child asked when he came to play. 'Why's your house so small?' asked another. My boys told a friend that we were renting and he offered helpfully, 'I know what renting is. It's when you own a house and other people give you money to live there.' It didn't occur to him that there was a flipside. 'Are you renovating?' asked another child, the only feasible explanation he could think of as to why you'd live in an apartment.

Many of my sons' peers travel overseas every year (or at least they did in pre-pandemic times), eat out at restaurants and their mothers (it's mostly the mothers who do the shopping while the dads work) would rarely have to weigh up the specials at the fruit and vegie section. Their friends have TVs (and Apple TV and PlayStations and Wiis) and have never slept on mattresses while their mother paid off the lay-by on a set of bunks.

But we're not poor – far from it. We have everything we need. That's what I tell my boys (and myself), anyway.

'We have a roof over our heads, don't we?' I asked to put their minds at rest. 'We've got food on the table and a car to take us where we need to go' (so long as I keep up the repayments – I don't say that bit). 'How about all the adventures we go on together? And check out that overflowing bookshelf!' I enlightened them that some people had nowhere to live and no money to feed their families. They needed perspective.

Things were not dire. Not at all. Not compared to countless other women in the same boat. Even though I had lost my job, we were staying above water. Rent and food got skimmed off first so my boys would never be knowingly impacted by my financial situation. I had the essentials covered: electricity (although not without a 'warning'), phone bills, car repayments, petrol, school uniforms for their ever-growing bodies, doctor and dentist. And then some: soccer registration, soccer boots, books, birthday parties, Christmas presents, child psychologist, health insurance, zoo membership, Disney Plus subscription, even the occasional holiday (subsidised by my hustled-for travel writing, granted).

Yet, it was a pretty precarious balance sheet. And it still is. As is the case for many single mothers, the sum of outgoings exceeded the sum of incomings. I had many nights lying awake, wondering how I was going to keep the wolf from the door.

It's hard to understand it unless you've lived it. Even if you have a job, as I did until recently, when raising kids as the sole adult, your salary alone doesn't usually cut it, with single mothers often working part-time. Child-support payments, if you're eligible, are simply not enough to cover Maslow's hierarchy of needs. (And single mums by choice and widows can forget about that altogether.) For those going through separation or divorce, it can take years (literally) to get a financial settlement if you happened to share assets with the other parent, with legal fees mounting sky high in the process.

I'm not bewailing. I would take my unsteady financial position any day if it meant my freedom. And I'm well aware of how fortunate we are in the scheme of things. But if my case is a best case, I can only imagine how desperate things must be for others.

Just Getting By

As single mothers, we all have to find ways to make our stymied financial situations work. We get resourceful, we cut corners, we go without. And we learn to accept help. Many women say they couldn't get by without their extended families.

'I would never be able to manage if it wasn't for my parents supporting me,' said Skylar. 'I don't get child support because my ex doesn't make enough money. I'm on a government carer's allowance for my son who has autism, which covers my rent, and my mum gives me an allowance from her savings. That's how I survive.'

'Mum and Dad helped me out at first,' said Zoe. 'I was working part-time earning sixty grand. My ex was paying my rent and my parents topped up the rest and helped with my legal costs. I couldn't have done it without them but I'd think, *I'm 40, I can't believe I'm having to borrow money from my parents. How have I got here?*'

'I have the immense good fortune of having a family that's not only emotionally supportive, but financially supportive,' said Neve. 'It meant that we could stay in our home, which is our safe place and our joy. We wouldn't have it without my parents' support. I have limitless gratitude for that.'

Sally sold her house to take the pressure off. 'I do worry I don't have anything to leave the kids,' she said. 'It hasn't been easy financially. There have been many times I've been very worried about money. But they can look back on their life and know I did everything. I'm giving them the best education. They haven't missed out on much.'

Becoming Financially Literate

I had always been pretty ad hoc when it came to fiscal matters. Yes, I'm a 'good saver', but I had flailed about in the woolly ambiguity of indeterminate balances and outgoings and arrears. I couldn't have told you if I'd been paid or what I'd spent on what on any given day. But when my Eftpos card bounced at the supermarket for the third week in a row, I couldn't keep up with the interest on my credit card and I ran out of petrol, I realised things had come to a head. It was time I turned my attention to the entire state of my financial affairs and got my house in order.

When going through separation, you are quite often expected to prepare a 'financial statement', an inexact science to determine who pays for what, which requires you to delve into the minutiae of expenditure – everything from toothpaste to movie tickets.

It was time to look at each of my six neglected superannuation accounts, some losing more money than they made. I had to update exact balances of my seven bank accounts in three different banks, amounts owing on the three credit cards I had at the time and the residual on my car lease (who knew I was paying all that interest?). I had to tally my weekly spendings on groceries, books, bandaids, health insurance and everything in between.

It was a disconcerting task. It was also excruciating. It took several nights – after the boys had gone to bed – poring over bank statements until well past 1 a.m. I went back in time to the electronic banking archives to stare years-old spendings in the face when I'd much rather have left them in the past where they belonged. Even more confronting was being reminded of the time I was the master of my own money, when I owned two apartments, had a fixed-term deposit and controlled my own cashflow and no one could take that away from me.

I felt queasy facing up to the perilous state of my finances after all I had done to ward against it. This was the very stark reality I had fought most of my adult life to steer clear of, saving and being sensible so I'd always have surplus for a rainy day. Yet that day was here and the forecast was bleak. My pragmatism in the past had done nothing to stop me paying the price for daring to design a new life.

When the incessant collating and calculating was finally over and I completed that dreaded financial statement, something came over me. I was forever changed. For the first time in my life I was getting about in the world as someone with clarity (for my finances, at least). I knew exactly how much money I had to my name. I knew precisely – almost to the cent – what I spent on sunblock, school uniforms and jars of Vegemite on any given week. I was across rugby registration fees, iceblocks after school, and luxuries such as a leg wax and theatre tickets. I knew what day the car lease, internet and health insurance direct debits came out of my account, and I put the dates in my diary so I would never again receive one of those passive-aggressive dishonour texts. I was even up to speed on the size of my modest retirement pool.

This financial clear-headedness brought elation. Those late nights hovering over my laptop, downloading long-forgotten bank statements and being accountable for my spending had altered my neural pathways. I was revelling in the sheer joy of being on top of things, of knowing for the first time where I stood with my own money. I felt responsible. Like an adult.

At a time when women often have so little power over anything at all – the very nature of divorce or separation – getting your head around your personal economic outlook (however dismal it might appear) can bring a sense of autonomy over your own financial destiny that, for many single mothers, has been missing for a long time.

Despite all the inroads on gender equality, so many women still hand over financial control to their husbands or partners, trusting they'll do the right thing by us and our kids. The storyline is embedded deep in our subconscious – that women are helpless (and hopeless) when it comes to money, and we're waiting for a man to rescue us. We follow the script without even realising. Then if we decide to – or have no choice but to – leave, or we are left, or our partner dies, we don't know where to start.

Divorce coach and divorce lawyer Prudence Henschke advises that, when going through separation, it's important to get legal advice early so you know what you're entitled to. 'A lot of the fear is about the unknown,' she said. 'Your ex-partner might be saying things that aren't right and that's perpetuating the fear. Get credible information to understand where you stand and what your entitlements are in terms of spousal support and child support. Then you can make informed decisions from there.'

I was in my mid-forties, looking down the barrel of starting again with hardly any money, certainly not enough to house myself and my two boys. This was despite working and saving diligently, doing all the 'right things' to secure my financial future. The 'nest egg' investment units I bought as a single woman had been offloaded for the family home I had just left. Any savings that I'd carefully accumulated by conscientious and scrupulous thriftiness had been chipped away at for general living over the years, exponentially so since choosing the path of single motherhood. On paper, the entire scenario appeared downright terrifying and if I thought about it too much (I tried not to) I would collapse in a quivering heap of dismay.

My situation, while unique in the details, is sadly not unique. Working hard, investing smartly, being sensible with money, being a 'good saver', are not protective measures in the face of single mother-hood and all the varying circumstances that bring us here. Many of us are, at best, back to where we started, except with dependents and far greater expenses in the bargain. The only thing we can take from this is to not repeat the mistakes of our past.

Becoming Money Conscious

As single mothers, we become adept at stretching a dollar. Life is not the same as it was when you come down from two incomes (in many cases, but not all, of course) to one, with children depending on you. And the pressures on single mothers by choice and widows are often even greater, with the financial burden all on them.

I'm aware that my circumstances make me far better off than many single mothers. I may have lost my job, but I receive regular mandated child-support payments, which may not cover the rent but is more than some get. And I have an education, a professional reputation and years of experience to help me get back on my feet. But I, too, know what it's like to have to rein things in. To buy the 1-litre milk instead of the 3-litre one despite it being more expensive in the long run, because that's all I can afford when I scrape the coins together from the bottom of my handbag, all I have to my name until payday ... in four days and counting. Begging Energy Australia to give me an extension on the electricity bill. Topping up petrol in ten-dollar increments, praying it doesn't run dry. (And it has.) Turning up to dinners after the actual dinner so the night out costs me nothing. I check the prices at the supermarket before lobbing food in the trolley, adding up the total in my head to make sure it comes in under the balance in my bank account. Many times I've had to sheepishly put items back on the counter because my sums were off. I occasionally see other women do this, too, and I wonder if they're single mums. This is new for me. When we had two incomes, I was in no way loaded but, when shopping for basics, if we needed it, or wanted it, in it went.

Single motherhood forced journalist Kelly Baker to realise, for the first time, that she hadn't been responsible with money. 'If I had ... I wouldn't be in the position I'm in right now – shifting cash from the credit card to cover the electricity bill and then back just in time to cover the gas', she wrote in an article for *9Honey* titled, 'I used to be rich but now I shop at ALDI'. 'What I will do is budget and be conservative. Because I now have the deep and terrifying awareness that life can spin on a dime. You can go from one end of the spectrum (rich fancy wife) to the other (where is Centrelink?) – just like that.'

Michelle's financial position forced her to work out her priorities. 'When my marriage ended I was desperate to keep the family home, but I had to make some tough decisions about what was important to me', she said. 'It's important to me to have quality time with my girls. We don't need to have a thousand things or this big supercalifragilistic house. So I made the decision that I wasn't going to fight for my home and I sold it. Most of my money goes on rent. I'm not earning anywhere near as much as I would if I was on a corporate salary, but it enables me to have time with the girls.'

There's a theory that less money begets less money. To flip it, it's easier for people with more money to save money by being able to maximise on incentives. You get a discount on the electricity bill if you pay by a certain date. But if your child-support payment isn't in yet and the rent is due that same week and your kid needs new school shoes because his toes are hurting, you can't make the early payment so you wind up paying more. It's the same with bulk buys at the supermarket. There are savings if you get two trays of sausages instead of one. But fat good that is if the budget doesn't allow it. It's astronomically cheaper to buy a car up-front than on a long-term lease with 6 per cent interest. But only if you have a spare fifteen grand or so sitting around.

'It's expensive to be poor,' said journalist Rick Morton, who wrote about this wealth bias in his powerful memoir, *One Hundred Years of Dirt*. It's the story of his own life growing up in poverty in rural Queensland. But the hero of the book is his mother, Deb, who raised Rick and his two siblings on her own in an enforced hand-to-mouth existence after her marriage ended and they were forced to leave the family farm. He observed his mum's meticulous accounting of her spending – noting every bus ticket, every coffee, every tin of baked beans – and thought this was normal. He described his mother's predicament as 'structural poverty'. Being 'poor' as opposed to 'broke'.

That is by no means my situation. But I do know what it's like to be cognisant of every last cent – to be broke, not poor.

Paying Down Your Debts

I have learned the hard way that debts come first. When money is stretched, this seems counterintuitive. It can be tempting to delegate debt to the bottom drawer. We shelve it as a low priority, way beneath supporting ourselves and our families, assuming liabilities can be put on hold – indefinitely – to be dealt with some other day, if there's anything left over. I resented the outgoings because it felt like money for nothing. But debt is not only financially costly, in terms of interest and penalties, it also takes a toll on your emotional state. Money owing – no matter the size – can wreak havoc with your conscience.

Ironically, it was when money was the tightest in my life – after first moving out of the family home with my two young kids – that I got better at dealing with debt, starting with credit cards. I didn't think it was possible to exist without a credit card. I'd been using them as my safety net my entire working life when, in reality, they were a never-ending vortex of deficit. Then I jumped on *The Barefoot Investor* bandwagon, a runaway bestseller teaching people how to get a handle on their finances. Author and investment adviser Scott Pape recommends that people 'detonate debt' by paying down their credit cards and then destroying them.

When I decided to give it a go, I had three credit cards with total debts of about $9000. I took out a 24-month interest-free card where I offloaded the debt, and paid the whole lot off in the requisite time, direct debiting payments each fortnight. I now have zero credit card debt. Because I have no credit card, I spend only what I actually have. It's liberating. I feel quite unencumbered.

Becoming Frugal

I have, by necessity, become a master of frugality. I'm getting quite good at making money last. Here are some of my findings (they'll be obvious to the initiated!):

- Mince meat is your friend.
- Eggs are also your friend. A dozen eggs can feed the whole family.
- Keep a box of Aldi chicken dinosaur nuggets in the freezer – around three dollars for a ready meal with some salad or vegies.
- Fruits and vegetables are seasonal – those in season are cheaper.
- 'School mum' coffee mornings are free if you go just for the chat and don't order anything.

- Save on your electricity costs by doing the washing during off-peak hours and on 'economy cycle'. It means I'm hanging washing on the balcony at 11 p.m., but it's quite pleasant at that hour.
- The same goes for fans or air conditioning in summer and heaters in winter: only switch them on after 8 p.m. and only if it's a heatwave/cold spell.
- There's no need to buy books – that's what libraries are for. I also bought myself a Kindle. In the long run, it's cheaper to buy e-books than the real thing.
- Avoid parking fines. That goes without saying, of course, but sometimes you don't have enough coins for the ticket so you decide to risk it as you're only ducking into a shop and you get slugged with a $272 fine. (If that should happen, ask the Office of State Debt Recovery to put you on a payment plan.)
- Avoid the shops on the way home from school pick-up or you'll be dragged into Bakers Delight for custard scrolls. Head straight home. A smoothie made out of the leftover fruit from the kids' lunchboxes will do the trick.
- Ask yourself with every cent you spend on anything, *Do I really need it? Will it change my life or my kids' lives for the better in some profound way?* If not, think again.
- Boring but vital: make a budget and stick to it.

Delaying Gratification

Once I started paying down debt, I found I wanted to keep it up. It was like a debt-reduction muscle that strengthens with use. Paying off that credit card by the interest-free deadline made me even more discerning in my spending. I've come to regard all purchases as 'risks', potentially hurling me back to where I started – a deep, dark well of arrears. It may have made me too cautious, but persistent restraint has a welcome side effect: delaying gratification has become my default.

We simplistically assume that getting what we want when we want it – instant gratification – is the stuff of happiness. But research shows that lasting happiness – happiness with substance – often comes from dreaming and longing for something that is unattainable right now, and the sense of achievement we gain from working (or saving) towards that thing down the track. We're more likely to appreciate rare indulgences – like a new bra (I've bought one bra in two years!) or lunch at a restaurant (similar odds to the bra) – when they're not on tap.

Since becoming a single mother and being required to pull in the reins more than before, no longer in a position to buy stuff that I 'want', many everyday items have become luxuries, deprivation escalating their worth. Such as new sheets – I was down to one set of sheets, which were getting threadbare, but instead of treating myself to a new set, I held off, waiting for a sale and until I had no other overriding expenses. And until my fitted sheet ripped fair down the middle. When I eventually got my hands on a set of new linen sheets and matching pillowcase, the delight was immense. I felt proud of myself for abstaining and couldn't wait to unfurl my new purchase. I stood at the door of my bedroom and fawned over my fresh manchester as if it were a thing of great opulence.

The sheets were on par with the thrill of new runners after five years. Or a cosy woollen jumper for winter, new pyjamas and a raincoat. These once run-of-the-mill purchases have taken on the aura of self-indulgent extravagance.

Buying Necessities

Delaying gratification can swing too far the other way. I once made do with a broken plastic jug, refraining from replacing it until I could justify it. That gratification delay was more about self-worth, flagellating myself with a handle-less jug as if reminding myself how low I'd come. I delayed my gratification to the extreme at times, tipping myself into virtual martyrdom. The sweet spot is to delay gratification on wants but not on necessities, and to have the wisdom to be able to tell the difference.

A necessity is something that makes your life easier and that you can afford (even if you have to use Afterpay). To clarify, a TV is a necessity. So is a washing machine. For me, anyway. Yet I denied myself both.

Within weeks of buying our first TV for our new home, the screen had cracked. (Plasma TV screens crack like iPads when a toy F1 Hercules people carrier 'flies' into them, it turns out.) I budgeted for six months before we got another one. Then it smashed, too! A ball, this time. It was bound to happen. A TV in a living room that serves as a playroom for two lively boys is not a good fit.

We went without a TV for a good while after that. And it wasn't good for any of us, not just because you can't really do without a TV when you have young kids in a small apartment with no yard, but because it made me feel 'less than'. Having no TV, an item as indispensable as hot showers for most Western families, played into my poverty narrative, the story I was used to telling myself – that I was struggling, and that I wasn't deserving.

When I eventually tried our luck with TV number three – as a family Christmas present – I realised what we'd been missing. I'd been depriving myself and my boys of this essential contemporary apparatus. Once I'd enlisted my friend's husband, Gus, to hook it up, life improved instantly, our new TV engaging the boys while I cooked dinner, meditated or finished off a writing deadline. It allowed for 'family movie nights' as we leaned on each other on the couch, working our way through kid classics with all the sequels: *Night at the Museum*, *The Incredibles*, *Toy Story*, *Free Willy*. If we finished dinner in time, we sat down together to watch *The Voice*. And I had a giddying array of Netflix to trawl through after the boys had gone to sleep. Such was my joy, it was as if TV had just been invented.

There were other household items that I decided to class as necessities after abstaining: a washing machine, a fan, a vacuum cleaner with proper suction, dining chairs that don't break when you sit on them and, yes, definitely a plastic jug.

Budgeting

Rather than draft a budget with regimented spending requirements that I can never stick to and then feel guilty and abandon the whole mission, I prefer to budget by depositing a certain percentage of my incomings into one bank account for daily expenses, while siphoning off the rest into savings accounts for splurges (another *Barefoot Investor* strategy). Then I spend only what I have, while the savings start to gradually mount (in theory).

Bronte has worked out a few budgeting hacks over her nineteen years of parenting, the last seven as a single mum. Including:

- **Be an economical cook:** 'I'll do a big gourmet dish a couple of times a week and make it last: shepherd's pie, risotto, quiche. If you've already got the basic ingredients at home, you can feed the whole family really cheaply.'
- **Shop at Aldi:** 'Aldi is so much cheaper. You can spend $120 at Aldi and for the same amount of stuff in Woolies or Coles it's $300. I've done the maths.'
- **Shop with a list:** 'And stick to it so you only buy what you need. I got strict with myself and stopped getting a six-dollar smoothie when I'm at the shops.'
- **Where possible, make your own:** 'I never buy cakes. It's cheaper to make your own cakes and they're better for you. I also make pizzas, including the dough.'
- **Never shop when you're hungry:** 'Everything looks more delicious when you're hungry. You end up buying twice as much.'
- **Eat out only on birthdays:** 'It makes it more special.'

- **Buy second hand:** 'I'm a shopaholic but I rarely buy new. I love going to second-hand shops. Half my clothes are from Lifeline and most of them are labels. I set aside money for second-hand books as well.'
- **Buy small luxuries:** 'I think it's really important that you indulge yourself occasionally because it makes you feel good. Even if it's just a five-dollar lip gloss.'

Shop from Your Pantry

My friend Tory told me about a tip that a friend gave her when she was lamenting her household money woes. 'Eat down the house,' her friend suggested. It means eating food only from your own pantry or fridge and buying nothing new, aside from fresh fruits and vegetables.

We all have a stash of food that never gets eaten and winds up getting chucked out when it's way beyond its 'best before' date. If I look closely at the frozen goods in my freezer, there's usually a meal to be made. If you go for a week or so without replenishing stock, you can save a packet.

Shop from Your Wardrobe

A similar concept to eating down the house is shopping from your wardrobe. It's a tip from Michelle Broadbent, who runs a business supporting overwhelmed female entrepreneurs. 'Each season I pull every item out of my wardrobe and decide if I'm going to keep or chuck. I mix and match all my clothes and write down every outfit. The first time I did it, I didn't need to buy a single item of clothing because I had six months' worth of outfits. I do it with the kids' clothes, too. I replace things I really need instead of roaming around the shops. Shopping centres are a great place to kill time and then, before you know, it, you've bought a ton of stuff you don't need.'

Wearing clothes we already own is also more sustainable. We can all do our bit by not adding to the estimated 92 million tonnes of unwanted clothing that ends up in landfill each year around the globe. Accepting hand-me-downs helps, too. My sister-in-law, Lucy, occasionally bestows on me a giant bag of clothes that her two boys have grown out of for my boys. School mums often present each other with uniforms our kids have outgrown. At the end of every season, I'm handed piles of school gear, and I do the same for others. It's not only good for the budget, but also for the environment.

Use What You Have

In an episode of her *Happier* podcast, Gretchen Rubin discussed the concept of 'using what you have'. She and her co-host, sister Elizabeth Craft, shared tips like those above, including 'shop your closet' and 'cook from your pantry', along with reading books you already own and using up the half-empty containers of lotions and shampoo in the bathroom before heading out to buy new ones.

I get a thrill out of making things last. I cut the toothpaste tube, moisturiser and sunblock to scrape out the last remnants and extend their life. I add water to surface spray. It buys me another week. And I wash the resealable sandwich bags and hang them on the clothes line. It's quite satisfying getting holes in my socks because it means I have used them to the death for the purpose they were intended.

Spend Well

Financial adviser and author Melissa Browne, who runs financial education courses for women – many of them single mums – says she's 'not a fan' of the word 'budget' as it has too many rules and can make us feel like we're failing. In her book, *Budgets Don't Work (But This Does)*, and via her Instagram page @moremoneyforshoes, she helps women become conscious of their spending while setting money aside for essentials.

'Single mums are already in that mindset of lack so instead of thinking about lack and deprivation and budgets, it's about spending well,' she told me. 'It's setting up your finances in a way that serves you, not sabotages you.'

Melissa is also not a fan of credit cards or 'buy now, pay later' schemes, which, research shows, cause us to overspend. She advises using apps such as MoneyBrilliant and Pocketbook to help track your spending and 'bring awareness to your spending choices'.

Adjust Your Spending Habits

Melissa has noticed many of her single mum clients are stretching themselves to try to hang on to the life they had before they were raising kids on their own. 'Too many single mothers get into a trap of "my kids used to have this life and I want to keep that up", she explained. 'It can be everything from the suburb they live in, the rent, the school the kids go to, the brands they're wearing, the devices they use. But is that a need or a want? They need to decide what life they're going to *choose* and make conscious spending choices rather than defaulting to the life they used to lead, which is keeping them in debt.'

Indulge in Small Luxuries

I followed Deepak Chopra's '21 Days of Abundance' daily meditations and mantras, sent via my friend Juliet. The intention was to eliminate money blocks and hopefully shift me into more elevated ways of thinking. I bought a pack of coloured Post-it notes for the abundance affirmations, sticking them on my bedroom wall.

Day 11: I expect and accept abundance to flow easily to me.
Day 17: I move through my days lighthearted and carefree,
   knowing all is well.
Day 21: Every moment of every day I live my life abundantly.

Day 20's theme was 'Living Luxury', with the accompanying mantra, *Today I treat myself to moments of luxury*. I was surprised at first to see it in the mix, such is my own aversion to spending on myself. But I decided to hear Deepak out.

'The more we bring small luxuries into our life', said Deepak in his trance-like timbre, 'the more we will recognise ourselves as a worthy, spiritual being deserving of love and abundance.' When we value ourselves, we surround ourselves with 'luxury', which doesn't have to equate to great expense but rather small pleasures beyond what we 'need'.

As it was a challenge, I complied. I bought myself a By Charlotte lotus necklace to replace the one I'd taken off at work and never saw again. It was a small gesture but I felt like a queen, honouring my worth. The whole exercise helped me to chill out, trusting that I am supported and all will be well.

When we indulge ourselves in big purchases often, the gloss wears off. When we're on what Gretchen Rubin calls the 'hedonic treadmill', it 'transforms delightful luxuries into dull necessities'. You run the risk of that when you allow yourself to have everything you desire at the exact moment you desire it. But when we make 'small luxuries' a habit, as Deepak prescribes, even the most modest acquisitions can feel like pure indulgence. Books are like that for me now. So are pedicures and breakfast at a cafe. I weigh up each purchase as if it's a special occasion. Luxuries can also be use of time, a decision to defer one thing for another. Like reading a book, going for a long bushwalk or talking to a friend on the phone instead of trawling through the backlog of 6000 emails or sending that pitch.

A luxury doesn't have to be expensive to have the effect of making us feel indulged. A bulk packet of Maltesers every time I go to Aldi is my go-to luxury any day of the week.

Accepting Generosity

My kids may not have a pool or a PlayStation or do tennis lessons or go to restaurants that much, and I regret that they haven't been able to learn a musical instrument (the cost of tuition cut that venture short), but we're getting by just fine. However, when offers of assistance come, I'm immensely grateful. At first I felt shame in that, the very idea of being perceived by anyone as a 'person in need'. But I've come to see the spirit in which this giving is intended – just as I feel when I lend a hand to someone else. The succour that comes from the kindness of others far outweighs my own pride and discomfort.

My school-mum friend, Lisa, knows how to tread that fine line of support without making it awkward. She once casually handed me a bag with a returned pair of runners from our boys' recent play date and at the bottom was a still-warm lasagne, fresh out of her oven. 'To save you cooking tonight,' she said. Once I returned to the car from school drop-off to find a parcel on my windscreen – afternoon tea for the boys. At a particularly difficult time, Lisa and another school-mum friend, Brigitta, gifted me a voucher from The Dinner Ladies for ready-cooked meals. It was a godsend – not so much for the money saved, but for the reprieve from having to think about what to do for dinner. One less decision to make.

Another friend, Sophie, handed me a huge batch of her home-made pasta sauce after we'd met for a bushwalk, enough for a week of dinners. Kristin paid for my fruit and vegetables at Harris Farm when we happened to be there together, tapping her card at the checkout before I could protest. My school-friend Juliet tried to cover my electricity account when I had no means to pay it. While it was such a kind gesture that it made me cry, I drew the line there. She has also lent us her house when her family is away. With a pool, a trampoline and a backyard to shoot their Nerf guns, my boys call it 'the resort'. My friend Bronte, a single mother herself to three kids, once tried to send me a supermarket voucher. I flat out refused because she needed the money more than me but, my goodness, the big-heartedness!

Sometimes strangers step in, like the time I took my boys to Dubbo Zoo. We camped in the zoo overnight, getting to feed the animals at dusk and dawn, for a story I was writing on the experience. The next night we headed out for pizza with a lovely family we'd met at the Billabong camp – a mum and her two kids, similar ages to mine – bonding over meeting the resident snake that was handed around at dinnertime. When the bill came, she swooped in and took care of it and wouldn't hear another word about it. We had only just met. I hadn't discussed my financial situation with her at all, but she knew that I was a single mum who had recently moved out of home with my two little boys and wanted to ease the load. Her kind deed warmed my heart.

I've never needed to ask for financial help (except when I asked my brother to borrow money to pay the bond on our apartment when we left home). But many single mothers don't have a choice.

Eva used to earn 'big money' as a banker but she was forced to quit when she had her second baby on her own, as she simply couldn't keep up the hours, and has often found herself short of cash. 'I've been in financial crisis a few times and I've actually had to ask friends for money,' she said. 'It's weird but it gets easier. I've paid them all back but it's humiliating to be in such dire straits. I've been down to my last dollar. Even now I still live week to week. It's a shocker.'

Teaching Kids About Money

Shakti said that she's open with her son about her financial situation so he can understand the concept of priorities. 'I don't show him my financial stress but if I'm unable to pick him up from school if I'm working, I'm transparent with him, saying, "I have to work so we can have a roof over our heads." He's aware we live in a small apartment compared to some of his friends and I've explained to him that's the trade-off. We went to Disneyland, lots of kids don't get to go to Disneyland and we can only do those things while we live in a little apartment. I like the ritual of going to a cafe together, but that means there's other things we don't do. I'm like, "I can't afford a box of cherries but we can get a handful." We can have things that we want within limitation. It's a life lesson.'

I take my boys to the local bookstore sometimes. They're allowed to choose one book each. Sure, I can afford more books (most weeks!) but I want them to delay gratification and learn to budget – to understand that there's a finite pool of money and we must make wise decisions about how it's divvied up. I drag them to the supermarket almost every time I go. When they're not building a fort with the toilet roll stacks, I ask them to help me choose the items based on what's on special and what's the best value for money: 'Let's hold off on the Nutri-Grain this week because it's full price ... Get the bulk pack of sausages and we'll freeze the rest.' And then there's more money for books. They've learned to scout for the 'on special' signs and to read how much items are per gram, not the end price. I want the boys to be involved in the family budgeting decisions, and also, as they get older, to understand that I'm here to sustain them, but not to serve them.

Putting a cap on spending also teaches our kids to value what they have. It's impossible to keep across this when you're co-parenting and have no say in what stuff your kids get when they're with their other parent, especially when there's an undeniable wealth disparity. However, where possible, we owe it to our kids to set limits.

I only allow my boys to get toys for birthdays or Christmas. They protest this often, stating their case for a more regular rollout. But what I know, and they don't, is that they treasure these toys far more, knowing they're not on tap. Buzz Lightyear and Woody still take pride of place in the toy basket several years after their arrival. Otis begged me for 'army guys' for months. I finally got him a set for his eighth birthday and he loves them so much that he keeps them in a 'special place', separate from the cavalry. A large military plane was Jasper's Christmas present in 2016 and it's still taken for regular joy flights around the lounge room, the army guys clinging on for dear life. The handmade wooden toys made specifically for the boys by 'The Swiss Toymaker', Armin Koch – including a firetruck, bi-plane, two police cars and a farm – are hallowed.

'It's great to be comfortable in this world, and I work hard to give to my children,' said Aisha. 'But a bit of poverty and struggle vaccinates them against arrogance. It's been instrumental to my children's personal growth. According to my values as a Muslim, it's what you leave behind, raising children as leaders for the next generation, that matters most. I'm teaching them to be humble so when they come into abundance, material or spiritual, they will always remain grateful.'

One thing I didn't want to pass on to my kids was my fear. I look around me some days and I wonder, *How did I end up in a worse financial position than before they were born?* I had been sensible and discerning and future focused. I had worked hard to protect myself against the exact scenario where I now find myself: renting and watching my money, weighing up even the most modest purchases, depriving myself and my boys of some of our greatest joys (such as holidays away), not sure how to navigate my way out.

At times like this, when practical solutions prove elusive and you have so little control over the outcome, the only way out is to go within. I had to delve deep into my role in this financial mess and get honest with myself about my contribution. It wasn't so much in terms of spending or even handing over my power like I had, but in the entrenched beliefs I had around money that had led me here. The time had come to shift my 'money mindset'.

SINGLE MOTHER WISDOM

- It serves you to become financially literate, educating yourself on your financial position: incomings and outgoings, debts and direct debits and superannuation. This might sound obvious but it often takes a life change – like raising children by yourself – to make you get a grip.

- Get rid of credit cards – spend only what you have.

- Become accountable for your spending and look for ways to be frugal. Ask yourself if each purchase will really change your life or your kids' lives for the better.

- Pay down debts as a matter of priority.

- Delay gratification – lasting happiness comes from anticipation, not in getting what we want when we want it.

- Don't deny yourself necessities – they make your life easier and help to enhance your self-worth.

- Indulge in small luxuries – they don't have to cost a lot, but they help you to feel worthy and deserving of greater prosperity.

- Develop budgeting hacks such as never shopping when you're hungry and using what you already have before you restock.

- Accept generosity. People don't give unless they want to.

- Be mindful that your money habits are important teaching moments for your children – they are watching and absorbing everything you do.

CHAPTER 13

Money Mindset

I have come to understand – although I am still working out how to apply it in practice – that one of the greatest things we can do to impact our financial future, along with making money, sticking to a budget, saving and investing, is developing an 'abundance consciousness'. In order to make real and lasting change, it's important not only to educate ourselves on sound money management, but also to overhaul our deeply rooted subconscious attitudes about money – to shift our money mindset.

Advice from the Experts

I spoke to two dynamos in the field of financial abundance who have helped countless women to reframe their approach to money and wealth. These women both have a particular desire to help single mothers to break free of limiting money patterns, which are so easy to fall into. Denise Duffield-Thomas, founder of Lucky Bitch, has built her own multi-million-dollar empire via her books and Money Bootcamp, inspiring women, many of them single mothers, to release their money blocks and shift their money mindset. Canna Campbell is the founder of SugarMumma.TV, a financial adviser and bestselling author. She has built a mass following through her practical hacks demonstrating how to create financial freedom, as she has done.

Our Money Story

Denise Duffield-Thomas believes that we all have a 'money story', usually formed in childhood, which informs our beliefs and attitudes about money and, ultimately, how much we have. Our money story has a profound impact on our financial situation, often holding us back from generating wealth. Everything from our family to the city where we grew up and, of course, gender affects our relationship with money.

'We're born into a lineage around money,' Denise said. 'All families have unofficial mottoes about money which are drummed into us and which we inadvertently take on. In my case it was, "It's nice to be important, but it's important to be nice," meaning, "You can't have a good job and be nice at the same time. It's one or the other." It could be that you have to work hard for your money or money makes you selfish.'

My own money story, which I picked up somewhere along the way, is that wealthy people are inauthentic. And I'm not that – authenticity is one of my defining values. Growing up as one of six kids, I also somehow took on the delusion that there wasn't enough to go around (money, food, clothes, love, whatever), even though in our home this was far from the case. Deep down I feared everything was finite – it would all run out someday so I must hang on tightly.

I have work to do to unravel these misconceptions if I have any hope of becoming financially independent.

Single Mother Money Story

It was Denise's own childhood, being raised by a single mum who struggled financially, that helped lead her to the work she does. 'Having those experiences of powerlessness around money has given me a drive to help women break free from their money stories and make their own money and have financial independence.'

In her workshops, Denise has observed that single mothers often have specific money stories, universal scenarios that get 'dialled up' in the circumstances, such as:

- 'There's never enough.'
- 'I can't trust anyone.'
- 'I have to work hard to make money.'
- 'I'm not good with money.'
- 'Other people have it all.'
- 'It's all on my shoulders.' (I added that one!)

There is also the guilt factor, often exacerbated for single mothers. 'There's that sense of, I can make money or I can be a good mum, but I can't have both,' said Denise. 'We've got that selfless mother story that "everyone's going to think I'm a bad mum", which is heightened for single mothers who are already feeling like they're not enough.'

My single mother money story runs along the lines of, *Everyone else is better off than me* (the old victim narrative strikes again). It plays like a loop in my head – like background noise, only it sinks in.

One of the most insidious, subconscious money stories we need to watch out for is 'scarcity thinking'. Usually ingrained in us in childhood, it permeates not just our attitudes around money, but everything. Denise recalls with sharp clarity the exact moment this idea took root for her: 'I overheard my mum saying to her friend, "I don't know what I'm going to feed them this week." I was eight. That was my first inkling of scarcity, that sense of, *Oh my God, we're not going to have enough to eat.* For many of us that becomes, *How dare you ask or desire or articulate what you want.'*

Denise helps people to identify their beliefs and conditioning around money, and consciously decide to rewrite the story. 'There's one thing we can control and it's our own personal mindset around money,' she said. 'A good money mindset is improving the stories and beliefs that we have about money in relation to our ability to earn it, keep it, and be a good person with it.'

If our beliefs inform our thoughts and our words, then it serves us to also watch how we talk about money as it perpetuates more of the same.

Creating a Positive Money Story for Our Kids

As we become conscious of our own damaging money stories, the tales we've told ourselves and bought into for most of our lives, we can at least be more mindful of the financial credo we're passing on to our kids. Denise advises that we aim to 'create neutrality' with our children around money. Instead of telling them we can't afford something, say, 'We're just looking today', or 'We're saving for a holiday', or suggest they put the desired item on their birthday list, so as not to shame them for wanting it.

As single mothers, we do often reprimand our kids for asking for things because of our own frustration and shame at not being able to provide them. Instead of focusing on lack, we can reframe it to focus on our values.

'I straight up say to my kids, "It's not in my values to buy you heaps of plastic junk. I'm not going to buy stuff for the sake of it,"' Denise said. 'Our kids are watching how we talk about money and how we spend money. That's how they learn.'

Whenever my boys ask for something, which is every time we go to the shops, as kids are wont to do, I say, 'I don't mind you asking and thanks for letting me know what you'd like, but we're not going to get that today because you may not value it.' This goes for LEGO, gaming arcades, toy helicopters, hot chips and whatever else catches their eyes. Every so often I oblige. We line up at the Boost Juice counter and order two 'original' size Mango Magics, and my boys are beyond thrilled. But I bet they wouldn't react like that if it was a regular occurrence.

'They're going to have their own money stuff. It's impossible not to,' Denise concluded. 'But a really good lesson to teach them is money doesn't make you a good or bad person, it doesn't make you happy or unhappy. Money's just money. It's hard with single parenthood because there are circumstances beyond your control. Ask yourself, *What values do I want my kids to have?* If you can instil that in them, they're going to be fine.'

Creating a Side Hustle

Canna Campbell was a single mother to her young son after her marriage broke up. She has since remarried and had another child but, through her own experience and advising clients in her financial planning practice, she understands all too well the struggle to keep afloat on one income. 'It was a really frightening time and I had no idea how it was going to work,' she said. 'But I knew I was making the right decision and I had to continue on. I had to follow my instinct and do what was best for my child and myself.'

Like Denise, Canna also believes that single mothers are often hampered by their 'money story'. 'For a lot of single mums their money block comes from a place of scarcity, fearing that they won't have enough, that money will run out,' she said. 'That may be because of the way their previous relationships worked, where they might have had lack of access to money or lack of control with money. There are so many different forms of financial abuse.'

Canna created The $1000 Project, hacks for making extra cash on the side. It was borne out of her own attempts to pay off her home loan as a single parent, a technique she shares on her heavily sub-scribed YouTube channel, SugarMamma.TV. 'I wanted to show people the power of taking one big goal and breaking it down into bite-size steps, and I thought the best way to do this is to lead by example,' she said. 'I was in a position where I couldn't afford to invest because I was on such a tight budget, but I thought perhaps I can do extra things in my spare time when my son's at his father's house or when he's asleep to bring in extra money to put towards investing. And that's what I did.'

Canna did market research and took on extra projects, 'racking my brains for as many different weird and wonderful ways to make money'. Every time she 'hustled' an extra thousand dollars, Canna would invest in shares. It's now a six-figure portfolio, the dividend income going to charity, fittingly the 1000 Girls project through World Vision.

Mindful Money

Canna is on a mission to teach women, in particular, to be more mindful with money. Her motto is: 'Only buy what you love, value and appreciate.'

'I'm never going to be a financial planner that says you can't spend, but spend on things you value because it means you're living your best life,' said Canna. 'Have mindful financial goals while putting money aside into savings and an investment portfolio and understand how your superannuation works.'

Despite being financially savvy, Canna is of the view that we take money too seriously – that it's a human construct to which we add meaning. 'Some people are intimidated and scared of money, but money is just energy,' she said. 'The more money you've got, the more energy you've got, the more choice you've got. Money's always flowing. Just like the ocean is always moving. People are great at having it flow out but they aren't great at having it flow in.'

Canna also suggests that we become conscious of how we were programmed about money as a child, challenging ourselves to rewire these misconceptions and to create a new money mindset: 'When people say, "I'm bad at money", I tell them to change it to something like, "Previously I've had troubles with money, but I'm working on fixing this."'

Budgeting and Goal-setting

'Having a budget isn't about being poor,' Canna said. 'A budget is a playground with a fence around it so you can play to your heart's content as long as you don't go outside the boundaries. It's a really empowering tool.'

Canna said it's important not only to budget for now, but also to prepare for the future. 'Many people focus purely on saving money. There's a lot of talk about budgeting food and putting money aside for holidays. But saving can only take you so far. We've got to learn how to invest, how to get our money working for us to set ourselves up for financial freedom and independence.'

Canna believes that having financial goals is especially important for single mothers. 'It's not just about the next five years, but what happens when the children turn eighteen and there's no more child support,' she said. 'What have you got in superannuation or investments? How will you keep your head above water in the long term? You have to plan ahead.'

Acting Abundantly

I'm working to cultivate a 'prosperity mindset'. It's much the same as an abundance mindset, only with more of a focus on attracting financial wealth.

I started with loving my bills. I used to resent paying bills, holding out until the last minute and then some. I hoped if I ignored them they might go away. As a first order of business, my life-coach friend, Alexandra Andrews, instructed me to get on top of my accounts owing. By paying others what they're owed, I'm signalling that I expect the same for myself.

Who would I be if I was financially abundant? How would I act? I'd go to cafes for breakfast and restaurants for dinner. I'd take my kids on holidays without trying to get story commissions to fund them. I'd buy more books, a bedhead and go to the theatre more often, paying for a babysitter to make it possible. I'd buy that dress, that handbag and a new pair of trainers (my current ones have holes in the toes). I'd replace the ten-year-old mattress that's starting to slope. I'd buy more gifts for friends, art for myself, get a cleaner, get my boys a desk (perhaps one for myself, too) and – pipe dream – move to a bigger home with a backyard, maybe even a swimming pool. I'd go skiing every year, both in Australia and overseas (when international travel eventually returns to normal). And I'd get my kids a dog.

I may not be able to do all of that right now. But acting abundantly doesn't mean living beyond our means. It's shifting into a prosperity mindset and acting accordingly. One thing I can control is how I feel. With an abundance consciousness, I would feel safe, secure and grateful. I'd be lighter. I would stop being so cautious and splurge on things I can afford, not weighing up every cent, such as takeaway dinners, flowers and good olive oil. I'd pay bills on time and invoice as soon as my work is published. I'd stop saying 'money is tight' and being resentful of those who seem to have it all. I would live for now instead of waiting for my life to begin.

'I feel tremendous relief in recognising that I do not have to wait for the money or the things to materialise before I can feel better,' wrote Esther and Jerry Hicks in *Money and the Law of Attraction* as an example of an empowering money story. '. . . When I do feel better, the things and experiences and money that I want must come.'

I'm rewiring my financial beliefs, rewriting my money story and acting abundantly. On a practical level, I'm getting a handle on my own finances. For the first time ever, I am hovering more in prosperity consciousness than not. I'm living in hope, not fear. This is a giant leap forward.

SINGLE MOTHER WISDOM

- It's up to us to determine our money mindset.

- Once you become aware of your subconscious beliefs about money, you can rewrite your 'money story' and change any limiting 'money blocks' and patterns.

- We can help shape our kids' 'money stories' by being open with them and watching our language around money.

- Act abundantly. This doesn't mean living beyond your means, but thinking and behaving like someone who is abundant, which will attract more of the same.

- Shift from fear to hope to trust to expectation – this state is fertile ground for inspiration.

Part Three:
CREATION

'All of the joy in my life has come from going towards the hard thing. And then there's the hard thing and then there's after and the after of the hard thing is the real joy.'

GLENNON DOYLE,
Interview with Sarah Kanowski,
Conversations podcast, aired 26 June 2020

CHAPTER 14

Single Mum Evolution

I realise now, some four years after I left home with my boys, that everything that had transpired to this point had to happen – the tumultuous union that became untenable enough for me to leave home, the rocking of my foundations, the thwarting of a vision of a united family of four, the single motherhood and all the doubt, fear, struggle and sheer panic that went with it. The rug had to be pulled out from under me, because this is what it took for me to wake up. Before all this I was more of a passive observer, letting life unfold around me as if I had no say in it. I was existing, not creating, bracing myself for the next inevitable hit. But in choosing to swim (not sink), I was making a conscious choice that this would be the making of me, not the breaking of me. If I couldn't do it for myself all these years – step up and take responsibility for my life – I could do it for my children.

Big life circumstances alter us, but only we get to decide in what way. They can deplete us and knock us about, leaving us jaded, resentful and cautious about life. Or they can be the catalyst for transformation, an opportunity to heal our wounds and become aware of who we are in the world. I had taken the first route many times – pretty much every time – and it only brought me back to the same place. My despair and displacement had become so unbearable that at last I was ready for an alternate reality.

I'm certainly not the woman I was before it all began. However, this was not a given – growth is not a happenstance of nature or an inevitability of passing time. It's a gentle unfolding of our own doing.

As the late Debbie Ford wrote in *Spiritual Divorce*, the choice is ours to make. 'In each moment many different futures are available to you,' she wrote. 'All of them are trying to lead you back to your divine nature.'

For a good couple of years after leaving our family home, I was far from myself. I had allowed myself to meander so off course that it was at times a bit of a stretch to recall, no less reignite, the woman I knew myself to be. I was on top of the day-to-day logistics of raising my boys – I never missed a beat there. But at the same time, I was often on edge, jittery, confidence sapped and humourless. I was uncharacteristically withdrawn. It was entirely possible for these two states – competent, ever-present, loving mother and lost woman – to coexist. Wasn't I once upbeat, engaging and social, commanding a room, aware of my passions and proclivities, interested in the world beyond my own? Or maybe that was just the blurry vision of who I hoped to be. Nevertheless, it was an alluring prototype to adopt for what possibilities lay on the other side of where I was.

Getting back to myself wouldn't just happen. It would require work, as it does for anyone who has been thrown off kilter. First, we must get quiet – quiet enough to know that we're exactly where we're meant to be, to understand and to accept that everything that has happened has brought us here. It's often a prerequisite that we go through the fire, where the heat becomes intense enough to compel us to find another way. 'You can look back and regret or you can look back and say, "that's what got me here",' said author and spiritual teacher Gabrielle Bernstein to a room of two thousand people at a seminar I attended in Sydney.

If leaving home and ending my relationship was 'destruction', day-to-day living and raising my boys (cooking bulk spaghetti bolognaise while doing sight words and times tables and hanging out washing at 11 p.m.) was a 'reset' – adapting to a new rhythm – then this (where I got to decide to heal and learn and evolve) was surely 'creation'. The foundations I lay in this phase will set the course for the rest of my life. I have a say in it. I don't need to be a passenger.

While my journey has been rough going at times and I have endured those lost nights on my bedroom floor, I'm thankful for all of it because I am forever altered (in a good way) and have learned vital lessons along the way – about life and about myself.

Here are some of my new understandings.

1. There Are Gifts in Suffering

Matt, my chiropractor and kinesiologist (who I started going to regularly to help ease the tension in my neck, flare-ups coinciding with Christmas, electricity bills and the kids being away), suggested that I write a list of the 'gifts' in my suffering so I could see clearly how it had served me. 'Ask yourself what's good about this,' he advised. 'The universe is working *for* us, not against us.' It was a tall order because at that point, I couldn't see much good in it at all.

'It's put you on the hero's journey, for starters,' said Matt. By that he meant the 'journey' all of us choose to go on when we decide to evolve beyond our suffering. When presented with a 'disturbance', instead of ducking and weaving or blaming others – or our circumstances – we opt for self-discovery and transformation. It's the arc for every ripping story ever told.

I had already worked out, through trial and error, that avoidance and blame only brought me back to the start. So this time I decided to take the *heroine's* journey, a path well worn by single mothers. Here are some of the gifts in my suffering, the 'silver linings':

- It led me to learn to meditate and become more conscious.
- It led me to take responsibility for my life.
- It helped me to generate more self-love and self-worth.
- It gave me the opportunity for a clean slate to create my future.
- I have learned to come from love, not fear, more often than not (and when I don't, I try again).
- I am more appreciative of small joys.
- I have greater empathy, strength and compassion.
- I have firmer boundaries – for me and for my boys; I tolerate less.
- I know that I am capable of much more than I realised.
- I have accepted that I am enough.
- I have stepped up my motherhood game because there was no one to pick up the slack.
- I can cope with my boys' 'big emotions', like sadness, anger and fear – I had faced them in myself so they no longer scare me.
- I shape my life from my own hopes and dreams, not from others' expectations.
- I am less afraid of suffering, seeing it as an instigator of growth.
- I have more hope.

Although the catalysts for becoming single mothers are divergent and our circumstances are all manifestly different, one thing most of us have in common is that we all face immense challenges. These can be the making of us.

'I wouldn't be the person I am today if I hadn't been through all that trauma,' said Tory, who has sole custody of her daughter. 'It's allowed me to step into my true power and potential because I've owned it, I've conquered it, I've marinated in it. I never once said, "This is a bad thing that's happened to me." It was very stressful and I cried a lot as the lessons kept coming. But once you get through that tunnel to the other side of the light, your whole being becomes this higher vibration. I feel like my life has begun all over again. I'm on this whole new path and I can't wait to see what happens next.'

'My entire journey has been incredible and I don't regret any of it because I've arrived here,' said Danielle, whose own growth has been so profound it inspired her career as an integrative life coach. 'This person wouldn't have needed to rise from the ashes, to find all the resilience, gumption and strength it takes to survive and thrive. It's important to recognise that tipping point where you don't need to be in survival mode anymore, and allow yourself to thrive. You can let fear ride roughshod over you or you can ride in.'

2. Thank Your Enemies

We all have them: people who have let us down, abandoned us, betrayed us. But our so-called 'enemies' are our teachers. We can be grateful for everyone on our path, including those who've hurt us deeply. People who might appear to be causing suffering are there to help us grow. 'Bless them,' said Wendy, my other kinesiologist, without a hint of condescension. 'Thank them for the lessons. People teach you a lot when they're un-evolved.'

Thankfully, we don't have to actually pick up the phone and thank our enemies. It's enough to acknowledge to ourselves their contribution. But I'm willing to try on the concept of seeing the bigger lessons in my interactions. We attract people and situations that mirror back to us the way we see the world; it's this that needs to shift before anything else will. It's the paradox of forgiveness – it doesn't so much free the one we're forgiving, it frees us.

In *Spiritual Divorce*, Debbie Ford suggested that we make the 'life-altering choice' to reinterpret our experiences so that they 'empower rather than disempower' us: 'Our resentments are like a steel cord wrapped around our past, forever binding us to those we see as our opponents,' she wrote. 'We must become willing to step through the constricting door of blame into the unbounded world of forgiveness.'

'Life is way too short to hold grudges,' said Inez. 'I've wasted so many years crying, being on antidepressants, seeing counsellors and lawyers, sitting in courtrooms. It's taken two failed relationships, good therapy and learning to meditate to be able to forgive and put it behind me. That's ten years I won't get back, but at least I'm stronger for it.'

'I'm really grateful to my ex, even though he drives me crazy,' laughed Julia Hasche. 'I'm a mum because of him, and I have my business because of him. I'm glad I'm having this experience. Being a single mum is hugely empowering. It's made me a better person and it's made me stronger.'

3. Be a Warrior

'There's time to be a yogi and there's time to be a warrior,' my meditation teacher, Tim Brown, said to me just weeks after I officially became a single mother and wasn't sure how I would cope with all the pressures bearing down on me. 'Right now you need to be a warrior.' He was referring to a scene from the famous Hindu text, the Bhagavad Gita, where the god Krishna tells the warrior Arjuna that, despite his resistance, he must fight on the battlefield and stand up for what's right. It's a metaphor for the internal battles we all wage, and it was the perfect metaphor for my life circumstances back then. The time had come to rise up and step into the breach, to do what was required of me as a woman and a mother, for my sake and my boys. To be a warrior, I could no longer be a victim. It's impossible for the two to coexist.

'I got this illustrator to draw me with a cape because anyone who's a single parent is a fucking superhero,' said Zoe.

'It's tempting to think, *I'm the one who's being wronged here, I'm the victim*,' said Lara, whose ex-husband doesn't contribute financially and rarely sees the kids. 'But you have to look at, "Okay, how did I end up in this situation?" I came to the conclusion that I'd actually committed a crime against myself by not being true to myself.'

'When you're a single parent, you're going to drop the ball and make mistakes and you're gonna see icky sides of yourself,' said Shakti. 'And there comes a time where you can't blame anyone. You actually get stuck with yourself. Then it's like, I can either keep doing what I've been doing, or I can resolve this stuff. When you've got a kid who hasn't slept properly for eighteen months, when you're in the midst of separation with a newborn and trying to figure out how you're going to financially survive, that's when you see parts of yourself that aren't so pretty. It was a real opportunity for me. I'm kinder, more resilient, I'm way more self-sufficient and, at the same time, I know how to ask for help when I need it.'

4. Rewrite the Script

We get to choose what story to tell, to ourselves and others. Not in any way to glorify our role in it, but because of the power of words to influence our reality. I could easily run with the narrative of being powerless and choice-less, holed up in a small rental apartment with my two young kids, forever shackled to my past, unable to give them the life they deserve. Or there's this version, which is equally true: I'm an empowered 'warrior woman' who took brave steps to move us forward so we can live in harmony in a home filled with love, respect and understanding. The rest – and the best – is yet to come. That's a much more conducive launching pad from which to create our brighter future.

Lisa said that she's rewriting her own narrative around being a single mum: 'If I was to say, "It's so hard being a solo parent" and got into worry all the time, then that's what I'd be living because wherever our attention is, is where we're at. So I flipped it. Many women think their happiness relies on everyone around them being okay, when really we get to choose that for ourselves, we get to set our vibration. As soon as I fall into that victim-hood speak of "woe is me, this is so hard, this is relentless", I cut off the possibility of it being anything other than that.'

Selwa, who bravely left her emotionally abusive husband with her two young daughters in the mid-seventies, said she was motivated by the desire to create a better life for her children: 'I wanted to be the best possible person I could as a woman and a mother for them to have someone to look up to.'

5. Create a Life You Love

So long as we're writing our own script, let's make it a good one. Yes, this may not be what I had in mind for my life, but what if it's even better? I live with two beautiful, wise, funny, big-hearted boys, who I get to learn from every day. They need me as much as I need them (for now, anyway). When I read them a story at bedtime, one cuddled up on each side of me, I couldn't be happier. 'Everyone I love most in the world is in this room,' I say to them. I love this life we three have created.

'We should all be thinking how to create a life we don't want to escape from,' said Lisa. 'I see it as another adventure, as evolution. My life is right here, right now. I can make it mean whatever I want. So why don't I choose to make it mean something positive for myself that I get to evolve, grow, find out how strong I am, how resilient I am? And I get to witness my kids' lives every single day.'

6. Find the Pride

'You should be so proud of what you're doing,' my friend and life coach Alexandra said to me one afternoon over lemon tea in her sun-filled front room. I glanced down at my teacup, my eyes welling with tears because no one had really said this to me before – not about me as a single mother. 'You moved out of home with two young kids, you're holding down a high-pressured, high-profile job, you're paying the rent and bills, with very little support, and you're managing to give your boys a great life. Focus on that.'

Alexandra's offering shifted something in me. For several years, I'd been so engrossed in scrambling to keep my head above water and shield my young boys from any fallout from their two-homes situation, striving to give them as 'normal' a life as possible, that I hadn't stopped to consider it from this perspective. That rather than *compensating* in the life I was etching out for us, I was delivering. I had been in survival mode, forever feeling deficient for not doing enough or being enough. I didn't look up for long enough to realise that I was in fact a *warrior*, carrying out a role that might trip others up at the pass.

I was gradually coming to accept that I'm stronger than I ever knew, determined and fiercely loyal. I'm resourceful, capable, tolerant, malleable, patient (sometimes), positive (eventually) and, when I remember, I come from love. But until then I hadn't been proud.

Another friend, Kristin, likes to joke that I'm like Princess Diana. Aside from the fact that Diana had several nannies and houses and cash to burn (she would hardly have had to save up for her sons' haircuts), I warmed to the analogy. I flicked on the TV one night and caught a documentary marking the twentieth anniversary of Diana's death, and I started weeping. It's the images of Di as a single mum that got me – on the waterslide with William and Harry, their three faces alive with joy. William on his first day at senior school with his beaming mum and little brother by his side. The trio on the ski fields in Austria. I'd never thought of her in this light before.

Diana may not have done it as tough as every other single mother financially, but she still knew what it was like to make do with scheduled time with her beloved boys and, presumably, make parenting calls on her own. That's to be lauded, no matter who you are. Diana seemed, from the outside anyway, to come into her own as a single mum – as if she got herself back. It's a familiar tale.

'I'm incredibly proud of myself because I think the hardest thing anyone can do is raise children on their own,' said Lara. 'Everything in our world is geared towards two parents raising a child. When you're doing it on your own, in my case with zero help, no co-parent, no family support, it's a huge achievement. My kids are teenagers now and we've got into a groove. But at first I was just, "Wow! I'm doing this!"'

'I did a big thing,' said Stella. 'I left my marriage and moved a family of three into a house by myself. I've done a pretty good job navigating two children through it all. I've screwed up plenty of times. But it's important not to be too hard on yourself. I'm proud that I'm raising good men: polite, outspoken, colourful personalities.'

'It's even more important for me to be a good parent as a single parent 'cause no one's going to pick up the slack,' said Bek, a mother to a son via a donor.

'I wear my single mum title like a badge of honour,' said Aisha. 'Because whatever I have achieved, I did it through my strong work ethic and my drive. And I did it on my own. Being a single mum has taught me to be more forgiving and compassionate and show kindness because I've been through the darkness.'

7. Back Yourself

As a single parent, we have to do most things. We can view this as a burden or a wonderful opportunity to test our limits. I have taken a five- and six-year-old overseas on my own and on several long road trips since they were even younger. I have assembled an IKEA outdoor table and a tent with no assistance (save from said kids), and pulled off the extraordinary feat of crumbing fish fillets while simultaneously assisting with an eleventh-hour Ned Kelly project, offering considered feedback on a poetry recital, registering for the swimming carnival and ironing the next day's school shirts all before getting my boys to bed and writing an article due the next morning. I've got us covered!

Katrina said that being a single mum has helped her to see what she's made of. 'I feel a bit ashamed that I handed over so much responsibility in my marriage for adulting. I've had to dig deep from that spiritual perspective of trusting that all the answers are inside me, trusting that I can steer my own course.'

8. Be Grateful for What Brought You Here

I doubt I would have the solid relationship I have with my sons if I wasn't a single mother. Because they rely solely on me (when they're with me), we are uncannily tuned in with each other (most of the time) and I can help turn their upsets and disappointments into teaching moments. My youngest once told me how he was asked by his Year 2 classmates to mediate their playground disputes. 'I ask to hear one side of the story and tell the other kid to not interrupt, then I let the other kid speak, and then I ask them to be the bigger person, forgive and move on,' he explained. And I was flushed with pride and the realisation of how this split family scenario – and all my boys have been through – is serving them. I don't want to change a thing because it's brought us here. I have no doubt that I'm right where I'm meant to be to learn the lessons I need to learn to move us to the next phase of our lives.

'Everything happens for a reason,' said Zoe. 'I'm very lucky that I have my son and he has two parents who love him. The family thing just wasn't to be for us. But I've had experiences I wouldn't have had if I was still married. You can become this bitter angry person or you can look to the future and see how you can make a better life for yourself and be a better mum. Realising I have no control over anyone apart from myself was a really big moment. It's what's got me through.'

The Making of Us

So many single mothers have told me that the experience of bringing up children on their own or as co-parents has been the making of them. 'My load has lightened,' said Emily, a mother of two who endured an extremely acrimonious divorce. 'I feel free as a person. After this long, stressful marriage I feel like time stood still for twenty years and now I'm asking myself, "Who am I?" I'm making choices for myself. I can do what I want, within reason. I'm still a single mother with two kids and carry all of those responsibilities. But things are much brighter.'

Despite all Neve has been through – the shock and heartache of finding out her husband had been unfaithful for the best part of their marriage, leaving her to raise three grief-stricken children on her own, on top of the devastation of losing a child – she says there's no doubt the experience has shaped her. 'Even though the loneliness can be debilitating and the self-doubt can cut you to pieces, if you can get past that and begin to remember who you really are, instead of having the edge taken off the joy in life, you can really sink into that joy and get thrilled at your own potential,' she reflected.

'I'm excited because I'm a person with a lot to give and I don't doubt that I'll make my life a good life.'

'For the first few years I was in reactive mode,' said Eliza. 'When you've got young children you don't have time to think about much else. Now I wouldn't change anything. Independence, freedom and self-reliance: they're my favourite words in the world. I've got an open slate to start again. That's a privileged position to be in.'

'It has strengthened my self-love,' said Fiona. 'I don't know if I would've got that if I hadn't become a single mum, because I would have been relying on my ex to give me that reinforcement. I look back now and think, "Thank God my marriage ended because I wouldn't be the person or the mother I wanted to be if it hadn't." It's given me a lot more faith in myself.'

'Single motherhood has shown me I'm capable of more than I ever imagined,' said Francesca. 'It's not a sprint, it's a marathon and I need to be really consistent in my approach to be able to get through. I've learned to be calm under pressure. If I lose it, we all go down. My daughter's going to be okay if I'm okay. I'm really mindful of that.'

Vanessa Roworth, a single mother by choice, said motherhood has changed her. 'I'm more resilient, resourceful and self-reliant. Raising Betsy has proved to me that I can stand on my own two feet, while also giving me the confidence to reach out when I need to. I'm swimming in the deep end and I feel so privileged.'

Wisdom from an Expert

'I've never seen a client who at the end doesn't think it was the best thing that ever happened to them,' said divorce coach Prudence Henschke. And she speaks with good authority, having parlayed her successful career as a divorce lawyer into divorce coaching after she realised it's not enough for her clients to 'get through it'. She wants them to be the better for it.

'Any challenge you're faced with forces you to grow,' she said. 'These things all happen for a reason, which may not be evident at the time, but most women, when they reflect on the end of their marriage and where they're at now, see it was a huge opportunity to change and grow. Without that catalyst that evolution probably wouldn't have happened. It's painful and challenging but there are rewards on the other side.'

Divorce coaching is a burgeoning field as women (mainly) recognise that, far from being the end of the road, it's just the start. Prudence helps propel women forward by sharing strategies to plan for the future. 'It's an opportunity to get to know yourself and move on. Ask "How do I want my life to look?" There's something better out there.'

While a married mother herself, Prudence's work in family law and divorce coaching – which she runs as two separate practices ('No one wants their lawyer to tell them to meditate,' she laughed) – has given her profound admiration for single mothers. She has started the Instagram hashtag #singlemothersvoxpop, collating the wisdom of single mums from around the world. 'I have enormous respect for single mums. I don't know how they do it most of the time,' she said.

As comforting and reassuring as it is to be seen by others, real transformation comes when we see ourselves.

SINGLE MOTHER WISDOM

- There are gifts in suffering. It's up to us to interpret how we view our circumstances and find the 'silver linings'.

- Big life changes alter us, but we get to decide whether they empower or disempower us.

- Our 'enemies' can be our greatest teachers. People who might be causing us to suffer might also be helping us to grow.

- Being a single mother is a time to be a 'warrior', to rise up and do what's required of us as a woman and as a mother.

- We can rewrite the script of our lives. We get to choose what story to tell, which in turn informs our perspective. Take time to be proud of where you're at.

- Create a life you love. As single mothers, we have the scope to do that on our own terms.

- Single motherhood gives you the chance to test your limits.

- Be grateful for what brought you here – everything you've been through has led you to this point.

- Single motherhood can be the making of you. It's an invitation to grow and evolve with a clean slate, from where you get to create your future.

CHAPTER 15

Self-care Revolution

NOTE: This chapter discusses spiritual concepts including meditation and trusting in a higher power. If this isn't your thing, feel free to skip it. If you're curious, read on. My spiritual practice is the thing that has sustained me more than anything on my single mother journey. Not only has it helped me make sense of how I got here, but it is also propelling me forward.

When Elizabeth Gilbert speaks, women listen. She inspired millions of women around the world with her seminal internal-truth-seeking memoir, *Eat, Pray, Love*, and her story of leaving her marriage and going in search of herself. We grabbed onto it as proof that if we follow our hearts and be introspective, we can create a life we love, too. This is the path to transformation.

One weekday morning I found myself, along with hundreds of other women, listening to Liz at a Business Chicks breakfast at Sydney's Luna Park. You would expect a woman as accomplished as Liz Gilbert addressing a captive audience of women in business – a roomful of goal-kicking, driven, multitasking women – might validate the doing-it-all versions of ourselves, commending us for our determination, resilience and competency. But she caught us all off guard. Her message, in no uncertain terms, was to chill out.

'I want to see a revolution of women who are relaxed,' said Liz. We laughed. We thought she was joking. 'You laugh because it seems so very out of reach.' Yep, it sure does. It also doesn't seem a very admirable thing to aspire to – not with the way we've been brought up. As Liz pointed out, women through the ages have always been strong, brave, resilient, wholehearted and courageous. That's our shtick. 'There's nothing radical or revolutionary about it.' But relaxed: now that would be something.

Relaxed doesn't mean lying around in bubble baths. It means shelving worry, anxiety and hyper-vigilance (default settings for women since the dawn of time) for being centred, calm and detached from drama. It means being at peace no matter what tornado is swirling. To, as Liz put it, 'drop into wordless one-ness in connection with the entire field of consciousness'.

I have experienced this when I meditate, which I do twice a day. Meditation is not only relaxing, but also a portal to this state of heightened awareness. I watch myself as if from above, staying calm, unruffled and in a state of love while all my tethers to security are being buffeted at their foundations. When I meditate, I'm relaxed. Not always, of course – I lose it often enough and I get trapped by my ego and desire to have things go a different way. But I also know there's an alternative. I know what's on offer when I let it all go.

This is what self-care looks like: making the time to remember who we are.

Create Boundaries

Liz suggested that one of the clearest paths to ignite this 'relaxed life' revolution is to set some boundaries. '"I don't care" are the three most powerful words a woman can have in her vocabulary,' she said.

The mistake women so often make is that we slip into 'toxic femininity', where we over-give to try to appease others or make them happy, without considering our own boundaries. Liz shared an anecdote of her own slide into toxic femininity after her divorce. 'I kept reacting by giving more so he wouldn't be mad. I was trying to see it from the spiritual point of view and be giving. I was trying to be Gandhi and Mandela – but those guys are lawyers,' she laughed.

Eloise King, a solo parent to a son, said that with her professional experience as a psychotherapist and founder of The Self-Love Project, she now sees clearly the trap she fell into. 'There's a danger for single mothers to kick into that mindset of, "I have to be father, mother, everything to this child,"' she said. 'That equates to being in survival mode rather than creation mode. That drive to look after my child and be the only one responsible for them, it's a very masculine energy. The danger is you can go too far in that direction and stop nourishing yourself. You have to be mindful to look after yourself as a single mother otherwise things can go south pretty quickly. If we don't manage our stress or take care of ourselves emotionally, if we're not mindful of having some level of balance, it seeps out sideways. And the people that bear the brunt of that are our kids.'

I must admit, my boundaries are a little blurry around the edges. I, too, am guilty of the common single mother tendency of overcompensating with our kids to make up for the life we have given them (coming from the ludicrous premise that it's deficient). It's one thing to see everything through the filter of what's best for my boys (as I do); it's quite another to make my life about theirs (as I also do), which leaves no room for my own. I will do whatever it takes to shield them from any harm – psychological often being the greatest risk in our world – working to erect impenetrable boundaries around their precious, impressionable hearts (an exercise that is futile in itself). But this doesn't mean I have to lose myself in the process.

Understand that We Create Our Reality

'Why is this happening to me?' I asked my chiropractor one day about an upsetting turn of events that rattled me.

'It's not happening *to* you,' Matt replied without a hint of irony. 'You have co-created it.' Like many in his field, Matt also practises kinesiology and Neuro Emotional Technique (NET). The modalities operate on the premise that we store emotional memories in our bodies, which are fused deep into our subconscious and which we repeat as patterns throughout our lives. We get stuck in a never-ending playbook that reinforces the unresolved emotions and unconscious beliefs we formed in childhood.

'Be aware that you created these circumstances so you can grow and learn the lessons you need,' he told me. 'When you come from the darkness you can appreciate the contrast.'

When I sit on that chair, miracles happen. Long-forgotten memories rise to the surface, providing context to how I wound up where I did. It's the basic spiritual law that we choose our thoughts, which inform our beliefs, which, in turn, create our reality. I baulked at this concept at first, railed against it, because it's affronting when you're more used to heaping the blame outside of yourself. *What does any of this have to do with me?* But it's an empowering position to take – if I created this, then what else am I capable of creating?

Since I have started to peel back these layers – via kinesiology and meditation (double dipping on introspection) – I have noticed profound shifts in myself. I'm less reactive, for starters. I can sit in the uncertainty about my future, yet not panic. I might occasionally feel adrift from human connection, yet no longer see this as a reflection of my worth. I'm more content and far more courageous, more future focused, not pulled asunder by the past. Synchronicity becomes a daily occurrence as the 'right' people cross my path. I begin to see with astounding clarity why I have been reacting the way I have for most of my life.

I still freak out sometimes. I get worried and despondent, mostly about single mother stuff, such as the seemingly impossible burden of creating a happy childhood for my kids. But I'm no longer running from the darkest parts of myself.

How to Self-care

Divorce coach Prudence Henschke started a blog called Mama's Me-time to promote the importance of single mothers prioritising regular time for themselves – what she calls 'practices to maintain your sanity' – in whatever form that takes.

'The last thing women want to hear is, "You need to be doing more self-care." Add that to the list. But they do need to find what fills their cup,' Prudence said. 'Sometimes self-care is just giving yourself a break, mentally letting things go, not being so hard on yourself, trying to quieten the inner critic, the negative self-talk. It's not the pampering. It's a lot deeper than that. It's a mindset.'

Sounds simple, only it's not. Friends bought me a massage voucher for my birthday one year; I accidentally let it lapse. I've been gifted scented candles and left them in the cupboard. It's not about time, it's about worth. I don't want to 'waste' those candles on me. As mothers we're conditioned to put everyone else first and we think that if we do something for ourselves, we're letting the side down. The neurosis is even more chronic for single mothers, constantly on guard fearing we might miss a moment if we avert our gaze. Co-parents want to make the most of the time when our kids are on our watch, not be dashing off to a barre class – especially when we're doing paid work that already takes us away from them.

Prudence believes it's imperative that we work through our 'blocks' to self-care. If not for us, then for our kids. 'It's about recognising you're important and doing things for yourself,' she said. 'For some women the easiest pathway to that is to think you're doing it for your children, otherwise you won't be able to continue to serve your children. If you let that go, everything starts to unravel. You have to counterbalance the stress or it just takes over.'

Meditate

I learned Vedic meditation when I was pregnant with Jasper more than a decade ago. It's been a non-negotiable ever since. At least twenty minutes, twice a day. Meditation is more than a relaxation technique. Countless scientific studies have proven that regular meditation alters our brain chemistry. It makes us calmer, more focused, and mentally strong. And, contrary to popular misconception, including my own false starts, it's stunningly simple.

Since my boys could talk they have commanded, 'Mummy, go and meditate' because it meant a rare session of TV or Roblox. No doubt they're also cognisant of the stark contrast between when I meditate and when I don't. We three have come to understand that if Mummy misses her meditation, it's not good for anyone. It's an investment in the boys as much as in me because they get me showing up in a way I simply wouldn't have the capacity to do if I was on edge. Of course, I get it wrong now and then. I raise my voice more than I am comfortable with. I snap sometimes. I spiral into old patterns of insecurity and self-doubt. But because of my regular meditation practice, I'm aware when that happens and can catch myself and make amends. As a single mother with all the extra demands placed on us (logistical, emotional, financial and the huge weight of responsibility), meditation is my vital secret weapon.

I'm not alone. Katrina Blowers learned to meditate after having a panic attack live on air while reading the news. She only managed to get out the words 'Good evening' before going blank. Realising something was wrong, the director cut to a story to get her off air and recover. It was this wake-up call, in front of hundreds of thousands of people, that led Katrina to learn Vedic meditation, which she now practises regularly. 'Other people perceived me to be calm, but I never felt that way inside, particularly through divorce. I felt like I had an internal storm brewing the whole time. I internalised a lot of stress because I didn't want to burden my children. I didn't want them to see that I was struggling or that I wasn't their rock. Meditation has enabled me to match my inside with my outside.'

Katrina said that meditation has also helped her to be less reactive. 'When my children do something that would normally make me fly off the handle, I'm able to take a pause between processing what's happened and reacting to it. I'm able to make better choices. It's been an amazing growth experience. I never thought I would become a daily meditator but it brings me a lot of clarity and peace. It makes me feel like there's a much bigger picture out there, which I'm a part of.'

'You still have the same problems but you frame them differently,' explained Tina. 'Meditation allows you to cope.'

Practise Mindfulness

For Francesca, her Buddhist mindfulness practice is vital for her relationship with her daughter: 'To be truly awake and present, you've got to be aware of your thinking and who you're being in the world. You're awake in a really loving way to everything that's happening in your life, which is so important for motherhood, especially when you're doing it alone. The greatest benefactor of that is ultimately my daughter because I'm more present for her.'

Practise Yoga

'Yoga held me,' said Shakti. 'I'm so grateful I had such a diligent yoga and meditation practice before all this happened. In my darkest hours there was always this light where I trusted I'd be okay in the end. I couldn't see how, I couldn't see when, but I knew there was a part of me that was indestructible. My teacher said to me, "You don't need to practise every day, but there'll come a time where you'll be grateful you practised every day." It's been my lifeline.'

Make Time

'I know I'm the best mother possible when I'm in the best space possible,' said Francesca. 'I need time out to reflect, recalibrate, process, to be thoughtful about my life and who I want to be in it. As a solo parent, I don't have that time. I don't get every second weekend off. I don't get the chance to replenish and restore what's been lost in my busy days as a single mum. I'm always compromised and I find that really challenging. Time alone remains for me that elusive elixir I'm dying to drink.'

Lisa also believes that it's vital we find a way to facilitate time to ourselves: 'If I'm starting to feel like it's relentless, then it's on me to call my parents and say, "I need a night free from the kids" or get a babysitter to stay overnight so I can have a night in a hotel. I'm lucky I've got those choices. I know that if I want to be okay, I need to ask myself the question, "What will make me happy today?" I make self-care a priority. Although I've got kids with me full time, I'm still okay because I choose to support myself. Don't put yourself on the bottom of the priority list, put yourself on the top and see how your life starts to change.'

Kelly is also learning that it's worth the effort of carving out time alone. 'It's really important for me to take time out from the relentlessness of solo parenting,' she said. 'I force myself to do things I know I "should" do, like going away on trips by myself, because the mental downtime and the ability to not have to think about anyone but myself recharges the batteries. I never want to go because I don't want to be away from the kids. But when I do go, I'm always glad that I did.'

Spend Time in Stillness

It's one of the paradoxes of single motherhood that we desperately crave the headspace to think clearly and re-energise, yet it's often impossible to find that time. Stillness is like an unattainable dream.

I've come to learn that there's always time to be still because it's a place we go to in our heads. We can be still before we go to sleep, on the bus, in the school pick-up line, in the shower. It takes no time at all.

'I used to be one of those people who said, "I don't have time to meditate. I never have any time on my own",' said Tory. 'Then this Buddhist monk in Thailand called bullshit. He said, "Who's in the shower with you in the morning?" Um, no one. I have no excuse. Every morning in the shower, I set up my intentions for the day. I make sure I have a really strong mindset. It calms everything down. That's my ritual.'

Divorce coach Prudence Henschke agrees that making room for stillness is especially important for single mothers. 'You've got to give your mind time to digest,' she said. 'I talk to clients about the importance of solitude, meditation and journalling in order to process the transition in their lives.'

Trust in a Higher Power

'At some point you have to decide if you're in or you're out,' Tim, my meditation teacher, said during one of his Facebook live group meditations. 'You either believe in the power of nature or you don't. You can't sit on the fence.'

For most of my life I was on the fence. I was dazzled by the notion of something greater than myself, intrigued by the concept of 'universal law' or 'nature', as Tim calls it. But I wasn't convinced. Despite the mountain of self-help books I'd devoured, twice daily meditations, kinesiology, yoga, seminars, podcasts and Instagram livestreams by spiritual leaders, TEDx Talks and Oprah's SuperSoul

Sessions, I still lived like I was the one in charge. As my father said to me not long before he died when I asked about his faith, I had been 'hedging my bets'.

But then my call to action came – to step up and raise two young boys on my own. I could cut corners all I liked when it was just me. Sink or swim, it wouldn't really matter either way. But with these great loves of my life depending on me, sinking was no longer an option.

Raising kids by yourself is an undeniable calling. We're required to deliver and call on resources beyond the realms of our knowledge and understanding. With nothing to lose, I decided to get off the fence, to trust in a higher power. The universe, God, my inner voice, divine intelligence. As spiritual teacher Gabrielle Bernstein said, 'I don't care what you call it, I just care that you call upon it.'

Trust that the Universe is Working for You

I've stuck a note on my fridge with the famous quote by the thirteenth century poet, Rumi: 'Live life as if everything is rigged in your favour.' It's an oldie. Seven centuries, to be precise. I see it every time I get milk, a reminder several times a day to trust everything is in divine order, even when it doesn't look like it. This was not the life I expected to be living – how is this in any way a good thing? As I delve deeper into my spiritual practice and strengthen my faith in a well-meaning higher power, I have come to see that all of my life happenings have served me in some way. It is, to put it simply, all for the best.

Go with the Flow

Our default setting as single mothers is a mad scramble to keep on top of it all. We're raising kids, often with little support, while holding down a job, bolting for school pick-up, playing Santa Claus, cracking the whip to get homework done and teeth brushed, sometimes managing tricky exes at the same time (or not having another parent to help share the load), all while keeping ourselves afloat financially. We strain and push, cajole and jostle in a desperate attempt to hold on for dear life and ensure we come out in one piece, preferably better than before.

But there is another way – one that doesn't lead to burnout. When we trust that all is as it should be and the universe is working for us, we can take our hands off the wheel and go with the flow. It's an art, a sweet spot between agitating for results and showing up. When we manage to 'surrender fear or desire', as my kinesiologist Wendy puts it, there's nothing else to do.

Pay Attention

The universe might have our backs, but we still have to do our bit. It's up to us to 'cultivate consciousness', to be aware of our thoughts and actions and pull ourselves up when we veer off course.

'Practise emotional discipline,' encouraged Marianne Williamson in a Zoom webinar I tuned in to. 'Say to yourself, *If I continue with that thought I'll spiral down.*'

Seek Therapy

Often it takes a momentous life change – such as raising kids on our own – to catapult us into a deeper inquiry of ourselves.

I don't need an excuse for therapy. I saw a spiritual psychologist named Sky for most of my thirties – pre-motherhood. Sky taught me to get out of my head and drop into stillness, a process she called 'stop and drop', which I use to this day. She was a loving, supportive, non-judgemental listener, providing respite from the sea of confusion and self-recrimination I was in back then.

I started psychotherapy as a new mum. I saw Melissa most weeks, bringing both my babies with me. A few years later I did group therapy, too. A group of women, all of us with young children, met every

Friday morning for three years. The power – and growth – lay not just in us nutting out what was going on in our lives, but also in the dynamics between us, which uncannily mirrored our 'real life' interactions. You can't hide in a room like that.

For many single mothers, therapy is their saviour. It's not cheap, but there are ways around that. In Australia, you're eligible for a Medicare rebate for several sessions a year with a mental health professional if you have a mental health treatment plan from your doctor. People in remote areas can access these services via telehealth video calls. Seeing a social worker is free when accessed via Centrelink. And services such as Relationships Australia often offer counselling with reduced fees, depending on your financial status.

'I started therapy after I split with my husband,' said Joy. 'It was a complete game-changer. I thought I was fine but when she asked me how I was, I couldn't stop crying. If you prompt me, I'll fall apart. It was basically grief counselling. She said to me, "You're being strong for everyone around you, you don't want your kids to see that you're upset. This is where you're allowed to let your shoulders down and cry and get all that grief out." I was resistant to therapy because my perception was, how can someone who doesn't know me help me? But I'd tell the therapist something and she would flip it back to me in a way I'd never looked at it.'

'My therapist helped me get to a place of accepting my situation and surrendering to the reality of it,' said Michelle. 'I was incredibly resistant. I was pissed off. I had become the worst version of myself. Having someone walk through the process with me was invaluable. It was a lot of going back into my subconscious mind and forgiving myself for my past so I didn't take it into my new life. I didn't want to be this bitter, twisted, woman. I wanted to be clear of it for me and my girls. That's when everything shifted. I hate to think how I would have turned out if I hadn't done that work.'

Practise Gratitude

At the end of each day, I scan my mind for a list of things to be grateful for because I've read the research: practising regular gratitude helps to build positive emotions, reduces stress and depression, improves health and builds resilience. Divorce coach Prudence Henschke encourages her clients to practise gratitude to see the positive in their circumstances. 'A gratitude practice turns your mind to things that are going well in life,' she said. 'It might be really basic stuff but it gets you to shift your mindset to what you do have, not focus on lack. There's a lot of science behind it.'

Michelle's therapist gave her a 'gratitude journal' and instructed her to write down what made her feel good. 'Some days were a struggle and I couldn't find anything,' she said. 'But soon I'd fill two pages. It's such a powerful practice, like an audit at the end of every day. It helps me to know myself better.'

'I often talk with the girls about being grateful,' said Tina. 'I'll say, "We're extremely lucky. We've got our health, clean air, good education, we're safe and happy. Just be grateful."'

'I include how it makes me feel because it hooks you into the emotional connection,' said Danielle, who writes a gratitude list each morning. 'Not only do you train your neural pathways to see the positive, you're actively triggering your happy hormones so it starts your day on a positive note.'

Writer Kerri Sackville is also stringent about her daily gratitude practice. 'A lot of it's about the kids because you're only as happy as your unhappiest child. When all three of my kids are happy, I feel like I've hit the jackpot. I have those moments where I start to think, *I don't have a partner, I haven't had sex in ages*, all that stuff. Then I look at what I do have: three amazing kids, great friends, a lovely home. I think how lucky am I to be able to lie in bed in the morning and drink my coffee at my leisure. Gratitude brings me back. It shifts my focus from what I don't have to what I do have.'

'When I wake up I set my intentions and clear my energy field because it's easy to take on negative energy when you're down in the dumps,' said Zoe.

Listen to the Whisper

'You have to listen to the whisper,' said Eloise. 'Your truth doesn't scream at you most of the time. It just whispers. You have to stop running and get out of survival mode to be able to connect with that space.' For her, having a spiritual practice is a non-negotiable. 'Spirituality is where the juice is,' she explained. 'When I stray from that I lose direction and things start to flip out sideways. If you're not nourishing your soul, then stress builds up and you snap and say something you regret. It's been incredibly important in terms of keeping a sane head and being able to have a quality relationship with my son.'

For Lisa, the tragedy of losing her husband after they separated led her to open herself to what she jokingly calls 'the woo woo stuff' and fully embrace her 'spiritual journey'. 'Picture this Australian girl at a mastermind retreat in Texas doing shamanic drumming and meeting my spirit guide and going into universal consciousness on a hotel room floor,' she laughed. 'Shifting at the subconscious level is where I'm at. For women it's about getting out of our heads, getting back into our body, choosing happiness and seeking joy and pleasure. It's important to be reminded of the insignificance of everything because we really do spend our lives caring about stuff that doesn't matter.'

Get in Nature

Where possible, I get in nature. I head to the bush straight after I've dropped my boys to school, to drink in the limitless beauty surrounding me. These bushwalks are part of my spiritual practice because when I pay attention to the twisted red gums crisscrossing a topaz sky, or a kookaburra soars so close to me I catch a glimpse of the blue shimmer on his wing before he lands to laugh with his mates on a branch, a bottle-green sea as their backdrop, it surely is a spiritual experience.

In her sublime book, *Phosphorescence: On awe, wonder and things that sustain you when the world goes dark,* Julia Baird cited studies proving what's not news to some of us: that bathing in nature is a salve like no other. Julia writes that, 'when we are exposed to sunlight, trees, water or even just a view of green leaves, we become happier, healthier and stronger'.

'I struggle to commit to things I would consider spiritual practices,' said Kelly. 'The closest I get is when I walk through bushland near my house. No music. No podcasts. Just being in nature. It calms my soul.'

Tina has taught her kids to observe nature: 'I say to them "Look at the light, look at that sunrise, have you noticed those flowers? They're starting to bloom." I want them to notice what's around them. I'm really conscious of the unfolding of nature and the seasons and the trees and the flowers. It grounds me.'

Choose Love Over Fear

When I remember, I ask myself the question, *What would love do now?* It acts as a compass for me.

We're always operating in one of two states: fear or love. Fear is emotional distress, resentment, the constricting stories of our past. Love – or faith – is hope and trust in the overriding positive force of nature.

'Faith and fear cannot coexist,' wrote Debbie Ford in *Spiritual Divorce.* 'Fear shuts us down while faith opens us up.' The choice is ours to make.

Do What You Loved Doing as a Kid

'I read that if you're struggling to figure how to make yourself happy, think about what you loved to do as a kid,' said Michelle. 'When I was a kid I loved dancing, so I went looking for a dance class. Doing dance classes not only makes me feel good, but it's helped unlock that side of me that thought I was unattractive without having to go and have sex with lots of people. I do at least one class a week. It's critical for my self-care.'

Set Goals

For Julia Hasche, the founder of Single Mother Survival Guide, it's setting goals that lights her fire. 'When I have time to myself I set goals because that's how I improve my life,' she said. 'Nothing's really going to change unless we plan. Otherwise it's whatever happens happens. There's always stuff to do as a single mum because we're running a home while working and raising kids and you're always thinking ahead. *I've got to pack the swim bag. Do I need anything for dinner?* You're not giving your brain space to be quiet. We get most creative when we can quieten our mind. When you have a clear plan, you can change your life.'

Make the Most of 'Alone Time'

For women who co-parent, it's important to make the most of that time when the kids are with their other parent instead of whiling the hours away. It can take a while to get into the swing of it.

'I didn't know what to do with myself at first,' said Michelle, whose daughters spend every second weekend with their father. 'I felt like a vagrant. I'd roam around shopping centres, not knowing how to fill my time. Then I thought, *This is ridiculous. You've got this time to yourself and you need to maximise it.* Now I see the weekends as 'me time' and I do things that fill my tank. Spending time with my girlfriends is super important to me because I'm fuelled by that connection. I like a bit of solitude, too, particularly being with the kids as much as I am.'

Model Self-care for Your Kids

Because my boys have grown up watching me meditate twice a day, pretty much without fail, not only do they get a calmer, more present mother (mostly!), they have also had it ingrained in them from day dot that me taking time out for myself is sacrosanct. I'm showing them that I matter. Often as single mothers, there is no one else to model that to our kids so we must be unambiguous about it.

'Some days I'd say, "I need some time out", and I'd lock myself in the bathroom and have a bubble bath with candles,' said parenting educator Maggie Dent. 'My boys would post notes under the door and I'd ignore them because I'd told them I just need half an hour and then I'll regroup because it can be really hard juggling the needs of four kids.'

Maggie says it's important as single mothers that we model self-care for our kids. 'My boys needed to know I wasn't their servant, I was their mother. And I needed to look after me because I was holding this ship together. As a single parent we can't tag team with another parent. We have to prioritise looking after ourselves because if we fall over, everything goes down.'

Julia Hasche is also a huge advocate for 'me time', encouraging her thousands of followers to make these practices a daily habit. 'Single mums often carry a lot of guilt for wanting to have time to themselves,' she said. 'They feel like their children are suffering enough because of their situation and they don't deserve to look after themselves. But it's more important than ever because you're going to come back refreshed and a better version of yourself and you're going to be a better mum so your kids benefit. When you have self-care, you're telling yourself that you matter. That's really important to your self-esteem and it flows on to your kids.'

Neen said that it was her children who realised she needed 'time out' after her husband died, and stepped in. 'I was so caught up in keeping busy and over-scheduling so we wouldn't feel alone,' she said. 'Then my son, Jett, eventually said to me, "You're holding us too tight; we need a break from you." He arranged for my sister to babysit for two weeks and 'made' me go on a holiday. It was like an intervention. It forced me to to be alone with my loneliness.'

Finding Religion

Many women find strength in their religion. Either the religion of their birth, which some say they returned to after they became single mothers as it brought comfort and continuity. Or others have turned to a new religion seeking clarity and a sense of purpose, a guiding set of principles to help right the ship after veering off course.

Even though I was raised Catholic, I did a runner for several years as soon as I left my Catholic high school. I've now found myself back in the fold, not so much because of my beliefs (which are more spiritual than religious), but because I appreciate the perk of being able to present Jesus as a role model to my boys. As far as good men go, Jesus is up there. And, on a less esoteric note, as a single mother I appreciate the structure. Having somewhere to be one Sunday of every month (for 'family mass'), followed by morning tea with the families from my boys' school, provides a sense of community that I am in no position to offer.

Buddhism

Fiona credits Buddhism with helping her to meet the challenges of being a single mother. She discovered Buddhism through *The Tibetan Book of Living and Dying*, recommended by another single mum friend who, Fiona observed, seemed 'zen and calm'. 'As I read I started sobbing tears of joy and recognition. I was like, *This is it.* I'd never seen it articulated this way before.'

'I love the Buddhist tenet to "tread gently on the earth", to stop grasping,' she said. 'I was attaching to things that aren't even real. It made me feel free. It doesn't mean I don't struggle as a single mum. Buddhism helped me to forgive myself, to know that I'm doing the best I can.'

Christianity

Bronte says her Christian faith has helped pull her through tough times. 'I prayed all through my marriage falling apart, asking God to guide me, to help me make the right decisions,' she said. '"Please help me do the right thing in the face of turmoil." I don't know how anyone gets through without faith. It's very comforting to know there's a higher power watching over you, making sure everything will work out for the best. That even though you're walking through troubles, he will carry you.'

Bronte also has taught her kids to do 'arrow prayers'. 'When you find yourself in situations where you're in panic, shoot an arrow prayer up to the sky. "Please, God" and "Thank you, God" are the easiest prayers in the world.'

Delilah also finds solace in her Christian faith – from the support in her church community, who provided her with prams and everything she needed for her baby, to her faith in God: 'It helps me feel less alone and it straightens out my priorities 'cause I kind of get stuck between going, "I really want to be a twenty-year-old, but I'm a mum." I have to find that balance. It helps me realise how much love I have in me to give to another person.'

Islam

Aisha attributes her Muslim faith with helping her pull through. 'I feel humbled that God has my back,' she said. 'I didn't lose my way and I could have. I always come back to what I know. We call it holding on to the rope of Allah. I had support from my community, who reminded me to put my faith in God and don't lose hope because my boys are watching me. I wanted to show them I could do it, to demonstrate that even when we're struggling to hold on to that rope, even if there's just a thread, hold on tightly and ask for help.'

Aisha explained the significance of mothers in Islam: 'In our religion, we say that the "dua" or the "supplication" of a mother is one of the most powerful forces in the universe. Mothers are highly respected because it's through our wombs that we give birth and that's the miracle of life. God says: "Revere the wombs that bore you." When we reach out to our creator, especially when you're a mother, God always hears.'

Judaism

Kerri attributes her Jewish religion with helping her feel supported as a single mother to three kids. 'It's not so much the faith but the culture around being Jewish, with its focus on family,' she said. 'We share every Friday night as a family for Shabbat dinner – we light candles, say prayers – so you always know that's there. It was important for the kids and me to have that consistency when our whole life had been turned upside down. Everything about my family had changed but we still had Friday night dinners, we still had Passover, Yom Kippur, Rosh Hashanah, which is Jewish New Year.'

Kerri said that one of the intrinsic parts of the Jewish religion is the sense of belonging, that no matter what happens, you feel a part of something. 'It's a really tight-knit community. You look out for each other and no one will let anyone in the community fall. If somebody is forced to leave their home or flee domestic violence, or there's a marriage breakdown, people will gather around and find somewhere for them to go. People come through for each other. Secular Judaism is very much about family, raising kids, community, taking care of each other and respect for women. I don't think anything inoculates you from loneliness. I have lonely moments like anyone else but, being part of the Jewish community, I don't ever feel like I'm completely alone.'

Going Within

I don't want this – all the turmoil, anguish, struggle and effort – to be for nothing. I want it to be for something. I have worked out, through being stuck in inertia and repetition, that the only way to reach states that I aspire to – states of peace, presence, acceptance, awareness, contentment and evolution (what Gretchen Rubin calls 'the transcendent values that underlay everyday life') – is via a spiritual practice.

I am in the role of my life, a single mother to two young boys who need me, and I can't wing it. I had to outsource, which turned out to be an 'in-source'. I had to go within. My spiritual practice is no longer a chore, it's a reprieve.

Gabrielle Bernstein said, 'Let prayer become a habit that is stronger than your fear. When we pray, we temporarily suspend the fear-based beliefs of our wrong mind.' Our 'wrong mind' is the part of our mind that still believes we are separate. I constantly have to yank myself out of there, remind myself I'm part of something bigger, bringing me back into alignment with who I was before I got so drastically sidetracked. I'm no longer seeking to be understood, but to understand.

SINGLE MOTHER WISDOM

- The greatest revolution for women is not in doing it all but in doing less. We owe it to ourselves – and our children – to detach from drama and cultivate inner peace.

- Self-care is not necessarily bubble baths and facials (although they're always welcome), but coming back to ourselves.

- Self-care is a mindset; it's quietening the negative self-talk that runs our lives.

- Trusting in a higher power can bring great comfort. Many single mothers return – or turn – to religion, both for guidance and to be part of a wider community.

- Therapy can also help you feel supported and find the growth in what you're experiencing.

- If you make self-care a part of your daily routine, it will not only fill you up but also allow you to be at your best for your kids.

- If we 'do the work', we are more likely to come out the other side of this better than before.

CHAPTER 16

Collective Wisdom for Thriving

Whether you're co-parenting, parallel parenting or solo parenting, single motherhood is a big ask. It's also relentless. But it's doable. Actually, it's beyond doable – being a single mother can be the greatest role of your life.

Lara sees being a solo parent as a blessing. 'At first I harboured this core of resentment where I felt it's so unfair I have to raise these children on my own,' she said. 'The turning point for me was one day when I woke up and thought, *Wow, I'm so lucky I get to raise these children by myself.* They were teenagers by then and I realised they were growing up. It was like a light bulb. I'm so lucky I get every day of that.'

Here's some collective wisdom from single mothers on the ways they have learned not just to get by but to thrive, for the ultimate good of their kids and themselves.

Know that You Are Enough

One of the things that held me back from taking on single mother-hood sooner was the fear that I wasn't enough. Not that I wouldn't be good enough, but that I wouldn't *be* enough – loving enough, calm enough, present enough – to be able to single-handedly com-pensate for the life I was unable to give my boys. I wasn't worried about logistics as, like many mothers, I'd been doing the lion's share of the work anyway. In fact, the load would be lessened as I'd be getting every second weekend 'off'. It was about my worth, that in stepping into the role of single mother I was taking a rather risky punt that I had what it takes to carry my boys through.

I may have had doubts at the start, but I have proven to myself, through getting in there and doing it, that I am well and truly more than enough for my boys. Sure, there are challenges and extra demands in raising children by yourself. It takes being resourceful, cutting corners, stretching yourself, going within and endlessly com-promising, but so does everything that's worthwhile.

Be Present

Our children want and need nothing more than our presence, to stop what we're doing and *be here, now*. That can seem especially hard as a single parent when there's so much on your plate. But many single mothers say they find it easier to be present with their kids with no other adult to sap their energy or divide their attention. Our kids get all of us.

'I look for expansiveness in small moments,' said Milly. 'I take my kids into the bush to hunt for lizards or climb a rock. It turns small things into significant moments. It's even more important to me now that I'm a single mother because I don't have them with me all the time so when they are, I try to make time slow down.'

Louisa is also conscious of being fully focused on her kids when they're not with their other mother. 'I try to give them as much support, love and affection as I can and be really present. To stop and observe and tune in to them, really hear their voices and what they're concerned about, rather than jump the gun and assume. I'm working on that.'

It's Okay to Overcompensate

When your child forgets to take something to school (library bag iPad, lunch), you have a choice: you can leave it (they'll be right!) or you can move mountains to make sure they get that thing. In 'normal' circumstances, the advice is to do nothing – our kids must learn to fend for themselves. But, as a single parent, different rules apply. The inclination is to race back home and get that thing, over-compensating, as we so often do, in an attempt to mitigate any deficiency our life choices have afforded our kids. We don't want them to feel any less assimilated than they already do. Which is why I drove across several suburbs one morning – trailing the charter bus – to deliver my eight-year-old the 'right' goggles for swim week when I'd accidentally packed the 'wrong' goggles. I have circled back many times after school drop-off to deliver homework diaries, hats, drink bottles and the rest. And there will be no stopping me.

When Annabel's daughter accidentally smashed her phone on school camp, Annabel drove a three-hour round trip to deliver a replacement, without hesitation. 'People say we should teach our kids resilience, but my kids have been through enough resilience building in their lives already,' she said. 'If it's possible for me to make things easier for them then I will. So long as I don't overdo it.'

Eat Dinner at the Table

It's conventional parenting wisdom that eating meals together as a family (whatever the configuration) is hugely beneficial for kids, a chance to bond at the end of each day, to talk and be heard, to sink into the same rhythm. But it's particularly pertinent for single-parent families, with dinner around the table acting as a touchpoint for kids who know they can rely on at least this one consistency in an often unconventional family routine.

Countless studies show that children who sit down for family meals are less likely to abuse alcohol or drugs and they do better at school because they feel more bonded to the family unit. I insist on it, even though it means the hassle of clearing our dining table, which doubles as my writing desk and the kids' homework desk. It's not so much about the meal itself, but taking the time to check in and connect. We talk about 'the best bits of our day'. With that, the not-so-great bits come out, too, as they should.

Get a Pet

Bronte has a cavoodle called Milo, guinea pigs and a rabbit. She said she acquired this menagerie for her three boys, partly to give them comfort during the huge changes in their young lives. 'Having pets teaches them responsibility like feeding, cleaning out bowls and guinea pig hutches,' she said. 'The love you have for your pet is a different kind of love because they're your responsibility. I tell my boys if they don't want to tell me about their problems, put your arms around the dog and tell him. I'll often catch them giving the dog a hug and whispering to him.'

We have a goldfish. Jasper would love a cat and Otis wants a pug. I wish they could have both but in a rented apartment, it's not an option. So a fish it is. My brother Ticka's family gave us their fish tank as soon as their last fish died. Miles, Jasper's young trumpet teacher, came with us for fish selection. He knows about this stuff; he has a pet snake. (We're not getting one of those.) We left Aquarium World with three fish – Mango, Spotty and Jeff (none named by me). Otis was so craving pet interaction that he'd do star jumps in front of the tank. 'Look, Mum, Jeff's copying me!' he'd say, seeing what he so desperately wanted to see.

When I came home one night to find Spotty and Jeff floating in the tank, I froze their little bodies in a takeaway container in the freezer 'morgue', then we buried them at sea off the rock pools with a small tribute. 'Thank you, Spotty and Jeff, for being our first pets.' The boys were a bit melancholy as we stood on the headland, which I thought was really healthy.

'Get your kids a dog so that when it dies they'll learn about death and the cycle of life,' advised Maggie Dent. Or a goldfish.

Play Team Sport

'Get your kids into sport. It's a must,' said Skylar. 'It builds community, teamwork, mental health. And it's really doable.'

I'm not sporty. I played netball for one season at high school because the teachers made me. My team didn't get one goal. And I couldn't have cared less. Yet as a mother, I'm all for sport. As soon as Jasper was old enough, I enrolled him in soccer and ferried him to games and training. In the summer, I got my boys up to the oval by 8 a.m. every Saturday for Milo Cricket – me and all the dads – tough going after a night shift at work. Sport wasn't Jasper's thing at first and he tried to wriggle out of it, but I have persisted because it isn't actually about soccer or cricket. It's about participation. By the time Otis was old enough, he needed no convincing.

My ulterior motive with the sport drive is that I want my kids to learn the value of commitment and teamwork, being an integral part of something, turning up on time even when they don't feel like it. These are vital life skills at the best of times but, as a single mother, I was especially conscious of them having a consistent place to be, of being part of a team where they not only belong, but are needed.

Author Glennon Doyle came around to the value of sport for her kids, too. It helped that their stepmother is US soccer supremo Abby Wambach, who enrolled Glennon's kids in soccer – not for the competition but for the life lessons it would teach them.

Seeing the change in her kids, Glennon has now morphed into a self-confessed 'soccer mom'.

My boys do drama classes, too, which is also a team sport of sorts. They've become part of an ensemble that writes scripts and performs. They're indispensable to that unit, an inherent part of the collective that wouldn't be able to function as it is without their input. (For the term, at least.) These are fundamental understandings I want them to absorb whether on the stage or field, or life in general.

Make One-on-one Time (Where Possible)

If you have more than one child, it's difficult to make one-on-one time with them when you're a single parent because there's often no one to leave the other one with. On the rare occasions it happens in our home – usually when one of my boys is at a sleepover with a friend – I make a big deal of it for the one who's 'left behind'. They get to choose what's for dinner and pick a movie. When Jasper had his first solo sleepover at his friend Joshua's house, Otis and I watched *The Cat in the Hat* and he fell asleep in my bed and he's never forgotten it. When Otis went on his first sleepover without his brother, Jasper opted for a bike ride in one of those pedal cars at the park and a meat pie from his favourite bakery. We had such a special afternoon riding around together. It's a very different dynamic when it's one on one.

'My kids really value it when I have one-on-one time with them because it's a novelty now that there's only one parent in the house,' said Joy. 'We carve out tiny niches of time. We cook together. That's our thing.'

Let Kids Be Kids

'It's unbelievable how much you do when you're a single parent and you don't have that second person,' said Sally. 'My kids often say to me, "I'm not your staff." My son even said to me, "I'm not your husband, Mum." I have to let them be kids. And I have to watch the gender stereotype thing. They accuse me of being sexist because I'll ask my son to take out the garbage, and my daughter to cook. But I say, "But hang on, I do all of it.'"

Early on, I learned that I needed to lighten up. I was driving myself crazy trying to stop my boys from jumping on my bed (the closest thing we had to a trampoline), kicking a ball indoors or pulling all the shoes out of my wardrobe for hide-and-seek. I had to accept that when you live in a small space with young kids, the same rules can't apply as for those with a sprawling backyard and a rumpus room. I occasionally had to take a deep breath and surrender to the shambles.

One morning when I was trying to get the boys out the door to school, I found them in a 'bus' fashioned out of all the cushions on the couch and most of the contents of the kitchen drawers. I started rousing on them to put it all back immediately. All I saw was the disarray. I didn't see the bus.

I mentioned the incident to the boys' child psychologist. 'What should I do in that moment?' I asked, seeking guidance.

'Get in the bus with them,' she said, as if it was the most obvious course of action.

The couch bus was a turning point. After that I let the boys disassemble the couch to build a 'fort' or a 'streetsweeper' or, one rainy Sunday afternoon, a 'mobile cafe', complete with 'ice-cream maker' and customised signage. I let them play tip in the stairway and even kick the soccer ball inside, ricocheting off every surface, even though it tests my mettle. They can jump on my bed, too, if the mood takes them (and me). I try not to notice the size of the place and see only their childhoods playing out.

Model Being Imperfect

'I have moments where I could have handled things better, and I'm honest with my son when that happens,' said Shakti. 'I have days where I go, "I'm doing my best and my best isn't wonderful but that's as good as it gets right now." I can only model an imperfect human trying to do their best. And I hope that's all he is in his life, an imperfect human trying to be the best person he can be. He sees me meditating, but he also sees me losing my shit sometimes.'

Fake It till You Make It

'I used the tool "fake it till you make it"', Jess said. 'When I had bad days, I pretended they were okay when they weren't. If you put a smile on your face and get off the couch and keep going, opportunities come to you. When you don't, you keep spiralling down. I would pretend it was all okay and then it eventually was.'

Hire an Au Pair (If You Can Afford It)

'I've had many au pairs and treasured each like a wife,' said Lauren. 'I was 1000 per cent reliant on the girls as co-parents, helping with my son who's autistic. It was written in the job description. I'm "head of autism operations". I'm responsible for the moral, financial, emotional and mental wellbeing of my son. I couldn't have coped without these au pairs when my son was younger.'

'I hired an au pair to give me freedom,' said Bek. 'I was given some career advice: Don't put your career on hold. Overinvest in child care when your child is young and don't look at what's going out versus what's coming in. Amortise it, like depreciation of an asset. I applied that concept to my life. With an au pair, I had someone who prioritised me. She interacted with my son while I was working. I've got a full-time job and the double admin of looking after the house. I just didn't have the headspace to play games on the floor.'

Learn as You Go

'I'm invested in evolving as a parent and understanding I'll make mistakes while working towards a positive relationship with my kids,' said Louisa. 'I like to learn and self-reflect. What worked, what didn't work, what can I try next time? It's a work in progress.'

Hold Your Children Lightly

'We have to watch we don't crush our kids with love,' Fiona said. 'It's easy as a single parent to grasp at our children because we're worried for them. Buddhism has taught me to hold our children lightly. To let go and trust that they'll be okay and you'll be okay.'

Take the Path of Least Resistance

This has become my single-parent motto and it applies to most things. My seven-year-old is refusing to have a shower: one night won't matter. I can't be bothered cooking dinner: cheese toasties it is. Kmart sold out of foam surfboards the week before Christmas (when I started my Christmas shopping): a note from Santa to say he'll make a special late delivery. (And he did.) So long as the kids feel loved and heard and understood, the rest can be made up as we go along.

Don't Sweat the Small Stuff

News presenter Juanita Phillips wrote an article for *The Sydney Morning Herald* called '10 things I don't worry about as a single mother'. 'Since I became the sole provider and carer for my two children, a wonderful thing has happened,' she wrote. 'I let myself off the hook.'

The things Juanita stopped worrying about – what she called 'normal parent worries' – include hairstyles, piercings and tattoos; school grades; what other people think of her; screen time: 'I don't want to tell you how many hours my kids spend watching YouTube, because you'd have to arrest me'; extracurricular activities (her kids don't do them); and volunteering at the school tuckshop: 'Thank you ladies, but I'll leave you to it. Feel free to hate me.'

But what keeps Juanita up at night is 'the darker stuff that surfaces at 3 a.m.', what she calls 'the crushing aloneness of full-time single parenting, the magnitude and precariousness of it. The feeling of being just one big life event – illness, job loss – away from crisis.'

That article went off. It was shared thousands of times and trended on Twitter. Mothers – single and not – were talking about it for weeks. Because we recognise ourselves. All that emotional energy spent on stuff that really doesn't matter in the grand scheme of life. Like the time my youngest, then six, missed his line in the Palm Sunday school liturgy. He had a meltdown about his socks ('too wrinkly') and refused to leave the house. By the time I convinced/ bribed/forced him to get to school, it was all over.

There were tears. From me, not him. My little boy took on an air of nonchalance. 'I didn't want to do it anyway,' he insisted with false bravado. I was crying because I didn't buy it. And because I blamed myself. Sure, it was the socks' fault, but if I was a better mother – not a single mother – this wouldn't have happened.

'It feels big now,' a fellow mum said to me when she saw I was upset. 'But it won't mean anything in the scheme of things.'

It was a reassuring thought because in that moment it felt very big indeed. My little boy missing his Palm Sunday liturgy had become, in my mind, a life-defining event shaping his view of the world, himself and me, forming neural pathways like highways of entrenched belief. I feared that he might shut down a part of himself to guard against future disappointment, like the kind he'd just felt. Until this mum's wise words snapped me out of my grand cata-strophising. *It feels big now, but is it really?* Maybe he'd forget about it altogether (probably already had) or fashion it into folklore – how he missed his stage debut because his socks were wrinkly.

We're all hyper-alert to the impact of 'things going wrong' on our kids' malleable young minds, but it feels particularly prevalent as a single parent where there's more room for error: favoured toys left at the other parent's house, alternate Christmases, no one to make a Father's Day card for when the father is absent, the other parent is a woman, or you're a widow, or solo mother by choice. Or maybe it's just the stuff of childhood that will shape them for the better. Not *big*, just different.

Forgive Yourself

We're all going to get it wrong sometimes. It's unavoidable, especially when you're a single parent negotiating all the extra demands on you, with no other adult in the house to back you up. Or take out the bins.

As much as I try to shield my boys from my frustration – meditation helps enormously – it sometimes seeps out sideways, like the time I had a meltdown over the table. Our table isn't just where we eat together every night, it's also the boys' homework desk, my writing desk and invariably the dumping ground for bills, library books, artwork and anything else that comes in the front door. To me that table represents the temporariness of our situation, a reminder that we're still living in limbo, waiting for our lives to begin. One night at dinnertime when there was no clear space to eat (because of my work strewn across it, mind), I lost it. I swept the papers onto the ground in a moment of sheer exasperation. 'I've had it up to here!' I cried. My boys looked at me stunned, not knowing whether to laugh or cry. It only took me a beat to snap out of it. I apologised, explained that I had not managed my emotions well (I had not been 'the boss of my temper', as their child psychologist would say). Then, more crucially, I forgave myself. For not keeping it together in front of my kids.

'Had I not been a single mum, I wouldn't have yelled as much,' said Fiona. 'Some mornings I'd be yelling, "Get in the car. I'm going to be fucking late!" I really regret that. Having said that, she's turned out amazingly as a teenager and we've talked about it. I've said to her, "I feel really bad about the times that I raised my voice and how stressed I'd get." And she said, "It seems like a big thing to you but I knew how much pressure you were under. You were always there for me, and I know you'll always be there for me. The respect I have for you is huge. You taught me that women can do anything. You're my role model." It makes me feel much better about it and I can forgive myself.'

Play the Long Game

Single parents with older kids often find the way they're turning out is 'proof' that they've done a good job, that it's all been worth it. It's vindication of sorts.

'I get a lot of compliments on my kids,' said Sally. 'It means so much. They're polite, they're empathetic. They're good kids. I so take credit for that,' she laughed.

Sally believes that our kids notice what we do for them, even though they may not say it at the time. 'One of the proudest moments of my life was when my son was going on a rugby tour. I suggested that his dad could go with him and he said, "No, Mum. You come to all of my games. If anyone's coming, it's you." I was given an award for being the only parent that had been at every game. He was very aware of that.'

Charlotte Smith is immensely proud of her nineteen-year-old daughter, Olivia, who she raised as a single parent since her little girl was eight. As an antiques dealer, Charlotte would 'drag' Olivia with her on buying trips, and can now see that the 'intense' relationship they share has influenced her.

'She's a mature, evolved young woman mingling with people of all ages and stages of life,' Charlotte said. 'I'm passionate about multi-culturalism and never wanting to see someone compromised because of where they're from. Olivia has embodied those values because that's what she heard in our household of two. She's very inclusive, with a strong sense of justice. It's become part of her philosophy and she's now studying Arabic and law. I don't know if that would have happened if I wasn't a single parent because I treated her more as an adult and respected her input from a young age. It was very empowering for her.'

My boys are still young, but I see it already – the little signs that they'll be okay in the end despite the turmoil they've been through.

'What did you do when we were at school?' my ten-year-old asked me at dinner (at the table, of course). It sounds like nothing major but it moved me to tears because he was asking of his own accord, genuinely interested in my day. In me.

This is what I hope for my children – that they'll care enough to have a stake in the lives of others from a place of curiosity and care. That they'll be kind and wise, capable and independent, ever evolving and expanding to their deepest potential. Not in spite of being raised by a single mother but, in part, because of it.

Lessons in Co-parenting

One of the hardest things about single motherhood for women who are separated or divorced is no longer being part of every aspect of your children's lives. Going from putting them to bed every night of their lives, preparing every meal, reading every story, being with them almost every waking minute, to suddenly not knowing what they're up to for sometimes days on end is a major adjustment. It takes surrendering to what is and trusting they'll be okay. As will we.

Family mediator Gloria Hawke works with separated couples to help them reach agreement over the best way to bring up their children and help them adapt to their new circumstances. She says it's important for single mothers not to be too hard on themselves.

'The healthiest scenario is to not judge themselves and not to expect to get everything right,' Gloria said. 'To be emotionally present with their kids, reassuring them that everything's going to be okay, while also letting them be sad or ask questions. There might be endless questions, or these might come out over time as reality sets in and new routines are formed.'

When I first became a single mother, I had grand intentions: to create a loving, stable and secure environment for my boys, knowing they belong in two homes; to do what I could to create the best life possible for them. It hasn't all been smooth sailing, but in terms of my own growth, I have come to understand that had things panned out the way I hoped, it might have brought peace, but not progress.

Here's some advice from other single mothers who have navigated the tricky and emotionally fraught path of co-parenting and are all the better for it.

Let Go

Inez has learned not to micromanage when her two kids are with their respective dads. 'I tend to be either all on or all off,' she said. 'I let the dads work it out and make mistakes. You have to leave them to it. It's hard to co-parent if you're not talking to the other parent so I always try to keep communication open.'

'When they're younger it's all about my time and dad's time and children can become a commodity,' said Zoe. 'Now my son's getting older you have to let go somewhat, knowing that it's about his time with his mates, whichever house that's in. One weekend he said, "Do you mind if I stay at Dad's because the surf's amazing?" I was like, "Yeah, no problem," but I put the phone down and had a mini melt-down. I realised he's growing up. Whether we were a happy couple or separated, that's reality. You're ever evolving as a single parent and not having that other person to bounce stuff off is hard, but there's a sense of letting go. I'm having to take a step back.'

Put Some Universe between You

'My therapist says, "Put some universe between you", said Lauren. 'I picture it as a blow-up Earth between me and whatever the issue is. Just sit out and let it blow over. I need this boundary because I have more empathy running through my soul than a football field of nuns.'

Put the Kids First

Never is this more called for than when our kids spend time with their other parent (if they have one) during holidays. No matter how in favour of it we may be, it never feels quite right. But as hard as it may be, we have to remember to put them first.

I write my kids notes when they go away with their dad, wishing them a wonderful time. I'm giving them 'permission' to enjoy themselves, to never have to bear the weight of guilt that in their joy and connection with one parent, the other one might be missing out.

'Even though there was a lot of emotion and hurt after the divorce, we decided to take a kids-first approach,' said Katrina. 'No matter what it took, we would get on in order to co-parent effectively together. Fortunately we see eye to eye on most of our parenting decisions but we went to counselling so that we could find a way forward in a new relationship as co-parents, rather than as ex-husband and wife. I'm really proud of how we're handling things.'

Melissa Hoyer is also proud of her and her ex-partner's 'healthy' parenting relationship in raising their teenage son 'long after we parted ways'. Glancing at her Instagram posts, the three of them look like a regular bonded and beaming family of three, Dad in the middle, accompanied by the hashtags #love #family #loveisallyouneed. 'The one major part of our lives that continued, well after our split, is and will always be our son,' Melissa said. 'So, that's exactly what we keep in mind when talking to each other now. We didn't come to any spectacular, thesis-type arrangement in regards to our co-parenting but, as we both pretty much have the same moral compass and ethical code, the way we co-parent has been on the same level. Like any relationship, it all comes down to good communication. We call each other to talk about any 'issues' and we make sure we're on the same page when it comes to advice and rules. That sometimes gets a little hard as we have totally different home situations, but it all works.'

Not everyone can make co-parenting work. Melissa Wilson recommends mediation to help facilitate a cooperative co-parenting arrangement and see things through the perspective of your kids. 'Mediation helped us cut through the emotions, anger and hurt,' she said. 'To have an independent third party was crucial in helping us set clear boundaries around communication and remember to always keep the kids front of mind. It's not easy but when you come from that premise, it helps you focus on who this is all about.'

Don't Diss the Other Parent

'I can lie straight in bed knowing that I've acted with integrity from the day my son's father walked out the door until every day in the future,' said Lauren. 'I would never denigrate him in front of his child. My son thinks his dad is golden, which is the way it should be. He has his own relationship with his dad, because he's his dad's family. Me and his dad are not a family anymore.'

'Children usually have the wool over their eyes when it comes to the idealism of their parents,' said Skylar. 'It's natural for kids to have a romantic view of their parents, and I don't think we should obliterate that because it destroys their sense of hope. They have to work it out themselves.'

'A counsellor told me that no matter what they do, don't denigrate their dad in front of the child because they believe, "I'm half my dad so if you say anything bad about Dad, you're saying it about me",' said Inez. 'Of course, little things come up, but you have to let it go and focus on the good. I might have chosen bad husbands, but they're great dads. I take myself out of the equation.'

'I sometimes play a game with my kids where we list all the positive things about their dad,' said Milly. 'I do this when he's let them down (which happens often) and they're telling me how angry they are with him and that they think he doesn't love them. It's a lesson in seeing the good in everyone – while acknowledging that people sometimes do things we don't like – and it also helps their relationship with their father, which is healthier for them in the long run.'

Be the Bigger Person

'I've become very good at being the bigger person, because life's too short,' said Inez. 'You want to fight for what's right but not to the detriment of the child because you still have to have a relationship with the other parent, whether you like it or not. That's co-parenting.'

Wisdom from an Expert

Divorce coach Prudence Henschke helps single mothers to create workable co-parenting relationships after separation. Here are her top tips.

Learn Communication Strategies

Become familiar with communication strategies around different conflict styles, including the 'BIFF' formula developed by family lawyer, therapist and head of the High Conflict Institute, Bill Eddy. It means writing emails that are 'brief, informative, friendly and firm' to help shut down conflict.

'It's about finding peace in yourself to be able to cope with what's coming at you because you're not going to be able to change it,' said Prudence.

Get Solid Parenting Orders

'When you're attempting to co-parent with someone with narcissistic traits, you need parenting orders that are so tight that there's no room for interpretation,' said Prudence. 'If orders are vague then someone with a difficult personality will use that as another opportunity to fight about every single thing. Solid orders help reduce problems down the track.'

Establish Communication Boundaries

Prudence tells her clients to create 'rules' around communicating with their co-parent if they are 'difficult', such as only corresponding via email, staying on topic, and not engaging if they are hostile. 'Some women give away their power too quickly,' Prudence said. 'Why respond to a provocative text from an ex-partner? You have to protect yourself so you can be there for your children.'

Neve found this to be the only way. 'I pulled up the drawbridge and dealt with my kids' father by email alone,' she said. 'Minimal contact in my case truly is the way to the peace and the light.'

Another avenue to peace and light – or at least a contented existence as a single mother – is to remind yourself that you're not the only one doing this. Take comfort and inspiration from those women who have skipped this path before you. You will come to see that single motherhood is a godsend, not to be resented but appreciated. It's an opportunity – to learn, to grow, to step up. One day our children might even thank us. But until then, we can decide to be thankful ourselves.

SINGLE MOTHER WISDOM

- Understand that you are enough. You have what it takes to raise your kids on your own (or partly, in some cases).

- It's sometimes easier to be present with your kids when you're a single mother because there isn't another adult to divide your attention.

- It's not so easy making one-on-one time with your children, but it's worth it when you do.

- There are ways to make life run more smoothly, including taking the path of least resistance, forgiving yourself (you're doing the best you can), not sweating the small stuff and having faith that it will all be all right in the end.

- Co-parenting (for those who are separated or divorced) is an adjustment, but you can help it to go more smoothly by always putting the kids first and establishing clear communication boundaries.

- Countless single mothers have paved the way before you, and their kids have turned out better than okay (as have the mothers themselves). Take heart.

CHAPTER 17

Collective Parenting

One of the most unhelpful pieces of advice that's proffered to single mothers, one that we get all the time, is to create a tribe for our kids to be part of. It's unhelpful because it accentuates the paranoia that's already front and centre – that we're not enough as we are. And it's unhelpful because it's harder than it sounds.

It would be wonderful to be part of a tribe. It's how I'd always imagined it would go – streams of kids flitting between gaps in fences into each other's backyards, group holidays with families with kids the same age, other parents to kick a ball with my boys or teach them to fish, or feed them around an overflowing table so they don't assume I'm the only one capable. Being included and validated by a bunch of good people who know them and want the best for them. Company and connection on tap without having to hustle for it. It's a particularly utopian idyll for single parents so often trying to be all things for their kids.

But how do you build a tribe? It's an organic process, surely – not something we can conjure up, yet another expectation on our over-piled plates.

Parenting educator Maggie Dent is big on tribes – 'collective parenting', she calls it. 'Our kids will pull away from us in adolescence, and we need to have tribes around the edges that have known our kids from when they were young that they can turn to,' she said. 'Boys especially need role models on their journey to manhood. But it's not up to the mum to deliver them. It's not their job. We need to look at children on that bumpy ride to adulthood as being all of our responsibilities, not just their parents.'

Thank goodness for that. So where do these elusive role models come from? Maggie has found in her research of 1600 young men that teenagers, especially boys, will often seek out their own role models, whether they're raised by a single mother or not. 'As they head towards manhood, they'll tend to look for men to model themselves on,' she said. 'But the research shows they need significant role models of either gender. They're in our schools, communities, sporting clubs, music, whatever. We don't have to go and find them. A boy needs to feel he belongs and have enough significant caregivers, to hang out with people who care about them. It's a privilege to be a part of another child's life. It's not about responsibility. It's about being present.'

My boys aren't on the 'journey to manhood' just yet. But Stella, a single mum of two teenage boys, the oldest now eighteen, is in the thick of it. She admits that navigating them through this time on her own adds another layer of complexity. 'In eighteen years of parenting it is without doubt the trickiest time of parenthood,' she said. 'And doing it by yourself makes it doubly tough. Your kids are up against everything from sex, drugs, cyberbullying, curfews. You get a lot of defiance at that age because they're hormonal. It would be great if someone was there to back me up and say, "Listen to your mother." My words don't have as much impact as I believe their father's would have, that authoritative male voice. There have been many times where I've tried to lay down the law and they've said "no". When I hit back with, "Would you say that to your father?", they'll say "no way". I'm trying to be the male authority figure and I'm failing miserably.'

Finding Male Role Models for Our Sons

The research shows that even boys with present fathers benefit from having solid role models outside of the family unit. I gently steer my boys towards men to emulate, drawing attention to their positive traits as they cross our path: kind, inclusive, good listener, present, patient, strong (emotionally more than physically), enthusiastic, involved in the world, philanthropic (I have to explain that one), interested in others. I bought them a copy of *Stories for Boys Who Dare to be Different* (volumes one and two), packed with tales of exemplary men, past and present, hoping they'll see what it takes to make the most of this life, often against great odds.

I point out men like my brothers, Ticka and Justin. Their older 'boy cousins' (my nephews), Dom and Tappy, stand-out young men who would sometimes look after my boys when I went to work, taking them jetty jumping and helping them with their homework. I would get home to find they'd cleaned the kitchen. At any opportunity, I would take my little boys to watch their older cousins in their element – Dom playing the French horn in the school orchestra, Tappy wowing the audience with a stunning monologue as Amadeus in all his madness, modelling for their young cousins that when you apply yourself (as they both do), and are good people (as they both are), you will find your place.

Miles the young jazz trumpeter, who we originally met when I went searching for a trumpet teacher for Jasper, has taken both my boys under his wing. He babysits occasionally (well beneath his skill set), packing their lunches and getting them ready for school.

He even stepped in for 'Grandparents' and Special Person's Day' at the school one year when it looked like my mum might not make it. 'Be kind to your mum,' I've heard him say to my boys more than once. One Christmas he gave me a present on behalf of my boys – a gift voucher to his mum Lyn's beauty salon. 'In case they don't get you anything,' he said. It was indeed the only present I was given that year. Miles was also raised by a single mum, who's clearly passed on a legacy of altruism to her impressive young son.

My kids also took a shine to my friend Suzanne's son, James, who we met on a weekend at their family farm. James and his delightful girlfriend Sophie (who the boys inexplicably nicknamed 'Tricky Sox') entertained the boys for hours before James and his dad, Mike, took them off to build a fire pit, showing interest and patience, while modelling what it is to be a good man.

I admit that I prefer getting male babysitters when I can. It's part of my mini campaign to bring as many fine men as I can into their orbit. These younger men – like Miles and my nephews – are not so far removed in age from my boys, meaning they can more likely imagine what it might be like to be there.

They need good older men in their lives, too – men like Tim Brown. Tim taught me to meditate when I was pregnant with Jasper and has kept a side eye on my boys since they were born. One pre-dawn morning, at 3.57 a.m., I was lying awake worrying about my boys (as I do), and in particular how my deeply empathetic eldest one would cope with what this sometimes harsh world might throw his way. The middle of the night is a lonely time – there was nothing to distract me from my incessant musing. I was stuck with my thoughts, with my fears and my grand catastrophising.

'Please help me with my boy,' I prayed, a desperate whisper into the darkness. 'Help me help him know how loved he is, how valued he is.' As if on cue, my phone vibrated on the floor beside my bed. At 3.57 a.m. It was a text from Tim. I hadn't spoken with him in months. It was an invitation for my son to join him for a morning at the beach near where he lives with his family. He was stepping up, without being asked. I was so stunned by the timing it took my breath away.

A few days later, I took my oldest boy to meet up with Tim. I watched them cling to the ropes of the ocean pool as they were buffeted by waves, before heading off to explore the clifftops above. That night Tim sent me photos of the two of them on their adventure with an accompanying text. 'He's a delightful, insightful, interesting, engaging, enthusiastic, smart, compassionate, aware young man. It was a pleasure and an honour to spend time with him. You should be incredibly proud of what a fine, conscious young man he's becoming. A tribute to you in many ways.'

I was putting the boys to bed when Tim's text came in. I read it out loud to them. The opinion of a third party might sink in more than mine, a list of my oldest son's finest attributes through the eyes of an unbiased role model. I wrote out Tim's words in coloured texta and stuck it to the bedroom wall. 'So you can remember who you are,' I said. Whenever my boy worries or doubts his worth (as all kids are wont to do), I retrieve that list and I read it out. 'This is who you really are,' I say. And he believes me, not because I'm saying so, but because a man he thinks is cool, who's not a part of his family, who has no vested interest in him, can see who he is. And took the time to say so.

Another time, a couple of years earlier, Tim took my boys for a walk in the bush reserve behind his meditation centre in Paddington, Sydney. He sat them down in the sprawling roots of a centuries-old Moreton Bay fig tree and shared a tale about good things always coming from 'bad'. It was a man-to-boys chat to ease them into the dramatic life change that had befallen them. It meant more coming from him than from me because he was outside of it. And perhaps because he's a man.

We don't get to see Tim that often. He has three kids of his own and runs a thriving meditation centre. Yet these interludes, these occasional check-ins with a man they look up to, are all it takes to cement the understanding that they're being looked out for – by someone who doesn't have to do so.

The boys have seen my chiropractor and kinesiologist, Matt, a few times, too. They emerge from their sessions energised and beaming. 'He's a magician,' Jasper once said. Aside from Matt's remarkable ability to 'clear' deep-seated emotions, what they're also reacting to is the power of having someone other than their parents give them their undivided attention and show a keen interest in their wellbeing.

My brothers, Ticka and Justin, also have families of their own, but when they carve out time for my boys it's the greatest gift. Ticka took them to watch the Big Bash League – their first professional cricket match – and on the longest bushwalk of their lives. One morning after I turned up to collect them from a sleepover they'd had while I was working, I found my older brother teaching Otis, then seven, to tie his shoelaces. Because here's another thing largely specific to single parenthood: our kids are often delayed at self-sufficiency, partly because we're so focused on getting by day to day that it slips our minds to teach them these milestones. And because it takes time and patience, which we don't have much of. It's the same with throwing a ball. Or using a knife and fork. Sometimes it takes an uncle to step in.

When Justin tosses a footy with my boys or plays Finska with them in his backyard, his two much younger boys joining in, too, it warms my heart. We don't see my brothers every day. But I make sure they're in our lives so that Jasper and Otis know what it's like to be held in high regard by good men. I hope my boys will look to them and take on the best of them.

Girls Need Male Role Models, Too

It's just as important for girls to have significant male role models in their lives, especially when being raised by a single mother without a consistent male presence in the home. Maggie Hamilton, author of *What's Happening to Our Girls?*, said we can only teach what we know. 'In many cases our knowledge is formed by stereotypes and our own limited experience. Studies indicate that girls who lack positive male role models frequently fall into risky, harmful behaviour, as they try to explore the male domain on their own.'

Maggie doesn't believe women need to seek men out for their daughters to look to, but to allow their circle of 'good men' to develop organically. 'Where a father figure is absent, for whatever reason, it helps if mothers reach out to the good men in their lives, to help bridge this gap. Their presence provides positive reinforcement for what girls can expect from men. It's important that mothers talk well of men, too, and of the qualities they most appreciate in them, to help girls find their way.'

Boys Can Do Fine
without a Father

Eloise believes that it's vital for our kids, especially those with single parents, to be raised by a 'village'. 'The saying, "It takes a village to raise a child", we've got to own that and look for support everywhere. Not being a life-sucking weirdo, desperate for people to take your kids. But being mindful that we need a village of people to raise our children. Lean on the school, friends, family, the football coach. Create opportunities for your child to be in relationships with lots of different people because the more people who love your child outside of you, the richer their experience of life is going to be. And the more people they'll have to lean on or to reach out to.'

As the solo but re-partnered mother of a son, Eloise also says it's important that our kids have role models. 'As kids get older, you can't be everything to them. Once boys hit a certain age, it's about finding men in the community they respect and can look to, to learn how to be a man. As a single mother, you can't be a male role model. I haven't jumped online looking for role models, but I'm aware of it all the time.'

Neen's husband was the one in the family who took her two boys camping, surfing and skiing – 'all that father-son stuff'. After he died she didn't want her boys to miss out on this dynamic so she approached other fathers at their school and asked if her kids could tag along. 'My boys' friends were doing activities with their fathers; it was a sacred thing and I wanted them to be a part of it,' she said. 'I took a deep breath and called the dads to ask if my kids could go on the camping trip. They always stepped up and it's now been going for four years. Now they text us first to ask if my boys are coming.'

Here's the good news for us single mothers: while the two-parent family is held up as an ideal, according to Maggie Dent, who raised four sons partly as a single mother herself, it's not everything. 'There's clear research that the significant, loving, consistent relationship of one parent is enough for us to become a decent human being,' she said.

'I got from one parent what most of my friends got from two,' said Suzanne of her beloved mother. 'Mum was so present with her children – physically and emotionally. When you don't have all the time-consuming responsibilities with keeping a marriage afoot, you can put that energy into the children in a more even-keeled way. Mum did that. I got the impression that she loved being in our company.'

Contrary to the belief that boys, especially, are better off with a man in the house, Maggie Dent says the research shows that many boys look to their mothers as their significant 'lighthouse figures'.

I was crying discreetly in the make-up room at work one evening. It was my go-to spot where I could hide away in between news bulletins if needed. In those first few months after leaving home with my boys, when it all seemed quite overwhelming, I retreated there a few times. There was a knock and Paul Murray walked in – a lovely, affable fellow with smiling eyes who hosts a contrary news opinion show and who's taken to fatherhood like he was made for it. I hastily explained my tears on account of the sometimes-daunting responsibility of raising two little boys on my own.

'My mum brought me and my brother up on her own after my parents divorced,' he said. 'I knew even then what she did for us. There will be a day where your boys will look back at the toughest decision you made and will admire you for having the strength to put them first. You are setting them up for the best possible life.' Paul's words have stayed with me, rising to the surface when I slide into worry about the impact this might have on my boys.

Journalist Rita Panahi, herself a solo parent to a young son, wrote an article for the *Herald Sun* about the strong bond between single mothers and, specifically, their sons. 'There are few forces in nature as powerful and prevailing as the bond between mother and son,' she wrote. She cited examples from the sporting world – testosterone-driven men at the top of their game, largely crediting their single mums for their success. One example was champion racing-car driver Mark Winterbottom, who wrote a heartfelt tribute in the newspaper to his mother June after winning at Mount Panorama in Bathurst.

'My mother raised me on her own. In a tiny house in Doonside, she loved me, cared for me and did her best to give me whatever I thought I had to have,' he wrote.

Sadly, Mark's beloved mother had died two years before he dedicated his win to her. 'Those fighting qualities come from my mum,' he wrote. 'She fought for everything she had, and fought for me ...

This win has been 32 years in the making. And it wouldn't have been possible without my mum.'

Rita also cited a roll call of AFL champions raised by single mothers, including Brownlow winners Jimmy Bartel, Adam Goodes and Shane Crawford. These men not only reached the pinnacle of their sport but also, as Rita wrote, 'are exemplary human beings who typify the qualities we all want to see in our children. It can be argued that growing up in a single-parent household strengthened the resolve of those young men to achieve great things.'

While single-parent homes are statistically worse off than the traditional two-parent model in terms of health, education and finances, these men are reassuring reminders that it's not always the way. Raising good kids is not determined by the quantity of parents in a family, but the quality of our parenting. As Rita said, 'The love and stability of a happy home can overcome just about anything.'

There are endless other examples of impressive men – and women – raised by single mothers: US Presidents Barack Obama and Bill Clinton, and US Vice President Kamala Harris; the late poet and civil rights activist Maya Angelou and her protégé, Oprah Winfrey; singers Barbra Streisand, Adele and Alicia Keys, and rapper Stormzy (who raps about how much he loves his mum); actors Naomi Watts, Cate Blanchett, Julia Roberts, Halle Berry, Guy Pearce, Keanu Reeves and Dax Shepherd (who often riffs about his beloved mum in his Armchair Expert podcast and calls her the love of his life); and author Trent Dalton whose book *Boy Swallows Universe* was loosely based on his own life.

Maya Angelou, who became a single mother herself at just sixteen, said her mother 'liberated her to life'. In *Mom & Me & Mom*, Maya wrote that when she left home with her baby son, her mother said, 'Remember this: When you cross my doorstep, you have already been raised ... You know the difference between right and wrong. Do right.'

Not that fame is any indicator of turning out well, it's just that these are the stories we hear about. I keep my eye out for others. When I meet someone who was raised by a single mother, I introduce them to my boys or at least make a point of telling the boys about them. There aren't so many examples where we live, a traditional 'pleasantville' suburb where intact families tend to stay that way, at least by appearance. So I look outside the village square.

I want my children to have a template of what's possible for them. And to know that even though it's just the three of us at the dinner table most nights of the week, that's more than enough.

SINGLE MOTHER WISDOM

- It's important for our kids to have role models to look up to, whether they're being raised by a single parent or not. But it's not our responsibility to recruit candidates. Our kids will seek them out, and we can also keep an eye out in our communities.

- Parenting educator Maggie Dent says that boys especially need male role models on the 'bumpy road to manhood'. We can steer our boys towards good men to emulate (young and old).

- Girls do well with significant male role models, too, especially when there are none in the family. It's important for mothers to 'talk well' of men to their daughters to help bridge that gap.

- Research shows that boys do just fine without a father, but they do benefit from having at least one consistent, loving parent (or guardian).

- Boys often cite their mums as their significant 'lighthouse figure' who has helped guide them along the way (but we single mothers of sons know that already).

- It's a privilege to be a part of a child's life and help guide them, in whatever small way; be that person if the opportunity arises.

CHAPTER 18

Making Rituals

When we lived in our old family home, my boys would eat dinner at their miniature orange table by the window in the kitchen. On a warm evening, I'd set the wooden picnic table in the courtyard and we would head out there. I was conscious from the get-go that I was instilling a tradition, kicking off a ritual that I hoped would be life-long, a non-negotiable nightly custom so long as I had any say in it.

When we moved into our new place, we left the orange table behind. There wasn't room in the apartment, and the boys had almost outgrown it anyway. We now gather every night at a bigger table in 'grown-up' chairs. Not just to eat, but to talk.

'What's your best bit of the day?' I will ask. Or they can list three things they're grateful for – it's up to them.

'My best bit of the day was when I didn't get nervous one bit when I did my "My Life as a Spy" talk in front of the class,' Jasper said once. Other times it's been 'Being cosy inside with you when it rained', 'Having Joshua for a sleepover then pancakes for breakfast' and 'Climbing "big foot" with my friends and one of our teachers jogged past' ('big foot' is a rock in the bush).

'Running through the sprinklers at Edward's house,' was one of Otis' 'best bits', along with 'That you let me roll in the mud with Alex and Edward in our school uniforms', 'Jumping off the jetty all by myself', 'Scoring a goal at soccer' and 'When you took me to the salt room' (it cleared up his persistent cough).

Katrina also talks about the 'best part of the day' with her two kids. 'It keeps them focused on the positives,' she said. 'I'm introducing them to gratitude by helping them think about whatever good has come from the day. I'm trying to build a positive mindset in them. It's important we establish routines and rituals to help them adjust to our life together in our new normal.'

We're not the only ones sitting around the table together every night. 'We eat dinner together no matter what. It's dedicated time to discuss your day, and to ask the kids to chew with their mouth closed five thousand times,' laughed Danielle. 'That ritual of sharing food together is really important in the bonding of a family. It's a good habit.'

Suzanne says food was one element that bound her family together when she was growing up. 'Mum was an amazing cook,' Suzanne recalled. 'She made our home a centre of gathering for our family and friends. She understood that food unites. Any time anyone wanted to come over, Mum's attitude was, "No problem to throw on some extra potatoes." She valued routine and rituals. We always knew where we belonged. Rituals centre you. They make you feel part of a continuum and they provide security. You know what's coming.'

'Scott Pape, in *The Barefoot Investor*, said that many single mothers fight to keep the house, when we should be fighting for the dining table,' said Michelle. 'Essentially that means we should prioritise having dinner with our children. Time with the kids is far more important than anything money can buy. That really struck a chord with me.'

I still read the boys a story every bedtime as well, even though they can both read themselves now. With me, they not only get all the voices, but also my time. Oliver Jeffers was a staple when they were little: *How to Catch a Star*, *The Incredible Book Eating Boy*. We've read *Charlie and the Chocolate Factory* and a roll call of other Roald Dahl books. My kids love all of David Walliams' books, leaping on them as soon as a new one hits the shelves, as well as *The Faraway Tree* series (taking me right back) and, their current favourite, the Kensy and Max series.

After the story, I wedge into bed beside each of my sons in turn – my youngest first in his bottom bunk, where we say a prayer of sorts, 'Peace, love and joy live in me', along with his own choreographed actions. Then I hoist myself up to his brother in the top bunk to talk about whatever's on his mind. Some nights I scratch their backs while they 'say goodnight' to their bodies. If they'll lie still long enough, I play a guided meditation from the Insight Timer app. They usually heckle throughout but the intention is pure.

Anyway, it's not so much about the attempted meditation or the read-out-loud stories or the sit-down dinners. It's about consistency. I'm attempting to impart rituals, to entrench habits as predictable as sunrise so my boys know that no matter what chaos swirls outside, when the world stops and it's just us here together, this nightly touchpoint will run as a constant.

Another of our rituals is ambling down to the rock pools at the end of our street via the bush track. The caves are a 'shop' selling burgers and milkshakes for $1000 each. There's a 'motorbike' rock that the boys ride in tandem, roaring off to it doesn't matter where. We fossick for sea snails, watching them retreat into their tiny shells when touched, count fish and startle crabs. We go after school and on weekends during any weather. One Easter I planted a choco-late egg hunt down there. I tell the boys that these rock pools are our 'special place', that when they're all grown up they can bring their own kids here and say, 'This is where our mum used to bring us when we were little.'

We can see the sea on our drive to school. 'What colour is the ocean?' I ask when we reach a high road where the view fills the passenger windows. It's a school drop-off ritual. Otis always says green, without fail. It's become an in-joke. Jasper indulges me by describing the more subtle hues of steel grey during a storm, diamonds after rain, blue sequins on a knockout mid-summer morning. But that's not the point. It's about teaching them to notice the beauty around them. And it's embedding this tradition as one of the unifying themes of their boyhood.

If I ever forget to ask – if we're running late for school and I neglect to look around me – they remind me: 'Wait, Mummy. What colour's the ocean?'

I'm consciously seeking to create small moments of significance, well aware that these seemingly inconsequential practices will all make up the fabric of their formative years. I'm also well aware that I'm compensating. My kids might miss out on the nuclear family and all that entails (in theory), but what I can provide is equilibrium, stability and dependability, infusing them with the understanding that they have a part to play in the world. That they are necessary.

Making Connections

Maggie Dent is also a big fan of incorporating rituals into family life. 'I cannot stress enough the importance of having regular connection moments with our kids, especially for single-parent families,' she said. 'It strengthens the sense of belonging and predictability. While that big predictability of "we all live in one house" has gone, these other things are still in place. The brain finds it easier to adapt to a new normal when we have rituals, and we can keep on creating new ones.'

Maggie says that rituals are often based around food. In her family it's the 'end-of-term treat'. 'I was teaching full-time and chasing four boys around and on the last day of term, I took them to a cafe for traditional chocolate sundaes. And I said, "This is going to be an end-of-term treat 'cause you've all done really well and I'm proud of you." We needed to celebrate that we'd done well as a little tribe. "End-of-term treat" became a thing in our family, which is still going, even though they're now adults. These things are really important in our families. It's coming together and letting the world go away while we share something. That's what rituals do. They're so powerful.'

Rituals from Other Single Mothers

Rituals don't need to be grand gestures. We may not even realise we're doing them. When repeated often enough, the simplest customs – unique to every family – can bind us and give our kids continuity. These small, 'no big deal' moments will make up the thread of their childhood, rising to the surface when other memories are long gone. They are a way of freezing time for our children, and also for us.

Drive the Kids to School (Where Possible)
Skylar used to drop her kids to school, even though they could have easily caught the bus, to ensure they had time together. 'Drive your kids to school as much as possible because when they get to teenage years it's the only time they'll tell you anything,' she said. 'My dad used to do that with us and I've never forgotten it.'

Not everyone's work or family situation allows for this, but it's a good strategy even if you can only manage it every now and then. The same goes with driving them home from school. My boys also do their best talking in the car. Research shows that boys specifically tend to open up more when they're side-by-side with you rather than front on. Like in the car. Maggie Dent says we should resist asking lots of questions and let them talk when they're ready, especially at the end of the day. It takes discipline and I usually forget, interrogating them as soon as they're in the car door. 'How did you go with your "Wright brothers" talk?', 'Who did you play with at lunch?', 'Did you include the new boy?' They've been to a Maggie Dent seminar with me so they know the deal. 'Mum, remember Maggie Dent said not to make us talk after school,' they say. So I wait. And then it comes. 'Mum, can I tell you something?' And the floodgates open.

Have Signature Foods

It's not just mealtimes that unite us to our children, but the food itself. I make banana smoothies as soon as my boys get in from school. It's a thing. They drink them with the swirly plastic straws in the same cups they got for Christmas the year we left home.

'Preparing traditional meals like my shepherd's pie or Sunday night roast is a nice routine and it's something my boys will always remember,' said Bronte. 'I still remember every Sunday night my mum would make her beautiful apple cider chicken dish. It's a comforting thing for the kids since my divorce.'

Set Intentions

Tory and her daughter, Bella, set intentions at the beginning of each year, reflecting on the year that was and what they want to attract into their lives. 'I've always done this by myself, then I started bringing my daughter in when she was four,' said Tory. 'It's important we share this ritual together because we are each other's family. One year we both declared we wanted unconditional love and a bigger family, and that was the year I met my husband.'

Where possible, I get into the ocean with my kids on the first day of a new year. We say our 'wishes' for the year out loud and send them out with the waves. 'To make new friends,' said Otis when he was starting a new school. 'To be a good leader,' shouted Jasper to the horizon. 'To know that you feel loved and safe and happy,' I said, pulling them close.

Keep Memories Alive (for Widows)

'I feel Nick is never far away,' said Lisa, a widow and mother of three. 'I hear them sometimes in the bath chatting to him. I buy cinnamon donuts from the bakery to remind us of their dad. We put on a stack of videos and watch him. He's got journals, and he recorded music and painted as well as being an aerospace engineer. So they've also got all of his art. He'll be present for them always.'

Kelly, whose husband died in 2017, says she struggles with being locked into the 'obligation' of rituals, but there's one they won't miss: 'One ritual that doesn't require too much effort from me other than showing up is the two State Basketball League teams my husband used to play for, when they play each other, they play for the Anthony Exeter Cup. That's a really lovely night where his friends take the opportunity to get together and see each other and touch base with us. It's such a proud moment for my kids.'

Coronavirus Made Me a Better Mother

While I'd long been conscious of creating rituals and memories to help make my boys' lives more meaningful, when the coronavirus pandemic struck in 2020, I went into overdrive. If there was one thing I thought I was tracking okay with in my otherwise off-track life, it was motherhood. All those gratitude lists at dinner, meditation apps, bedtime stories. Overt attempts at balance and presence – going about my aspirational 'connected' parenting ways – like ticking 'good mother' boxes. I thought I was all over it.

Until the unthinkable happened: we were confined to our homes almost 24/7. No school, no soccer, no play dates. No distractions.

It took this calamity to snap me out of my delusion. To realise I'd been giving my kids what I thought they needed – time and attention – but what they really needed was me. I had, for the most part, been going through the motions. I was there but not really there.

This was a wake-up call (homeschooling will do that to you). Sure, everyone from the Prime Minister to school principals urged us to lighten up. 'The curriculum can wait,' they said. 'The kids will catch up.' But I ran the home 'classroom' like it was the real deal, sticking to the lesson plan as if my children's futures depended on it. I crammed YouTube tutorials on 'unlike fractions'. I became an authority on the Gold Rush; the life of Aboriginal leader, Barangaroo; and Jesus' crucifixion; and helped prepare a 'persuasive text' on why books are obsolete – in the affirmative. We did 'P.E.' at the local oval, kicking a soccer ball in the cricket nets. I lost my patience often. I was frequently frazzled. But I was there.

Lockdown was extra tough on single mothers – being the only adult in the house exacerbated loneliness for many of them. But for me, this enforced time with my kids was the correction I needed. Coronavirus made me a better mother.

'What was your happiest time ever?' Otis asked me and his brother during one of our regular headland walks, the only time we were 'allowed' out of the house. He also asked about our 'saddest time' and 'a time we'll never forget'. When the kids were not being pulled from pillar to post, goaded out the door, there was time to ponder.

Yes, my boys were restless, rumbling like puppies. You get that after being cooped up together for weeks with no yard. But in abandoning their incessant badgering of me with 'What are we doing today?' (because what would the point have been?), the doors were thrown open to more meaningful discovery. They weren't pining for their other life because kids are masters at adapting to what is. No one else to see, nowhere else to be.

Downtime spurned mild innovation. Otis started sketching. Jasper and I replaced the batteries in the RC cars and revved them up again. They built a 'fort' and slept in it. In normal circumstances I would have insisted they put the couch back together. We baked banana bread. I never bake.

Time slowed. Our world expanded in its contraction. More importantly, I was paying attention. My boys might have protested when I dragged them for 'not another bushwalk', but as we walked I felt a small hand reach absentmindedly for mine. I'm quite often blindsided by my children's insights, as if they have unique and unfettered access to the bigger picture. But this time I could see clearly what was going on – that I was unfurling as much as them, reaching for each other across a divide I hadn't realised was there.

The challenge is to carry these new understandings with me amidst the invitation to revert to the habitual. To be reminded of what's of value when all else is taken away.

SINGLE MOTHER WISDOM

- Rituals are important for single-parent families as they serve as a constant, providing stability and predictability – for our children as much as ourselves – when so much else is uncertain.

- Rituals don't have to be big deals – it's about creating small moments of significance for our kids that will weave a thread of consistency through their formative years.

- Examples of rituals from other single mothers include: sharing dinner at the table, driving them to school, setting intentions together and keeping memories alive (especially for widows).

- These traditions strengthen both belonging and dependability, consciously connecting us with the people we love the most.

CHAPTER 19

Getting Back Out There

The first time a friend tried to set me up with a man, I froze. It was a text suggesting I meet her very nice brother-in-law's brother. I was so freaked out it took me a week to reply. And the answer was no. It wasn't him, it was me.

It had only been a few months since I'd moved out of the family home with my two young boys, and meeting another man was the last thing on my mind. Not even for dinner. I was touched my friend had thought of me, but even though I was technically single, I wasn't on the market.

In the years after that, there were others – offers, that is. Invitations to meet someone's recently divorced single dad or never-married friend or colleague, the well-intentioned assumption that mutual singledom is criteria enough for assured compatibility. The assumption that I must surely be seeking someone, anyone, as I was alone. I'm sure some of those men were perfectly fine, and they might even have made great partners for the right woman, but she wasn't me.

It's not that I had sworn off men. I wasn't jaded or suspicious. I wasn't permanently scarred or on guard. I still had faith in good men, lasting love and functional unions. But, like many of us who have suffered the fallout of a broken dream, I needed time to heal and I was also evaluating and dissecting my part in its demise. I was caught in a debilitating state of lament for what might have been, mourning the family unit that I'd come to accept my kids would never know. Not in the format I'd imagined, anyway. Had I gone on a date back then, I would have cried at the table, regaling my temporary companion with a sorrowful tale, and he wouldn't have got a word in.

Instead of going out, I went within. I knew I would be no good to anyone else – or myself, for that matter – until I processed the unravelling of my life as I knew it. To tag team with someone else, however suitable he might be on paper, would only distract me from the work that needed to be done. It's not like I stayed home sobbing every night, although there was a bit of that at the start. But I bunkered down with my boys, monitoring their adjustment to this path they didn't choose. Just as vitally, I bunkered down with myself, grateful for the latitude that being the only grown-up in the house afforded me.

A friend who'd ended an unhappy marriage a few years before led the way. She had gifted all of her furniture to her ex so that she could deck out her house the way she liked. A blank canvas, just like her new life. She downloaded customised playlists and cranked them with abandon. 'It was a time of great freedom and personal growth,' she said. 'There was something lovely about being on my own again, doing what I wanted and bonding with my kids. It took two years to distill it all. To work out my part in the relationship so I didn't attract it again. I thought if I never meet anyone else that's absolutely fine.' (Although she did happen to meet the love of her life not long after.)

I have had suitors and flirtations and been on the odd date, and I quite liked someone for a bit, but on the whole I, too, am revelling in my solitude. For now. I have a teetering pile of books on my bed-side table. I sleep in the middle of the bed. I eat dinner with the kids and watch Netflix of my choosing after they've gone to sleep. I meditate when I feel like it and do yoga on the lounge-room floor. I'm doing me, as they say.

I've done enough therapy to know that unless we explore the underlying failings of our past relationships, we'll keep inviting the same ones in. Rinse and repeat, as one friend puts it.

'I have fought my way to a deeper happiness on my own,' wrote single mother Drew Barrymore on Instagram, contemplating 'not being able to successfully date' for four years. It's the only route to authentically love or be loved by another.

At least there's no rush. The last time I was single – a good decade ago – the stakes were higher, driven subconsciously by a biological time limit for procreation. Now I don't seek a father for my children.

It'll have to be someone pretty exceptional to cut through. That's all I am up for.

Finding Love Again

My boys once asked me if I wanted a boyfriend. They were quite specific about the criteria I should follow: 'He needs to kick a ball with us, read to us, take us skiing, teach us to fish, help us with our homework, play Battleship with us. Just like you, but a man.' Jasper kindly offered to write my profile on eharmony. He says he saw an ad for it on TV while watching *Bondi Rescue*.

Dating as a single mother can be an emotional minefield. Most of us have already given relationships a good shot and the best thing we've got to show for it is our kids. Single mothers by choice often – but not always – arrive at that place because they haven't had much success finding lasting love. As playwright Alexandra Collier wrote in an article for *Good Weekend* magazine about her decision to have a baby on her own with donor sperm, 'my romantic life was out of sync with my reproductive timeline'. For widows, there's a mountain of grief to climb before they can even think about bringing someone else into the family. Then there are the pure logistics of trying to meet someone new, let alone conduct a meaningful relationship while raising kids on your own, as we grapple with how to integrate our two worlds.

'My life might not be how I planned it but I have a great career that I worked hard for, two gorgeous kids and a supportive family and friends network,' said Melissa Wilson. 'A partner would be an added bonus but I certainly don't need someone.'

Jess said that between working full time and raising her son, she had no emotional energy left for a relationship. 'When my son was with his father I would go on a date. They'd ask, "When can I see you again?" I'd say, "On a Thursday night in three weeks' time for half an hour,"' she laughed. 'There was no momentum.'

As author Theo Pauline Nestor wrote in *How to Sleep Alone in a King-Size Bed*, her memoir chronicling her divorce and entree into single motherhood, '. . . lately I've been wondering, "What about sex? Was that it for me, then? Will I never sleep with anyone again? Or might I meet someone – where? The children's section of the library?"'

On the other hand, finding love again (or for the first time) when you're a mother already can also be wildly liberating. The pressure is off to get the deal done to a biological deadline. We're free to make decisions on want not need. We already have everything we desire, so a new man or woman is an adjunct, not a vital component. We get to decide the terms of engagement.

Dating as a single mother – getting 'back out there' – is an opportunity for deep, authentic connection and true partnership with no ulterior motive, often for the first time in our lives. It's also an opportunity for unbridled free love, devoid of commitment and complication, a journey of self-discovery through the mirror of sex and intimacy, when having children is not necessarily at the back of everyone's mind. Even for those single mothers who'd like to have more children, it's not usually a driving factor the next time around.

As Eloise said, 'Dating as single parents is like bringing finished canvases together.' In theory, at least.

Take Time to Heal

Divorce coach Prudence Henschke agrees it's important that we 'take time to heal' before diving back into a relationship so we don't repeat the same mistakes.

'I don't think it's a good idea initially,' Prudence said. 'There's usually some healing that needs to be done. It's about rediscovering yourself and what's important to you. Many single mothers haven't thought about that for so long because they've been in a dysfunctional relationship. You need to get clear on that first before you enter into another relationship. If you can date without getting too attached then it's okay to do it sooner. It depends how you're coping with the separation. People tell you you should be out dating and it's been long enough but the only person who can judge when you're ready is you.'

Thoughts on Dating as a Single Mother

For those who do feel ready to meet a new partner – or even just to hang out with another adult – here's what some other single mothers shared with me about diving into the dating pool.

You're Not Damaged Goods

'A friend who has been a single mum for fifteen years said to me, "Don't see yourself as damaged goods or broken. If you meet someone, they're so lucky because they get you and your son,"' said Zoe. 'She was really empowering and I started to see it that way, too.'

Canna Campbell, founder of SugarMumma.TV, had similar reservations before she met her now husband. 'I thought, *Who's going to want to be with me? I'm 35, twice divorced, and a single mum.* I didn't have much faith in myself. But I learned to relax and go, *This is who I am. The right person will see that not as a hindrance but as something special.* And I met someone who loves my son like his own. It's an incredible relationship, a very respectful team, which I didn't know existed before.'

'I was 40 when I separated and that's not the end of your life,' said Zoe. 'You want to share it with someone or at least go out and meet people. You might not want to find the one but you can still go for a wine. And you want to have sex, too. I mean, we're not 85. You feel like you're the same age going back into the world as when you met your partner. I felt like I was 25 again. But I'm 40. Getting naked in front of someone again is layered and wonderful. And vodka helped, too,' she laughed.

Dating Apps Are the Go

'Dating apps are how we meet people now,' said Zoe, who met her new partner online. 'Get over it. Just put yourself out there and don't overanalyse. Things are going to work with some people and not with others.'

Canna also met her husband online and they've since had a child together. 'I was always with my son and didn't go out much, so being online allowed us to actually meet. Within a week of us meeting, he was on my doorstep saying, "I'd love to see where this goes." We've been together from that moment.'

Shift Your Mindset

'When I walked away from a toxic relationship, I threw myself into creating a healthy mindset,' said Tory. 'I was in a rut and I knew something had to shift. An energy healer said to me, "Tory, your bed's facing the wrong direction." I flipped my bed around and slept like that for three months. It might seem crazy, but it switched my thinking and it switched up the energy in my house, and things started to change. I was ready for love and for the family I'd always wanted and deserved and I set about attracting that into our life. Now we have this beautiful happy ending with my daughter, my husband and his son.'

'I just wanted a really good human who does it for me,' said Lauren. 'My son and I are a package deal. I have now met the most amazing man and we have blended our families. We were set up by friends on a blind date and we've been together ever since.'

Sexual Revolution

'I hadn't had sex for such a long time that I thought my body was broken and I couldn't orgasm,' said Danielle. 'Sharing my body with someone post-babies was fraught with all sorts of insecurities like, "Do I look okay?" The first time I orgasmed I cried. "My body's not broken!" It was a sexual revolution. Like stepping into the full goddess power of my physicality.'

Lisa, a widow, is also embracing the sexual side of herself. 'The whole idea of exploring your sexual identity beyond marriage: way to fast-track personal growth and your evolution and personal power!' she said. 'I'd been in caretaker mode for so long I forgot what it felt like for someone to have your back. There's something about being 40, giving zero fucks about your body and just seeking pleasure. It's thrilling and fun. I really enjoy that part of my identity.'

The Right Partner Is Worth Waiting For

'I needed more dating experience,' said Lauren. 'I only had one significant partner before I met my ex-husband. I kind of did my twenties dating post-divorce. I was totally attention starved. I suddenly had people filling my mind with, "Hey, you're amazing!"

But I didn't believe it myself. I loved being married and I'd love to be married again. I tried to make every post a winner after my divorce. As in, the next boyfriend could be "the one" and building up the scenario in my mind. In the end I realised I can be alone, I might always be alone and that's okay. An equal partner is worth waiting for and I can wait. That's the position I reached after a bit of heartbreak.'

Nothing Wrong with Staying Single

For many single mothers, the idea of another relationship is too much, and they are quite happy putting their energy into their kids and themselves.

'If I couldn't make my relationship work with my children's dad, there's no way I'm going to try to make it work with someone else,' said Jo. 'I have two special-needs children who need all of me and I need all of them. I've gone through too much to get to this position where I'm free to be the parent I want to be. Don't compromise it because of a moment of loneliness. When my kids are older I can date then. For now I'm happy being free.'

'It's super hard to meet someone when you've got two kids from two fathers,' said Inez. 'Try and find someone who doesn't mind that you've got two exes. It's a bit complicated to bring up.'

'I'm a bit jaded and cynical about relationships,' said Skylar. 'That's something I have to work on. I actually do better on my own.'

'I'm cautious because I haven't got a good track record,' said Louisa, who split with the mother of her kids. 'I'm wary of bringing someone new into my boys' life. I spend my time with wonderful friends instead.'

Blended Families

Blended families are quite the norm when you re-partner as a single parent – there's almost no avoiding it. They can be complex and complicated. Or they can work beautifully for all concerned.

When Lauren's ex-husband re-partnered, she couldn't have been happier for their son. 'I totally embraced my son being in a blended family with his father, his partner and her kids,' she said. 'As far as my boy's concerned, life is a lot better when there are lots of kids around. He gets to see his dad every second weekend. And on the other weekend, my partner's kids are with us. It's like the circus for him.'

Stella's new partner now lives with her and her two kids. She says it's difficult integrating their roles. 'It can be hard 'cause I think my way is right and I don't back him as much as I should. The kids and I are the unit, and he's a bit on the outer. The hierarchy is the kids, then me, then him. I adore him but they come first. It's a constant negotiation.'

'I re-partnered for three years with a guy who had three children of similar ages to mine and it was wonderful,' said Sally. 'My kids loved it, they had a "family". Sadly, it didn't work out but it exposed us all to how good a blended family can be.'

Wisdom from Writer Kerri Sackville

'I can't see myself living with someone,' said writer and single mother, Kerri Sackville. 'I love living by myself. It would be nice to have someone in the bed then kick them out. The freedom I have now, I can't imagine ever giving that up.'

Kerri wrote a book for women who are dating in mid-life, appropriately title, *Out There*. Here's some of her wisdom on dating as a single mother:

When Is the Right Time to Start Dating?

'It depends whether you've had time to mentally prepare for the end of the relationship. It's important to sort yourself and your kids out first. You don't make good decisions when you're in crisis and you can end up clinging to the wrong person like they're a life raft because you're not thinking straight. You don't have to have all your shit sorted. You can be in therapy, you can still feel angry at your ex. We all have emotional baggage by this age. But you know when you're in good working order. If we waited till we were completely self-actualised none of us would have relationships.'

What Is the Best Way for Single Mums to Meet People?

'Single mothers are often home raising kids or working from home, which makes it hard to meet people. I'm not going to meet a single man unless one crashes through my ceiling onto my kitchen table. The chances of meeting a man in a bar are slim at our age, and how do you know if he's married? Meeting people organically in a random "meet cute" way where you just bump into someone at a supermarket is pretty rare. If you've got a big social life where your friends are constantly introducing you to single people, that's great, otherwise it's apps. The good thing about apps is everybody's on there to meet someone. There's no playing games.'

Is It Preferable to Date People Who Also Have Kids?

'I'll only date men who have kids or who've been step-parents. Men without kids often don't understand that our kids always come first. It's ideal if you meet someone whose kids are around the same age as yours. I don't particularly want to hook up with someone who's got toddlers. It can even be difficult with men whose kids have left home because they might want to travel and you're at different life stages.'

Should Our Kids Be Our First Priority?

'For me, dating and being in the company of men and feeling like I'm vibrant and alive and sexy is really important. It makes me feel good about myself. But we need to be mindful of our kids and their feelings about what we're doing. I think we should always prioritise our kids, at least when they're young. But it's possible to have a dating life that doesn't impact on them. If I go on a date I'll say, "I'm going for a drink with a friend. It's unlikely to go anywhere but I'll let you know if it does." If it leads somewhere, I'd start introducing the concept gradually.'

When Is It Worth Paying for Babysitters?

'If possible, go out when your kids are with their other parent – if they have one. Or make a reciprocal arrangement with another solo mum where you look after each other's kids. Before you go on a date from an app, do your research. Do a reverse image search to make sure they're who they say they are. Talk to them on the phone first to get a sense of rapport and ask the questions that are deal-breakers to you. If you're just looking for a fling that's different. But if you're committing money to a babysitter, you don't want to come home thinking, *Not only did I waste an evening, I wasted $60.*'

When Is the Right Time to Introduce a New Partner to Your Kids?

'There's no point introducing your kids to anyone unless you're pretty sure they're going to be a long-term prospect. There's a school of thought that you should introduce them early to see if they get along, but I would have introduced my kids to 70 men by now.'

How Much of Meeting Someone Comes Down to Luck?

'I try to disabuse people of the notion that if you have the perfect profile and date enough men, you'll find your person. You might not. And that's okay. A lot of women who haven't found partners yet see it as like a problem they can't solve. "I've achieved in my career, I've been a good mother, I've managed my money. Why can't I find a man?" 'Cause it's luck. The right man could come around tomorrow.

But if he doesn't, that's not because you're deficient or you've done anything wrong. It's just your number hasn't come up.'

And if your number doesn't come up, if the right man – or woman – continues to elude you, then nothing is lost. You have all the time in the world.

SINGLE MOTHER WISDOM

- If you've come out of a long-term relationship, take time to heal and reconnect with yourself so you don't risk repeating the same pattern.

- Dating as a single mother is incredibly freeing because, with the biological clock no longer ticking, the pressure is off. You can date on your terms and dive in only when you're ready.

- Finding love again can be liberating because, especially when you already have a child and if you're financially stable, a partner is an added bonus. They're a 'want', not a 'need'.

- It's an opportunity for a relationship free of commitment or expectation; some women describe it as a 'sexual revolution'.

- Dating apps are the way of the world – get on board!

- Blended families can be tricky to navigate, but they can also be an enriching union, giving you and your kids a second chance at having the big family you might have thought you'd missed out on.

- If you don't meet anyone you like, or it's taking a while, it doesn't mean it's all over. You have all the time in the world.

- It can be just as thrilling to be single by choice – to fall in love with yourself.

CHAPTER 20

The Upside

I made an appointment with a child psychologist back when I first decided to leave our family home. I was hoping she could give me 'tools' on how to steer my young children through the change I was about to impose on their young lives by transforming everything they knew. She did help with that, but she was more interested in me. 'Your boys deserve to see the real you,' this woman said. 'They will get to experience you as empowered, in charge of your own destiny. They will get to see you happy and free, being true to your-self and following your heart. By doing that, you're modelling for them that this is the way to live.'

It was the clincher. Staying was no longer an option. As author Glennon Doyle said when she was deciding to leave her unhappy marriage with the father of her three children after falling in love with her now wife, Abby Wambach: 'I remember looking at my daughter and I remember thinking, *I'm staying in this marriage for this little girl, but would I want this marriage for this little girl?'*

It's one of the upsides of single motherhood – that we get to show our kids who we really are. We get to live as our authentic selves (if we so choose). It's a far superior demonstration of womanhood for our children to aspire to, whether they're girls figuring out who they want to be as women, or boys picking up cues on how to treat women. It's possible to do this in a marriage or partnership, of course – one that's supportive and collaborative and love-filled. But, if not, single motherhood is our chance.

I am slowly coming back to myself. It's been rough going at times in the years since I swapped one life for another, but I have created enough distance, enough of a buffer, that I've been able to unearth forgotten parts of me among it all. It's another one of the many gifts of single motherhood – the opportunity to not only rediscover ourselves, but also re-create ourselves. To re-create our families.

Suzanne described how her mother would put a positive spin on their circumstances when she was raising four children on her own in the 1970s. 'The best of a beach day is when the sting has gone out of the sun and the nor'-easterly has picked up,' she said. 'All the other mums would be packing up to get home and get dinner on the table and Mum would say, "How lucky are we that we can stay and have fish and chips?" She saw the upside in every situation.'

I try to do that, too – to consciously examine what's good about our lives, what benefits my boys and me in our current set-up. We, too, can stay late at the beach and often do. I join in, swimming and kicking a ball where I'm not sure I would if there was another parent around. I'd probably sit on the beach with a book, barely looking up. We have a closer bond because it's mostly just the three of us. With no other adult to defer to, I am all things.

I love the fact that my future is still unknown. Every day is filled with possibility because it could be the day that my life will change for the better. Of course, that possibility is available to anyone, but when you're not locked into a traditional family dynamic with a shared trajectory (which can be nice also), it seems more open to interpretation.

What We Love About Single Motherhood

Ask any single mother – co-parenting, parallel parenting, mothering solo (whether by choice or not) – and they're unilateral about one thing: that good comes out of all of this. Whether they have shielded their children through a storm (of varying magnitudes) or delivered them consciously into a one-parent, conflict-free world of love and inclusion, they are embracing all the perks that come with it. Here are some thoughts from other women on the many upsides of single motherhood.

Finding Your Strength

'You get to see how strong you are as a single mother,' said Julia. 'A lot of women in relationships don't get the opportunity to ask, "What do I want to do with my life?" We've got an opportunity to reset and live life on our terms.'

'As a single parent you have to become everything: the accountant, the gardener, the person who can put a picture up on your own, do a school lunch, take your child to a psychologist if they're having a bumpy ride,' said Zoe. 'You become a much stronger person and much more independent.'

Autonomy

'It's the autonomy that I love,' said Lauren. 'Being able to make every decision, whenever I want. I'll always consult with his dad but I'm the decision-maker.'

'I've often noted the lack of stress because I'm calling the shots,' said Eloise. 'When your child becomes a teenager, the nature of the relationship changes. I usually get the final say, but he gets a big say in things as well. It's that collaboration which wouldn't happen if there was another parent. We have our moments, but there's a very unique bond between a single mother and a child. It can be challenging and it can be beautiful.'

'I know that I'm a good mum but it's hard when you're not in sync with your partner, especially as I have two kids with special needs,' said Jo Abi. 'Now I'm the mother I want to be. My whole life is managed to the kids' schedule. We're a little team and I am so much happier.'

Even Kelly, whose husband passed away, said she appreciates being able to parent freely, and 'being able to make decisions about things you know would ordinarily be contentious without all the talk and needing to bring the other parent around to your way of thinking'.

'As a single parent you get to create your own traditions and experiences with your kids,' said Louisa. 'We go for a walk-and-talk and have thickshakes and share hot chips with chicken salt. I sit with them and watch the crazy YouTube videos they want to show me or listen to the latest music that they like. It's just us three.'

A Better Relationship with Your Kids

'I was struggling in the marriage, which was taking up so much of my energy and I wasn't in a good place,' said Joy. 'Now we're so tight. It's like living with three messy flatmates. We wouldn't have that bond if it wasn't just us thrown into this together. You become a team. We're like four moving parts. We can't do well unless we're all pulling our weight.'

'Because you have to be mother and father to your children, you become so much closer,' said Katrina. 'They share things with me because I'm the go-to person. I really treasure that. It's a lot of responsibility, but I've formed a much closer bond with them. It's us against the world.'

'When I was married, my son always wanted to go surfing with his dad or kick a ball so I felt a bit like the person who made breakfast and got him to school and his dad did all the activity stuff and I was a bit unsure where I fitted in,' said Zoe. 'I have a much deeper connection with my son now, finding things that we love to do together, just me and him.'

Being More Present with Your Kids

'Since being a single mum, I'm a better me and I'm a better mum,' said Zoe. 'I'm much more present. I realise that blink and he's going to be eighteen and he might want to go surfing around the world so it's just enjoying where we're at right now.'

'When I'm with them, I'm with them,' said Inez. 'I want to make the time that they're with me special and fun and not too busy so we can catch up on lost time.'

'So much of my energy had been invested in the marriage so when it ended I couldn't believe how much more energy I had to be the crazy, zany, fun mum I'd been years before,' said Maggie Dent. 'I had more energy to shoot hoops with my boys, go for a bike ride together, to be the mum I wanted to be. I became a better mother. That was one of the gifts.'

Being a Role Model

'Divorce is sad but it's much sadder to be in a relationship with someone where you're not happy or being true to yourself,' said Katrina. 'It's sad when things end, but it also opens up new opportunities and new beginnings. I don't want my kids to think they have to settle for something that's "good enough". I want them to strive for the absolute, to suck the marrow out of life. You get one shot. I don't want to die with any regrets and look back and wish I'd done things differently. Even though it seems scary to take the leap, it's not so scary on the other side.'

'I'm aware of the immense privilege and responsibility in modelling being a woman to my daughter,' said Francesca. 'She sees a woman who left a relationship because I was unhappy and it wasn't working and there wasn't enough love or intimacy or harmony. She sees a woman saying, "I don't accept that, that's not how I choose to live my life."'

As the solo parent via a donor, Bek said she's modelling to her son that 'women can do anything'. 'When he gets older, he'll respect women as strong and independent because that's all he sees. He's unlikely to take on the default gender divide of most traditional households with "inside jobs" for women and "outside jobs" for men because that's not how it is in our home.'

'I want my son to see me strong and capable, but also soft,' said Shakti. 'That's the challenge for single parents. To be both is really hard. That's the dance. Hopefully by him seeing me be imperfect but also kind of whole and okay with that, he feels like he can be that in the world. And when he grows up he'll let women be messy and imperfect and strong and capable.'

Time to Yourself (for Co-parents)

'Every second weekend when my kids go to stay with their father I can choose to have that time by myself, with friends, or take a lover or two. I have the autonomy to make all those decisions,' said Anika.

'On the days that I don't have to do the school run or pack lunches, I book things that are for me – yoga, exercise, coffee with friends,' said Inez. 'I try to switch off.'

'I had so much guilt at first for how hard it was on my children,' said Danielle. 'Then it started to be frickin' awesome! I think every mother needs two days off from their children every couple of weeks, because otherwise you forget you. No grown person really wants to spend three hours at the park. They want to do things that feed their soul. But you can't take the kids to the museum because they'll have a massive meltdown at the Frida exhibition and totally shame you,' she laughed.

It Helps Shape Your Kids

'The relationship you have with your child as a single parent is so strong and the understanding and the partnership you form is unbelievable. I wouldn't change that for anything,' said Tory. 'It's a blessing not only for myself but for my daughter because she's become this very independent, empowered woman. She's a teenager now and she knows exactly what she wants and she's fearless because she's been exposed to a variety of circumstances throughout her life.'

'I love how female our home is, two generations of women, my daughter and I growing together,' said Francesca. 'She has a wonderful relationship with her dad, too, which is so important. But I'm also thrilled that we get to be in a really female space. Unafraid to be emotional and heartfelt. Whatever we're talking about, it's always with that beautiful woman's take. I come from a strong tribe of women, many of whom were also single mothers. And I'm proud of that.'

'It's nature versus nurture,' said Jess, who's been a single mother to her eighteen-year-old son since he was eighteen months old. 'I look at him and the nature is definitely there. He's very sweet, empathetic and kind. He's a good egg. But I also see my part in it. I've kept my calm and always been upbeat, positive and supportive, even when I didn't feel like it. I've tried to be a good role model by working hard and teaching him good values. I have a strong moral compass and I can see that he's learned that. I'm proud of how I've raised him. I pinch myself when I look at the wonderful man he has become.'

My children may not be old enough yet for me to see how this is all going to play out. But I can already make out promising hints that my brave choices are helping to shape them.

They seem to understand that hard feelings are legitimate and that most people are well intentioned even though they sometimes don't appear to be. It's better to be alone than to spend time with people who don't see you. They see that it's important to be the bigger person. And they know, because they're living it, that life can also be fun and joyous, with endless adventures to be had.

I hope they will come to accept that there are times when they will be required to be a warrior, and other times when they just need to sit still and take it all in. I want them to know that everything happens for a reason and that there's learning in everything. And most importantly, that I am, and always will be, their safe haven.

When Otis was seven, he wrote me an acrostic poem for Mother's Day. His list of adjectives to describe me included 'cheerful, nice, amazing and beautiful'. 'The best mum.' I'll take all that. But the line that meant the most to me was: 'Never gives up.' He also wrote a 'descriptive text' about me when he was eight. As well as describing me as having 'hair as thick as a horse's mane and golden like straw,' he wrote, 'She's generous and as kind as Buddha. She makes me feel special like I'm the only kid in the world. She's as calm as a cucumber. I love my mum as much as all the seeds in the seed vault.'

Jasper referred to me in a school project (one that I didn't help with) as his 'strong, loving mother'. 'You can do anything,' he said to me once.

I am immensely relieved that my boys perceive me in this way. Because had I not changed our course, there's a good chance they may not have. It's the single mother in me who is strong, calm as a cucumber (sometimes) and never gives up. Who can do anything (or at least appear that way to my kids). This is one of the upsides of single motherhood – that we get to be better than before, and therefore our kids are, too.

I don't have it sorted. I don't know all the answers. But I am asking the questions. And that is worth everything.

SINGLE MOTHER WISDOM

- The best thing we can do for ourselves and for our children is to live bravely and truthfully; this might mean making tough choices and causing our kids to suffer momentarily, but it's preferable (for all concerned) to losing ourselves.

- As single mothers – whether we're co-parenting or parenting solo – we model to our children strength, courage, resilience, super-human capability and unconditional love.

- We show our girls what an empowered woman looks like; we show our boys how to treat them.

- Single mothers have autonomy over how we raise our kids, spend our time and shape our lives.

- Single motherhood presents an opportunity for you to re-create yourself, and your family.

- Other benefits of being a single mother are that you get to be the mother you want to be, and you have the chance for a better relationship with your kids.

- Being raised by a single mother will help shape our kids and teach them valuable life lessons. They might not like it now, but they will appreciate it in time.

CONCLUSION

Our Unmapped Future

From the outside, it all looks the same. We still live in the same 'temporary' apartment where we moved when we first left our family home, when I began my life as a single mother. Our 'code of conduct' is still stuck on the stainless steel fridge, buried but not forgotten beneath a mountain of merit awards and other such passages of time. Jasper's acrostic 'THINK' list remains on the back of the front door, faded but legible. The angel wings that my mum gave me when we moved in – to 'watch over' us – still hang on my bedroom wall.

So little has changed. But also, so much has changed. Both my boys can read and write and do long division. They can shower themselves and tie their own shoelaces (thanks to their uncle). I can no longer carry them up the stairs. New friends have been made and countless fierce rounds of Uno and Trouble have gone down on our lounge-room floor. They can both crack eggs and use the blender. We three have danced and cried and rumbled and got back up again after we've fallen, a great swathe of my boys' childhoods played out between these borrowed walls.

I have grown up, too. I needed to. I arrived here lost and a bit broken. Not that I knew it. I fashioned myself as the fierce lioness protecting my cubs, taking a heroic stance – a leap of faith – for the good of us all. I assumed moving out and moving on was the final chapter and all that was left to do was to get on with our new life. In reality, it was just the start.

I had to crash and burn before I could rise again. I had abandoned myself so fully for so long, kept myself so tightly coiled that there needed to be an unravelling before I could recall who I was. I had to suffer properly, surrender fully and be cast adrift so I would know what it's like to have nowhere to turn, to be backed against a wall and be forced to find solace solely within myself. I'm glad I didn't know this back then or I might not have braved it. And I needed to brave it. Not just for me, but because my boys need me. The best of me.

The changes are small, unnoticeable to anyone but me. Because I'm the only one who knows where I've come from.

'Can I play a song?' Jasper asks. He syncs Spotify from his iPad to the speaker I gave him for his tenth birthday and blasts 'A Million Dreams' through our apartment. There are sausages on the grill and school shirts on the line with the weather app showing rain and Otis needs help with his 'ghost towns' project. I might have once demanded that they turn the music down. But I don't. Not this time. I recognise that this cacophony – in all its suburban mayhem – is a precious moment that will slip by if I don't pay attention. I turn the stove off, leave the kitchen and dance. Feigning embarrassment at first, Jasper eventually joins in, then Otis. We three bounce about, making a memory instead of an altercation.

That's what's new: my ability to choose. Again. And again. I can choose to dance. And I can choose to be hopeful, proud, at peace. To be cool with chaos. To see how far we've come while looking to our unmapped future and being thrilled by it.

I spot a post on a single mother Facebook forum: a photo of a wooden cubbyhouse with steps. 'I built this today, all by myself with no help from absolutely anyone,' the caption read. 'Single mum, 4 boys.' Building cubbyhouses is one thing. And then there's rebuilding ourselves.

Single mothers have got this down pat, too. First destruction, then a reset and now creation. No matter what brought us here, we get to create something else. To imagine it, then choose it. We do this by refusing to settle for 'good enough' and instead riding the trajectory of our authentic vision. Of our truth. We have the opportunity to start again with our children as our witnesses, holding us to account in our evolution. For their sakes – if not our own – we must locate the greatness within ourselves. To once again become vibrant and aware, curious and wholehearted. Sink into genuine joy. Be who we were always meant to be. Build a beautiful life.

My boys have no idea of the transformation that's taken place in their honour, and nor should they. So long as they feel held and free to be kids.

I would like to deliver more. A bath, for starters. And a puppy. Until then, I'm happy so long as they come to know that their mother is more than enough to carry them through. In case they haven't worked that out already.

Recommended Resources

BOOKS

Divorce and Separation

Aftermath: On Marriage and Separation, by Rachel Cusk

Falling Apart in One Piece: One Optimist's Journey Through the Hell of Divorce, by Stacy Morrison

How to Sleep Alone in a King-Size Bed: A Memoir of Starting Over, by Theo Pauline Nestor

The Hungover Games, by Sophie Heawood

Spiritual Divorce: Divorce as a Catalyst for an Extraordinary Life, by Debbie Ford

Split: A Memoir of Divorce, by Suzanne Finnamore

Empowerment

Letting Go: The Pathway of Surrender, by David R. Hawkins

The Power of Now, by Eckhart Tolle

The Universe Has Your Back, by Gabrielle Bernstein

Untamed: Stop Pleasing, Start Living, by Glennon Doyle

The Untethered Soul: The Journey Beyond Yourself, by Michael A. Singer

When Things Fall Apart: Heart Advice for Difficult Times, by Pema Chödrön

Parenting

The Conscious Parent, by Shefali Tsabary

From Boys to Men: Guiding Our Teen Boys to Grow into Happy, Healthy Men, by Maggie Dent

No-Drama Discipline, by Daniel J. Siegel and Tina Payne Bryson

What's Happening to Our Girls?, by Maggie Hamilton

The Whole-Brain Child, by Daniel J. Siegel and Tina Payne Bryson

Money

The Barefoot Investor: The Only Money Guide You'll Ever Need,
    by Scott Pape

*Mindful Money: A Real Guide to Building and Managing Financial
    Independence in a Busy World*, by Canna Campbell

Money: A Love Story, by Kate Northrup

*Money, and the Law of Attraction: Learning to Attract Wealth,
    Health, and Happiness*, by Esther and Jerry Hicks

*The Soul of Money: Transforming Your Relationship with Money
    and Life*, by Lynne Twist

For Kids

Blueback, by Tim Winton (ages 6–12)

It's Not the End of the World, by Judy Blume (ages 8–13)

Just the Way We Are, by Jessica Shirvington and Claire Robertson
    (ages 2–5)

Kisses in Your Heart, by Sonia Bestulic (ages 3+)

Mum and Dad Glue, by Kes Gray (ages 3–5)

My Super Single Mum, by Bronwen Fallens (ages 2–7)

The Suitcase Kid, by Jacqueline Wilson (ages 9–14)

Two Homes, by Claire Masurel (ages 3–5)

Was It the Chocolate Pudding? A Story for Little Kids About Divorce,
    by Sandra Levins and Bryan Langdo (ages 2–6)

For Kids of Single Mothers by Choice

Happy Together: A Single Mother by Choice Story, by Julie Marie

The Pea That Was Me: A Single Mom's Sperm Donation Story,
    by Kimberly Kluger-Bell

The Special Two: An Enchanting and Heart-Warming Tale of How a Precious Boy Came Into the World, by Sarah Kissane

Why Don't I Have a Daddy?: A Story of Donor Conception, by George Anne Clay

Empowerment for Kids

Good Night Stories for Rebel Girls, by Elena Favilli, Francesca Cavallo

I Think, I Am!, by Louise Hay and Kristina Tracy

Kids Who Did: Real Kids Who Ruled, Rebelled, Survived and Thrived, by Kirsty Murray

Stories for Boys Who Dare to be Different, by Ben Brooks

Stories for Kids Who Dare to be Different, by Ben Brooks

WEBSITES

Support, Inspiration and Life Coaching

beanstalkmums.com.au

champagnecartel.com

divorceandseparationhub.com

lisacorduff.com

powerful-steps.com

prudencehenschke.com

singlemothersurvivalguide.com

singlemum.com.au

theselfloveproject.com

yourgoodlife.com.au

Finance

luckybitch.com

melissabrowne.com.au

sugarmamma.tv

PODCASTS

Beanstalk Single Mums

Single Mother Survival Guide

SugarMamma's Financial Foreplay with Canna Campbell

FACEBOOK FORUMS

Australian Separated, Single & Divorced Mums

Beanstalk Anonymous Single Mum Forum

Single Mother Survival Guide

Single Mums Support Group Australia

INSTAGRAM

@champagnecartel

@kyliechamps

@letsgomum

@mamasmetime

@mumpacktravel

SUPPORT SERVICES

1800Respect national sexual assault, domestic and family violence counselling service: 1800respect.org.au

Council of Single Mothers and their Children: csmc.org.au

National Council for Single Mothers and Their Children: ncsmc.org.au

Relationships Australia: relationships.org.au

Solo Mums By Choice: smcaustralia.org.au

Victorian Assisted Reproductive Treatment Authority: varta.org.au

A Note of Gratitude

This book began – as they so often do – with a conversation. When I mentioned to my publisher, Kelly Doust, the dearth of books on single motherhood, she suggested I write one. And so I did.

So, to Kelly: thank you for backing me and believing in me, giving me the freedom to riff off an idea and run with it. And for indulging me with missed deadlines (homeschooling during a global pandemic will do it) and keeping me on track during this epic marathon with your invaluable advice, support and care.

My friend Juanita Phillips came up with the title, *The Single Mother's Social Club*, and was generous enough to allow me to use it. A title can make a book, so I'm most grateful.

I feel immensely fortunate to have aligned with editor Justine Harding, who treated my words like her own with remarkable attention to detail, making hefty word cuts pain free.

Editorial Manager Julie Mazur Tribe is a big-picture visionary who helped me adjust my lens accordingly. I thank her for her vigilance, precision and eye on inclusiveness.

And huge thanks to the rest of the Murdoch Books team, including Emily O'Neill for that work-of-art cover, and publicist Sarah Hatton for getting *The Single Mother's Social Club* out into the world.

Thank you to Selwa Anthony – my agent, mentor and friend – for standing by me all these years.

To my wonderful 'writer friends' who make a solitary pursuit seem far less so, including L.J. Charleston, Suzanne Daniel, Karen Fischer, Angela Mollard, Natalie Murray, Juanita Phillips, Cat Rodie, Tracey Spicer and Nicole Webb.

Those friends who 'check in' regularly, which means the world when you're the only adult in the house, including all of the above as well as: Juliet Andrews, Tory Archbold, Amanda Blue, Kate Cliff,

Bronwyn Curran, Caroline Horsley, Juliet Horsley, Sophie Hoskin, Alex Luffman, Fiona Nilsson, Nat O'Dea, Ineke Rapp, Julia Reynolds, Lauren Rose, Giulia Sirignani, Kristin Sweeney, Kat Vidovic, Neen Weir, and my dear sister, Cait Tynan.

I couldn't have got by in these single mum years without the 'school mums', from making sure I knew when it was mufti day to minding my boys while I met deadlines. These thoughtful women include: Antonia Collopy, Carolyn Maloney, Bridget Moroney, Lisa O'Hea, Agnieska Senderowicz, Elsa Van Wijk and Julia Vitali.

Special mention to my former neighbour, Terry Duff, for inviting me in for endless writing break 'cuppas' while she lived downstairs, and handing out treats to my boys like a grandmother.

Enormous gratitude to my 'spiritual mentors', Tim Brown, Dr Matthew Bourke and Wendy Procter, who taught me that growth is the only worthy option, while guiding me gently towards it.

And to Justine, Joanna and Rachel for making me feel held – and hopeful. You give family law a good name.

Heartfelt thanks to my mum, who raised six kids pretty much on her own, and who is always there on the end of the phone.

To my dad, who left me with the legacy of knowing that I could write – or do anything, really – if that's what I wanted.

I am incredibly grateful and indebted to the many women (all single mothers) who divulged their experiences and insights for this book, trusting me with their stories – in person, over Zoom and via email. Vulnerability and open-heartedness are generous acts.

And thanks beyond measure to my beautiful boys, Jasper and Otis, for allowing me to share their anecdotes, perspectives and acrostic poems, for giving me the space to write and edit (albeit with occasional bribery), and letting me off the hook when it was Chargrill Charlie's for dinner again. But mostly for being my living proof that love is the path of least resistance. You boys are my incentive – to do better, to evolve, to create.

Index